The American Eve in Fact and Fiction, 1775-1914

The American Eve in Fact and Fiction, 1775-1914

ERNEST EARNEST

University of Illinois Press

URBANA   CHICAGO   LONDON

FOR MY WIFE MAUDE

LIBRARY OF CONGRESS CATALOGING IN PUBLICATION DATA

Earnest, Ernest Penny, 1901–
   The American Eve in fact and fiction, 1775–1914.

   Includes bibliographical references.
   1. Women in the United States—History. 2. Women
in the United States—Biography. 3. Women in literature.
I. Title.
HQ1410.E17   301.41'2'0973   74–19339
ISBN 0–252–00448–5

Acknowledgments

It is with gratitude that I acknowledge a grant-in-aid from the American Philosophical Society during the preparation of this book.

I thank also the Schlesinger Library of Radcliffe College for permission to quote from the journal of Louise Stoughton; the Historical Society of Pennsylvania for making the diary of Adele Biddle available to me; and the Haverford College Library for the use of the diaries in the Quaker Collection. The librarians of all these institutions have been most helpful.

The lines from "Wild Nights—Wild Nights," "Title divine is mine," and "What soft, cherubic creatures" are reprinted by permission of the publishers and the Trustees of Amherst College from Thomas H. Johnson, Editor, *The Poems of Emily Dickinson*, Cambridge, Mass.: The Belknap Press of Harvard University Press, copyright 1951, 1955, by the President and Fellows of Harvard College. The lines from "Title divine is mine" are reprinted with the permission also of Houghton Mifflin Co., publishers of *The Life and Letters of Emily Dickinson*, edited by Martha D. Bianchi.

Contents

Prologue

"... of all womankind no variety better repays sympathetic and discriminating study than the American."

Hjalmar Hjorth Boyesen,
"Types of American Women,"
Forum, VIII, 1889–90

From the earliest days of the republic European visitors were fascinated by the American girl. Here was a new kind of woman: beautiful, self-reliant, fashionably dressed but competent in housework, desirable but innocent, and above all enjoying a freedom unknown elsewhere in the world.

During her visit to America—1818 to 1820—Frances Wright noted: "The liberty enjoyed by the young women often occasions some surprise to foreigners; who contrasting it with the constraint imposed on the female youth of Paris or London, are at a loss to reconcile the freedom of the national manners with the purity of the national morals."[1] She commented on women's manners, "peculiarly marked by sweetness, artlessness, and liveliness; ... there is about them a certain untaught grace and gaiety of the heart equally removed from the studied English coldness and indifference, and from the no less studied French vivacity and mannerism."[2]

Tocqueville, who visited the United States from May 1831 to February 1832, wrote:

Long before an American girl arrives at her marriageable age, her emancipation from maternal control begins, she has scarcely ceased to be a child, when she already thinks for herself, speaks with freedom, and acts on her own impulse. The great scene of the world is constantly open to her view; far from seeking to conceal it from her, it is every day disclosed more completely and she is taught to survey it, with a firm and calm gaze.[3]

He came to the conclusion that "the singular prosperity and growing strength of that people ought mainly to be attributed to their women."[4]

It was not only the earlier travelers who found the American girl superior. David Macrae, who came in 1860, described American and Canadian women: "Pale features of exquisite symmetry, a delicately pure complexion, eyes radiant with intelligence, a light, graceful, often fragile form—this is the vision of liveliness that meets the eye in almost every American drawing room. I never saw in all my life before so many fairy forms which it would have surprised me no less to see shooting out wings and floating up into the empyrean."[5] He had the curious notion that hot bread and pie caused the women's paleness (Lowell told him it was climate), but "Paleness and pie notwithstanding, the American girls are very delightful. And in one point they surpass the majority of English girls—they are all educated and well informed."[6]

James Bryce, who at fifty did not see them shooting out wings and floating up into the empyrean, nevertheless wrote in 1889: "In no country are women, and especially young women so much made of. The world is at their feet."[7] Like Tocqueville a half century before he thought that "no country seems to owe more to its women than America does nor to owe them so much of what is best in social institutions and in the beliefs that govern conduct."[8]

Even Kipling, who was hardly pro-American, and who in 1886 had written "a woman is only a woman, but a good cigar is a smoke," became enthusiastic about the American girls he met three years later. After commenting on the charms of the girls of Devonshire, France, and India, he added, ". . . but the girls of America are above and beyond them all. They are clever, they can talk—yea, it is said that they think."[9]

Early American novelists, with the exception of Charles Brockden Brown and Nathaniel Hawthorne, were less perceptive about the American girl's unique qualities. Under the influence of Richardson a host of sentimental novelists, including the "scribbling women" excoriated by Hawthorne, pictured a series of heroines threatened by seducers before they discovered true love. A favorite device was to picture two protagonists: the sensible, downright, self-effacing heroine temporarily outshone by a pretty, shallow sister or cousin. The pattern goes back to Jane Austen and appears as late as Howells's *The Rise of Silas Lapham* (1885).

Eight years before that, Henry James published *Daisy Miller*. Like so many figures in American literature she became more than a character; she became a mythic symbol. A writer in *The Times Literary Supplement* in 1960 noted this quality in American protagonists:

> The American heroes that we think of as characteristic—Natty Bumppo, Melville's Ishmael, Huck, Isabel Archer, Milly Theale, Gatsby, English, Holden—seem to have an especial quality that sets them apart from the creations of any English novelist. It is obviously not a question of convincingness or vividness of delineation in any simple sense. It is rather that they are myth-figures as the characters of no English novelist are, myth-figures in that they recapitulate within themselves deep and apparently abiding national experience, and that they are conceived by their authors with a lyrical intensity that seems to confer on them a more than naturalistic stature. They can stand for more than the characters in English fiction are called upon to do.[10]

So much is this true that the larger-than-life symbolic character comes to be regarded as not only typical but universal. Babbitt is a case in point. *Daisy Miller* since the time of its publication has been discussed less as a story than as a valid or false portrait of the American girl. A study by Elizabeth F. Hoxie[11] shows the extent to which American books on etiquette used the story as a warning against certain kinds of behavior. She says, "Daisy Miller therefore came to be regarded as an authentic portrayal of all American girls in Europe." More than that, she came to represent the nineteenth-century American girl everywhere. Howells described Mrs. Lapham as one of those women "born to honor the name of American Women, *and to redeem it from the national reproach of Daisy Millerism*" (italics mine).

This concept was reinforced by a whole series of Jamesian women —Isabel Archer, Caroline Spencer, Mme. de Mauves, Milly Theale, Maggie Verver—who are all thrown into conflict with the more sophisticated and corrupt society of Europe. These women share certain characteristics. Leon Edel's description of Isabel Archer could apply to all of them: "A new kind of heroine, given all the freedom and innocence of the New World and made to confront the worldly-wise, the urbane, the civilized, but also deeply corrupt life of the old."[12]

The present study is not especially concerned with the nature of European society but rather with the authenticity of the portrait of the American girl. The novels of James, because of their power and influence, are central to the study but by no means the only fictional portraits to be considered. Next in importance to James for the purposes of this book is the work of William Dean Howells. However, a variety of stories and novels by lesser writers deal with the lives and characters of American girls and women—a number of them specifically designed as national portraits.

Partly because of the convention of the love story young girls are central to a great many of the novels; mothers and older women come in only incidentally. But it was also true that it was the young American girl who impressed both novelists and European travelers as a unique type. Her upbringing, her freedom, her grace, beauty, and innocence seemed to set her off from the girls of other societies. She is treated thus in William Wasserstrom's *Heiress of All the Ages.*[13]

Wasserstrom devotes most of his account to the fictional portraits. The present study, while considering these, is largely an examination of the actual girls and women as they are revealed in diaries, memoirs, and biographies. An examination of these suggests that the American girls of fiction were far different from the living models.

As has been stated, the American girl rather than the American woman engaged the attention of native writers and foreign visitors. It seems to have escaped their notice that a new kind of girl might grow into a new kind of woman. The evidence presented in this study suggests that this is exactly what happened. Thus, although this is not primarily an account of the struggles for women's rights, education, social reform, and the vote, these must come into the story. However, because many of the pioneers in these fields were exceptional in ability, dedication, and life style, this study will also examine the lives of more ordinary women as revealed in their diaries.

This, then, is not a history of American feminism; rather it is an attempt to answer the question: What were American girls and women like between the Revolution and World War I?

There are several reasons for confining this study chiefly to the years between the Revolution and World War I. Colonial society, although increasingly divergent from that of England, nevertheless preserved many of the laws and customs of the mother country. Thus Page Smith's account of the sexual mores of the New England Puritans[14] obscures the fact that these mores were largely transplanted. Such things as the considerable sexual permissiveness granted to courting couples and the social and economic status of married women to a large degree reflected the practices of the social classes who migrated to the new world. In particular, rural societies had long accepted premarital sex for betrothed couples or even for courting couples. It will be remembered that in the country town of Stratford, Shakespeare's first child was born six months after his marriage. According to Page Smith the records of numerous Puritan churches indicate that until at least the middle of the eighteenth century premarital relations were the rule rather than the exception.[15]

On both sides of the Atlantic adultery was a more serious offense than premarital sex, but Puritan records show that numerous cases of adultery occurred in New England. Hawthorne recognized the close links between colonial society and that of England by representing Hester as an English girl brought up in a poor but genteel home where her father still wore an Elizabethan ruff. She came to America as a married woman. Her illegitimate child Pearl married abroad.

Elizabeth A. Dexter's *Colonial Women of Affairs*[16] shows that in America women engaged in a wide range of occupations. Frequently they took over a dead husband's or father's business. They often became shopkeepers and teachers, but sometimes blacksmiths, innkeepers, silversmiths, tinworkers, shoemakers, shipwrights, tanners, gunsmiths, barbers, and butchers. Eleven women ran printing presses and ten of these published newspapers in America before

1776.[17] Franklin advised his sister Jane Mecom, married to a feckless husband, to take up the family business of soapmaking, and proudly presented samples of her crown soap to aristocratic friends in Europe. While John Adams was in Philadelphia attending the Continental Congress, Abigail ran the farm at Braintree so well that General Warren told John it had "never looked better . . . and that Mrs. — was like to outshine all the Farmers. . . ."[18]

All this is only partially explained by the emergence of a new social order in colonial America: it was to a considerable degree a matter of social class. American settlers came largely from classes used to supporting themselves in farming, trades, and small business. Thus many of the colonial businesswomen listed by Elizabeth Dexter were born abroad and came to America either with their husbands or on their own initiative to set up shop in the new world. They brought their skills with them. Thus advertisements read, "Lately come from London, Mrs. C. Atkinson, who designs the making of Mantos and Riding dresses . . ."; "Mary Marcomb, Mantua Maker from London . . ."; "Mary Cannon, widow of Charles Cannon, late from Manchester, Taylor . . . proposes to carry on the business of her late Husband with some sober qualified workmen they brought from England. . . ." "Jane Morland, from London" informed the public of her prepared sausages, tripes, and sheeps tongues.[19]

Mrs. Dexter's list of women who early in our history became landed proprietors, contains the names of English, German, French, and Dutch immigrants along with those of women born in America.

The first woman poet in America, Anne Bradstreet, came to Massachusetts from England as a married woman. Anne Hutchinson, sometimes pictured as the first American champion of woman's rights, was about thirty-four when she came to Boston with her husband.

It would be hazardous, therefore, to try to define a characteristically American type during the Colonial period.* But the soil and the seed were there. The theory of a selective migration is quite tenable:

---

* For similar reasons this study omits a consideration of the wives and daughters of those ethnic groups which have tended to maintain separate cultures. These groups require specialized studies and have been portrayed in special categories of fiction.

it was the more enterprising spirits who came to the new world: men and women who were cramped by state religions, repressive political systems, and a still feudal economy. For instance, Perry Miller and T. H. Johnson (in *The Puritans*, 1937) attribute the Puritan movement to the revolt of a capable middle class against a feudal society.

In the new world this class, whether Puritan or pagan, Quaker or Moravian, Dutch or Scotch-Irish, tended to develop a social system in its own image. The cliché, "Protestant ethic," so beloved by contemporary intellectuals, is fundamentally not a religious position but an economic one. Franklin's maxims such as "Keep your shop and it will keep you" were based on the hard experience of his class.

To a considerable degree the emergence of the new American woman was the result of the class structure of early American society. The upper-class attitude of English society toward women is reflected in Chesterfield's advice to his son: "Women, then are only children of a larger growth. . . . A man of sense only trifles with them, plays with them, humours and flatters them, as he does with a sprightly forward child; but he neither consults them about, nor trusts them with serious matters. . . ."[20]

On the other hand, the middle-class Defoe wrote sympathetically, "How hard it is for the poor industrious woman to be up early and late, to sit in a cold shop, stall, or market all weathers, to carry heavy loads from one end of the town to the other, or to work from morning to night . . ." only to go home to a brutal husband.[21] As early as 1698 he blamed women's follies on inadequate education and stated "I would deny no sort of learning. A woman well bred and well taught, furnished with the additional accomplishments of knowledge and behaviour, is a creature without comparison. . . ."[22]

It was this middle-class view which increasingly became institutionalized in America. A hundred and sixty-two years later an ill-educated Poughkeepsie brewer, Matthew Vassar, endowed the first great women's college with the statement, "It occurred to me, that woman, having received from her creator the same intellectual constitution as man, has the same right as man to intellectual culture and development."[23]

As with all social phenomena there can be no beginning or terminal

dates. Cultural changes do not happen overnight, nor do they pro-
ceed at the same rate throughout a society. Thus although some
characteristics of the new American woman had begun to emerge in
the colonial period, the Revolution helped to define the American
as a separate species. For one thing the more traditionally minded
elements tended to be driven out or to expatriate themselves. Various
aristocratic usages fell into disrepute, especially those relating to
rank and unquestioned authority. A people who could reject a king
became less tolerant of a patriarchal family head. Thus the period
of the Revolution is a useful beginning date for this study.

For similar reasons World War I is a good terminal date. It
defined the end of the Victorian era, especially for American women.
For a decade or two the sexual taboos had been relaxing, but America's entry into the war became a kind of watershed. As never before
girls left home to get jobs; they learned from secondhand Freud of
the dangers of inhibitions; novelists became more daring in their
treatment of sex. Across the Atlantic women increasingly won
economic and political freedom. Higher education for women no
longer remained an American idiosyncrasy. The upper-class institution of chaperonage, which had never taken deep root in middle-class
American society, largely disappeared everywhere. Daisy Miller
would not have been uncomfortable in Europe after 1914. The
American girl was no longer a unique species.

Since World War I, the American woman may have seen out-
distanced by her European sisters. In his study of American feminism, William L. O'Neill states: "It is not just in socialist Russia that
women comprise a large part of the professions and hold high public
office, nor only in social democracies like Sweden; even in fairly
traditional countries like England women make a more important
contribution to the public welfare than in America. Yet not long
ago conditions were just the opposite."[24]

Therefore this discussion will be concerned with the period between the shot heard round the world and the guns of August. The
evidence suggests that before social customs in the western world
became homogenized, the American girl and woman during that
period was quite a person, fully justifying the opinion of foreign
observers that the American Eve was something new under the sun.

NOTES

1. Francis Wright, *Views of Society and Manners in America*, London, 1822, p. 391.
2. Ibid., p. 32.
3. Alexis de Tocqueville, *Democracy in America*, ed. and abridged by Richard D. Heffner (Mentor), New York, 1956, p. 234.
4. Ibid., pp. 246–47.
5. David Macrae, *The Americans at Home* (originally published 1871), New York, 1951, p. 41.
6. Ibid., p. 42.
7. James Bryce, *The American Commonwealth*, London and New York, 1889, II, 592.
8. Ibid., II, 598.
9. Rudyard Kipling, *American Notes*, Philadelphia, n.d., p. 38.
10. "The Limits of the Possible," in "The American Imagination," *Times Literary Supplement*, Nov. 6, 1959, p. 39.
11. Elizabeth F. Hoxie, "Mrs. Grundy Adopts Daisy Miller," *New England Quarterly*, XIX (1946), 474–84.
12. Leon Edel, Introduction to *The Portrait of a Lady*, New York, 1956, p. xi.
13. William Wasserstrom, *Heiress of All the Ages: Sex and Sentiment in the Genteel Tradition*, Minneapolis, 1959.
14. Page Smith, *Daughters of the Promised Land*, Boston and Toronto, 1970.
15. Ibid., p. 51.
16. Elizabeth A. Dexter, *Colonial Women of Affairs*, Boston and New York, 1924.
17. Ibid., p. 166.
18. *Adams Family Correspondence: December 1761–March 1778*, 2 vols., ed. Lyman H. Butterfield et al., Adams Papers Series, Cambridge, Mass., 1963, II, 238.
19. Dexter, pp. 41–46.
20. Lord Philip Chesterfield, *Letters to His Son Philip Stanhope*, London, 1774, Letter of Sept. 5, 1748.
21. Daniel Defoe, *Augustus Triumphans*, 1728.
22. Daniel Defoe, *An Essay on Projects*, 1697.
23. Benson J. Lossing, *Vassar College and Its Founder*, New York, 1867, p. 91.
24. William L. O'Neill, *Everyone Was Brave: The Rise and Fall of Feminism in America*, New York, 1969, pp. 349–50.

One

The Revolutionary Women

> ... whilst you are proclaiming peace and good will to Men,
> Emancipating all Nations, you insist upon retaining absolute
> power over Wives.
>
> Abigail Adams to John Adams, May 7, 1776

George Washington appreciated and enjoyed the company
of witty and intelligent women. The same cannot be said of most
novelists during the next century and a quarter. Whatever women
they may have met in life, they have, with rare exceptions, portrayed
a gallery of nincompoops, self-righteous prudes, and naive innocents.
Certainly the founding fathers were associated with a remarkable
constellation of women such as no novelist of that era or later ever
discovered in America. It is small wonder that at Martha Washington's afternoon parties, the president devoted himself to the ladies.

One of them, Abigail Adams, is among the most remarkable
women in our history, far more interesting than her able but can-
tankerous husband.

In 1776 when John was attending the Continental Congress in
Philadelphia Abigail wrote him apropos of the pending Declaration
of Independence:

> I long to hear that you have declared an independency—and by
> the way in the new Code of Laws which I suppose it will be neces-
> sary for you to make I desire you would Remember the Ladies, and
> be more generous and favourable to them than your ancestors. Do
> not put such unlimited power into the hands of Husbands. Remem-
> ber that all Men would be tyrants if they could. If perticular* care
> and attention is not paid to the Ladies we are determined to forment

---

* Abigail's spelling was scarcely more erratic than that of her Harvard educated
husband, who often wrote *colledge* and frequently *Phyladelphia*.

a Rebellion, and will not hold ourselves bound by any Laws in which we have no voice, or Representation.

Here for the first time was the note which was to echo for over a hundred years in the demands for woman's rights: the principles of the Declaration of Independence should logically apply also to women. Abigail continued:

> That your Sex are Naturally Tyrannical is a truth so thoroughly established to admit no dispute, but such of you as wish to be happy willingly give up the harsh title of Master for the more endearing one of Friend. Why then, not put it out of the power of the vicious and the Lawless to use us with cruelty and indignity with impunity. Men of Sense in all Ages abhor those customs which treat us only as Vassals of your Sex....[1]

In answer to this, John, whose frequent letters—he sometimes wrote her twice a day—were usually affectionate, became harsh: "As to your extraordinary Code of Laws, I cannot but laugh. . . ." He went on to speak of the loosening bonds of government, of the disobedience of children and apprentices, and added:

> But your letter was the first Intimation that another Tribe more numerous and powerful—This is rather too coarse a Compliment but you are so saucy, I won't blot it out.
> Depend upon it, we know better than to repeal our Masculine systems. Altho they are in full Force, you know they are little more than Theory. We dare not exert our full Power in its full Latitude. We are obligated to go fair and softly, and in Practice you know we are the subjects. We have only the Name of Masters.[2]

Abigail was not taken in by this ancient masculine gambit. To Mercy Warren she said that John had been very "sausy" in return for the list of female grievances she had sent. "I think I will get you to join me in a petition to Congress." The traditional English laws were harsh to women in giving "such unlimited power to the Husband to use his wife ill . . . I believe I even threatened a Rebellion in case we were not considered, and assured him we would not hold ourselves bound by any Laws in which we had neither a voice, nor representation."

For the first time in her extensive correspondence she criticized

John: ". . . I will tell him I have only been making trial of the
Disinterestedness of his Virtue, and when weigh'd in the balance have
found it wanting."[3]

A few days after her remarks to Mercy Warren, Abigail, in a letter
to John, underscored this view. After giving him a report on the
political situation in Massachusetts she added: "I can not say I think
you very generous to the Ladies, for whilst you are proclaiming
peace and good will to Men, Emancipating all Nations, you insist
upon retaining absolute power over Wives." She warned that arbitrary power was the kind most likely to be overthrown "notwithstanding all your wise Laws and Maxims we have it in our power not
only to free ourselves but to subdue our Masters, and without
violence throw both your natural and legal authority at our feet—
'Charm by accepting, by submitting sway/Yet have our Humour
most when we obey.' "[4]

Two days later, after a parting shot, she agreed to drop the subject.
Knowing John's concern for the development of the sciences in
America she quoted from Joseph Wharton's *An Essay on the Genius
and Writings of Pope* a statement on the need for freedom if sciences
are to attain their full growth.[5]

John in turn became conciliatory: "I think you shine as a States-
woman, of late as well as a Farmeress. Pray where do you get your
Maxims of State, they are very apropos."[6] The fact was that despite
inflation, preparation for war, and the fighting in and around Boston,
Abigail was running the farm at nearby Braintree very well. By
September of 1776 she said that so many men were engaged in
privateering that the women might have to reap the harvests. "I am
willing to do my part. I believe I could gather Corn and Husk it, but I
should make a poor figure at digging potatoes." The following spring
Mercy's husband, General Warren, told John Adams that the farm
had never looked better and that Abigail "was like to outshine all
the Farmers."[7]

The description of General James Warren as Mercy's husband
is proper. He is so listed in *Webster's Biographical Dictionary*. It
is not that he was a nonentity: after all he was a political leader in
Massachusetts, paymaster general of the Continental army (1775–
76), member of the Navy board for the eastern department (1776–

81) and in the 1790s three times member of the governor's council. Nevertheless Mercy Warren (1728–1814) overshadows him as she does her able patriot brother, James Otis. It is only fair to record that a head injury cut short Otis's career; he gradually went mad. Although she was sixteen years older than Abigail, the two were kindred spirits. Their long friendship was not ruptured until late in their lives when the Warrens became supporters of Jefferson.

Like so many other able American women, Mercy had the support of her father and brother in gaining an education. Colonel James Otis, the presiding judge at the district court in Barnstable, kept his house open for friends and neighbors who came to discuss politics. The children were not excluded from the debates around the huge fireplace. Because Colonel Otis had no high opinion of the local school, he sent his two oldest boys and his daughter Mercy to be tutored by his brother-in-law, the Reverend Jonathan Russell. Russell, a Yale graduate, had a library containing Pope, Dryden, Milton, Shakespeare, and Raleigh's *History of the World*. Mercy read them all with enthusiasm while her brother was laboring through Homer and Virgil.[8] When James Jr. got to Harvard he became enthusiastic over John Locke, whose philosophy was to influence him throughout life. James interested his sister in Locke.

When Otis began the practice of law in Plymouth, he resumed his Harvard friendship with a young farmer and merchant, James Warren. On visits home Otis took Warren with him. Warren enjoyed the company of intellectual women and Mercy fell in love with him. After a long courtship they were married in 1754 when Mercy was twenty-six. For three years there were no children, then five boys within nine years. James Warren was well-to-do and had a good library. He and Mercy read books together and she kept up a literary correspondence with her brother. Warren bought a fine house where they spent the rest of their lives. In 1785 Abigail Adams described the grand salon in the house she and John occupied in Auteuil, France, as the finest she knew except for that of "General Warren's Hall."

Mercy, Abigail, and John kept up a voluminous three-way correspondence, much of it devoted to politics. John, who admired Mercy's neoclassic verse, suggested that she "describe the late frolic among the sea-nymphs"—meaning the Boston Tea Party. "I wish to see a late glorious event celebrated by a certain political pen, which has no equal that I know of in this country." She took the suggestion, wrote *The Squabble of the Sea Nymphs*, and sent it to John for criticism. Along with it she included some couplets about the abilities of women:

> For females have their influence over kings,
> Nor wives nor Mistresses were useless things,
> E'en to the Gods of ancient Homer's page,
> Could they neglect the sexes sage advice. . . .[9]

Adams compared the poem to *The Rape of the Lock*; probably it was he who sent it to the Boston *Gazette*.

Although she had never seen a play, Mercy Warren was an admirer of Molière, whose plays she had defended to Abigail, who thought the representation of human nature was too harsh. With her gift for satire Mercy anonymously published her first play, *The Adulateur: A Tragedy as It Is Now Acted in Upper Servia*. It was not much as a play, but it was immediately popular. The victim, the unpopular Tory governor Thomas Hutchinson, was represented as Rapido, a nickname Sam Adams gleefully picked up. An unknown writer added two acts covering the Boston Massacre. A year later Mercy wrote another play, *The Defeat*, again with Hutchinson as villain. It demonstrates the extent to which women like Mercy Warren and Abigail Adams were taken into the councils of the leaders of the Revolution. Franklin in London had got hold of Hutchinson's letters, which seemed to show that the rebels were only a minor faction. Franklin sent them to Thomas Cushing of Boston, a colleague of General Warren's. Warren took the letters to Plymouth, where his associates assembled to read them. Mrs. Warren's play and the publication of the letters helped to finish Hutchinson's career in America.[10]

Her third play, *The Group*, was published as a pamphlet in Boston, April 3, 1775, while that city was occupied by the troops of General Gage. The Group were the Tory leaders under such names as Sylla (General Gage); Brigadier Hate-All (Timothy Ruggles); his companions Hum Humbug, Esq.; Sir Sparrow Spendall; Hector Mushroom; Beau Trumps, Simple Sapling, Esq.; Crusty Crowbar, Esq.; Scriblerius Fribble. As Katherine Anthony says, it is not a play but a conversation piece. The descriptive names suggest Mercy's acquaintance with seventeenth and eighteenth century drama. She sent her unfinished manuscript to her husband who sent it on to John Adams in Philadelphia where John rushed it into print. He asked Warren to send his "regards to a certain Lady, tell her the God Almighty (I use a bold style) has intrusted her with Powers for The Good of the World, which, in the Cause of his Providence, he bestows on few of the human race."[11]

It was after Washington took command of the Continental Army in July 1775 and established his headquarters at Watertown that the Washingtons and Warrens became intimate. In that same month Abigail met Washington for the first time. She described him to John: "Dignity with ease, and complacency, the Gentleman and the Soldier look agreeably blenden in him. Modesty marks every line and feature of his face." She quoted Dryden:

> Mark his Majestick fabrick! he's a temple
> Sacred by birth, and built by hands divine
> His Souls the Deity that lodges there.
> Nor is the pile unworthy of the God.[12]

Martha Washington soon joined her husband at the Watertown headquarters. Despite her fear of the trip she had come by coach from Mount Vernon. Somewhat to her surprise the journey had been a triumphant procession. At Philadelphia the smartly uniformed First City Troop escorted her into the city. The patriot society proposed a ball, but after Sam Adams objected, Martha agreed that the expense should be spared. At Newark a mounted escort took her across the Hudson. All along the way she was greeted with pealing bells and cheering crowds. When she got to Watertown, she felt a bit strange among people of the North, but quickly became at home. There was a circle of officers' wives: Mrs. Thomas Mifflin from Pennsylvania; Mrs. Morgan, wife of the Philadelphia physician who had been appointed Director—General of the army hospitals; Mrs. Horatio Gates, a fellow Virginian whose mannish riding habit raised eyebrows in New England. General Greene's wife Kitty drove over from her husband's headquarters two miles away. She showed Martha the new baby christened George Washington Greene.

Washington's secretary, Colonel Harrison, discovering that Martha wrote a better hand than the General's aide, Colonel Baylor, set her to making copies of General Orders and letter-book entries of letters to Congress and the Provincial governors.[13] Washington ran an office like a modern business executive: everything was copied and filed except the confidential letters he wrote in his own hand.

Although Plymouth was nearly forty miles from Watertown, Mercy Warren came up frequently despite her dislike of riding through the camps at night. On the way she always stopped off at Braintree to visit with Abigail Adams, who wrote John that she wished she could as easily visit her husband "as Mercy can go to Watertown."[14]

At headquarters Mercy was delighted with Martha Washington's outgoing reception of her as if they were longtime friends. Apparently the officers' ladies were welcome at camp. The Washingtons and Warrens frequently exchanged dinner invitations. George, who got up at dawn, usually had his business out of the way by the then fashionable dinner hour of two. During the morning the women were treated with oranges and a glass of wine, then joined the men for dinner. With the women Washington, although rather formal, was always courtly and lighthearted. He believed that wine brought cheerfulness to his table. After dinner the women retired while the men discussed business.[15]

An important item for discussion was the almost complete lack of artillery. Lieutenant Henry Knox, the bookseller from Boston, had made cannon his hobby; he loved artillery almost as much as he did his plump bride, Lucy. Although he weighed two hundred and fifty pounds, he suggested an expedition to get the captured cannon from Fort Ticonderoga two hundred miles away. In a trek from November to late January, Knox and his brother William rounded up horses, oxen, sledges, and scows by means of which they transported sixty tons of artillery and supplies over territory which often lacked roads. A scow sank; the largest cannon broke through the ice, but they fished the gun out and went on. However, in the midst of all this

Henry, recently made a colonel, did not forget Lucy. At the start of the return trip he wrote that he expected to see her in two weeks: "Had I power to transport myself to you, how eagerly rapid would be my flight. It makes me smile to think how I should look—like a tennis ball bowled over the steep." [16]

When he finally got back to Cambridge, the ebullient and pregnant Lucy joined him and the circle of officers' wives. Knox's biographer, North Callahan, describes her as a young lady of high intellectual attainments. In any case it was her love of reading which had brought her to Henry's bookstore. Her Tory father, Thomas Flucker, royal secretary of the Providence of Massachusetts Bay, had originally forbidden the match, but once the couple had married, he used his influence to get Knox an offer of a commission in the British Army. Lucy's brother was already a British lieutenant. However, Henry had become friendly with Nathaniel Greene and Paul Revere. Before the Battle of Lexington, Knox was already under suspicion. General Gage gave orders that Henry was not to leave Boston without permission. [17] Like her husband, Lucy became an ardent patriot. Henry got her away to Worcester where she stayed until joining the other women at Watertown.

Under Washington's orders Colonel Knox and General John Thomas set up the cannon and mortars behind improvised barricades on Dorchester Heights, too high for the British guns to reach. In March the American artillery blasted Howe's army out of Boston.*

Mercy Warren rode over to see the evacuation of "women, children, soldiers, sailors, governors, councilors, flatterers, statesmen, and pimps huddled promiscuously either in fishing boats or Royal barks, whichever offered the first means of escape to the panic stricken multitude." [18] She felt compassion for the frightened loyalists, but Washington, preparing his triumphal entry, remarked that "One or two of them have done what a great number ought to have done long ago—committed suicide." [19] A few weeks before this, Abigail had written to John: "I heartily wish every Tory was Extirpated [from] America, they are continually by secret means undermining and injuring our cause." [20]

---

* General Howe had succeeded General Gage.

After the capture of Boston, Washington set out with the army for New York where he thought Howe might land. The women scattered: Martha and Mrs. Gates followed their husbands to New York; Kitty Greene went home with her baby to Coventry, Rhode Island; the Philadelphia wives went back to Pennsylvania,[21] and Colonel Knox took his protesting Lucy to stay with friends at Fairfield, Connecticut, where she bore her first child.[22]

Shortly after the British evacuation Boston was struck by a smallpox epidemic. Mercy and James Warren entered a Boston hospital for innoculation and Abigail Adams brought her children from Braintree for the same purpose. Unlike the vaccination with cowpox to be introduced by Jenner a quarter of a century later, innoculation, using smallpox virus, was a three-weeks ordeal. From Philadelphia, John wrote that he was unhappy not to be with his family and told Abigail to spare no expense.[23] Both the Warrens and the Adams family were undergoing the ordeal when the Declaration of Independence was signed and broadcast through the colonies.

After returning to Plymouth, Mercy used her experiences during Washington's capture of Boston to write *The Blockheads: or the Affrighted Officers: A Farce; Boston. Printed in Queen Street.* Mercy had not visited a military encampment with closed ears: she pictured the British soldiers hemmed in Boston by Washington's army and afraid to venture out. One soldier remarked, "I would rather s--t my breeches than go without [outside] these forts to ease myself." With eighteenth-century frankness, she represented the maid Dorsa telling her mistress about a suitor: "One thing I would mention (excuse my boldness) this Lord Dapper labors under the disgrace of *inability*." The lady answers that he may still "serve for a cully to fleece for my indulgences and fashion." "That he may do," says Dorsa, "but for anything else . . . I had rather marry my old grandfather."

Picturing the Tories' flight from Boston, Mercy has Simple advise his wife Jemima against the voyage: "I shall pity your modesty, when what is in will come out, perhaps at both ends. Pray, my dear, was you ever seasick?" To which Jemima replies, "I like no such coarse phrases; if I had fifty ends, my modesty would forbid anything from coming out of either. I know how to behave myself and keep all ends safe." Understandably the colonial troops roared with laughter.

In their letters back and forth Mercy and Abigail had discussed politics and the military situation. In 1774 Mercy wrote a satiric letter to Abigail on the theme that women's narrower sphere precluded them from the masculine hazard of making fools of themselves in public.

> If the Mental Faculties of the Female are not Concealed in the Obscure Retreats of the Bed Chamber or the kitchen . . . Whereas Man is Generally Called out to the full display of his Abilities but how often do they Exhibit the most Mortifying instances of Neglected Opportunities Advantages of what is Called a Liberal Education, as Barren of Culture and as Void of Every useful acquirement as the most Triffling untutored Girl.[24]

Two years later, just after she got over the innoculation, Abigail took up the subject of women's education. A few months earlier John had complained, "I wish I understood French as well as you . . . I feel the Want of Education every Day—particularly of that Language. I pray, My dear, that you would not suffer your Sons or your Daughter, ever to feel a similar Pain." It was to be over a hundred years before men's colleges offered regular instruction in modern languages. In August Abigail picked up the theme:

> If you complain of the neglect of Education in sons, What shall I say with regard to daughters, who every day experience the want of it. With regard to the Education of my own children, I find myself soon out of my depth, and destitute and deficient in every part of Education.
>
> I most sincerely wish that some more liberal plan be laid for the Benefit of the rising Generation, and that our new constitution may be distinguished for Learning and Virtue. If we mean to have Heroes, Statesmen and Philosophers, we should have learned women. . . . If much depends as is allowed upon the early Education of youth and the first principles which are instilled take the deepest root, great benefit must arise from the literary accomplishments in women.[25]

It was a doctrine which women would repeat for many years. In 1860 Matthew Vassar restated it in founding the first heavily endowed women's college. John Adams, possibly a little ashamed of his harsh reply to Abigail's woman's rights plea, hastened to say he agreed with her about education. The biographies of illustrious men usually showed "Mother or Wife or Sister to whose Instigation a great Part of their merit is to be ascribed. A smart Wife would have put Howe in Possession of Philadelphia, a long Time ago."[26]

There is a Philadelphia tradition that once Sir William occupied that city, a smart, or at least attractive, mistress so beguiled him that he dilly dallied about chasing Washington's ragged army. In 1776 Francis Hopkinson celebrated an occasion when the rebels launched powder kegs against the anchored British fleet. During the uproar:

> Sir William he, snug as a flea,
>   Lay all this time a snoring.
> Nor dreamed of harm as he lay warm,
>   In bed with Mrs. Loring.[27]

When they could, the officers' wives joined their husbands. Martha Washington, Kitty Greene, and Lucy Knox went to New York until the American army was driven out. Martha went back to Mount Vernon for a time, then joined her husband at the Morristown headquarters. Kitty Greene and Lucy Knox were kept away by childbirth. As a group, the Revolutionary leaders and their wives were relatively young people. In that summer at Morristown, George and Martha were only forty-five. Colonel Bland, bringing his Virginia cavalry also brought his lively young wife. Writing to Fanny Randolph, Mrs. Bland said, "Now let me speak of our noble and agreeable Commander (for he commands both sexes). . . . We visit them twice or three times a week by particular invitation. He is generally busy in the forenoon—but from dinner to night he is free for all company. His worthy lady seems to be in perfect felicity while she is by the side of her *Old Man*, as she calls him." Mrs. Bland went on to say that when the General threw off the hero he became a chatty and agreeable companion "downright impudent sometimes—such impudence, Fanny, as you and I like. . . ."[28]

According to Martha's biographer, Elswyth Thane, Martha was undisturbed by the various young women who fell half in love with her husband. Nor did she, like many military wives, try to wear his badge of rank. In Morristown some aristocratic ladies put on their finest rainment to visit "Lady Washington." They found her wearing a checked apron and knitting stockings for George, an activity she continued during the call. She talked much about the poor soldiers, especially the sick ones.[29]

When Washington was at Valley Forge Martha made a winter journey to arrive early in February and share her husband's cramped little house. Baron Von Steuben's French secretary, Pierre Etienne Du Ponceau, wrote of the ladies there:

> In the midst of all our distress, there were some bright sides to the picture which Valley Forge exhibited at that time. Mrs. Washington had the courage to follow her husband to that dismal abode, and other ladies also graced the scene. Among them was the lady of General Greene, a handsome, elegant and accomplished woman. Her dwelling was the resort of foreign officers because she spoke the French language and was well versed in French literature. They often met at each other's quarters, and sometimes at General Washington's where the evenings were spent over a cup of tea or coffee. There were no levees, or formal soirees, no dancing or playing, or amusement of any kind except singing. Every gentleman or lady who could sing was called in turn for a song. . . ."[30]

He could have added that it was all very American: husbands spending their evenings with their wives, an aristocratic Virginia commander-in-chief with a wife who knit his stockings and a New England Quaker general whose wife knew French literature—all of them drinking coffee and taking turns to sing. The New World had created a new breed: men and women who associated on more equal terms than in any previous society.

It was not only the upper-class women who had roles in the new Revolutionary society; those of all ranks participated. Sarah Bradlee Fulton, who lived to be 94, was called "Mother of the Boston Tea Party." There was of course Mary McCauley (Molly Pitcher), who carried water to the soldiers during the Battle of Monmouth, and who, when her husband collapsed from the heat, manned his cannon. She was honored by Washington and in 1822 granted an annuity by the state of Pennsylvania. In South Carolina, Dorcas Richardson, who lived to be 93, persuaded her husband to forego the pardon and promotion offered for loyalism. In North Carolina, Sarah Dickinson, mother of nine, captured five Tories and saw the British in revenge lay waste to her plantation. She died at 96.[31]

Some Boston women took matters into their own hands. Abigail Adams described to John the occasion when a hundred women with a cart descended on a profiteering merchant who was demanding six shillings a pound for coffee. When he refused to give up the key to his storeroom one of the amazons tossed him into the cart, where he was kept until he gave up the key. Then they dumped him out, opened the storehouse, and distributed the coffee.[32]

In 1775 twenty-two-year-old Deborah Champion, accompanied by a slave, rode from New London, Connecticut, to Cambridge carrying important dispatches to Washington. Her father, General Champion, unable to leave his post, had asked her if she would undertake the mission. At one point she rode all night. She was stopped at the British lines but somehow got through anyway.[33]

As their descendants were to do in the Civil War, the women of the Revolution collected funds, nursed the sick and wounded, made clothes for the army, and ran farms while their husbands were away. In Philadelphia the Marquis de Chastellux saw 2,200 shirts which the women had made for the Continental Army.[34] These represented not only sewing but also spinning and weaving.

However, not all the ladies were self-sacrificing patriots. While Martha Washington at Valley Forge was mending clothes, and taking her meals in a log dining room adjoining the cramped little house, the Tory girls of Philadelphia were enjoying the most brilliant social season that city had ever known. The young British officers, products of a system where rank depended on wealth and family, gave weekly balls at the City Tavern and frequently at other inns. They reopened the Old South Street Theatre where with the help of a few actresses they put on a series of farces, comedies, and some tragedies. But the crowning entertainment was a great fete, the Mischianza, in May 1778. Major John André, one of the leading spirits, described the affair. There was a parade of warships and boats and a tournament between the knights of the Blended Rose and those of the Burning Mountain, followed by a ball. It began with a display of rockets and bursting balloons. The ballroom was lined with eighty-five mirrors festooned with flowers and silk scarves. There were places for four hundred people. Each group of knights championed a number of ladies representing the aristocracy of Philadelphia.

Oddly enough two ladies of the Blended Rose and two of the Burning Mountain married Revolutionary officers. However, one of the latter was Benedict Arnold, whose defection was due in part to an expensive and possibly Anglophile wife, Peggy Shippin. There is evidence that Judge Shippen had forbidden the three Shippen girls places in the pageant, and that they had been bitterly disappointed.[35]

Naturally the Whigs disapproved of this lavish display. The next year James Warren wrote to John Adams of the vulgar display of Boston profiteers: "I am still drudging away at the Navy Board for a morsel of bread while others, and among them fellows who would have cleaned my shoes five years ago, have amassed fortunes and are riding in chariots. . . ."[36] Mercy Warren caricatured them in another short piece: *The Motley Assembly: A Farce, Published for the Entertainment of the Curious.* Her sharpest thrusts are against the snobbish ladies of fashion, although the greatest snob is Mrs. Bubbles's servant maid Tabitha. A Mrs. Flourish refers to Washington's men as the "rebel" army and to the patrons of the new Republican Assembly as "Cattle." When an American officer proposes that each of the ladies should make two shirts a week for the Continental soldiers, the ladies scorn them. Mercy's biographer, Katherine Anthony, points out that Mercy's target is very much the Whig *nouveau riche.*[37]

One thing that is evident in this account of some important women of the American Revolution is their close association with fathers, brothers, and especially husbands. Unlike most societies of the era, that of eighteenth-century America did not confine women to a kind of social and intellectual harem. Men encouraged their daughters to get an education, often teaching them themselves. Fathers and husbands often joined with their daughters and wives in reading serious books, especially histories. The women were permitted to listen in or often participate in political discussions. The letters of the Adamses and Warrens are filled with politics.

As has been noted, John Adams encouraged Mercy Warren to do her political satires. In the 1780s her son Winslow got her interested in writing blank verse tragedies: *The Ladies of Castile* and *The Sack of Rome*. Despite their historical subject matter Mercy embodied her libertarian views. In *The Ladies*, the heroine, wife of one patriot and sister of another, defies tyranny and appropriates church treasure to pay the people's army.[38]

Mercy again had masculine encouragement in her most important literary project, her three volume *History of the Rise, Progress and Termination of the American Revolution*. After she finished the main part in 1791, it lay dormant until James Warren encouraged her to continue it. Since her eyesight was failing, he acted as her amanuensis. In the third volume she extended the account to include the post-Revolutionary period. The work was published in 1805 when she was 77. John Adams, whose views were by then considerably to the right of Mercy's, did not get around to reading it until 1807. Sensitive as a boil to her restrained criticism of himself, he wrote her an angry letter which led to a two-months exchange of bitter recrimination—ten letters from him and six from her. She ended her last: "There must be some acknowledgement of your injurious treatment or some advance to conciliation, to which my mind is ever open, before I can again feel that respect and affection to Mr. Adams which once existed in the bosom of—*Mercy Warren*."[39]

It must be evident from the foregoing account that at least some women in the latter part of the eighteenth century were closely associated with their men in war and politics. What may not have appeared in the discussion so far is the shared love, the warm sexual attraction between so many of the partners. Even before they were married, John and Abigail were exchanging provocative letters. Addressing her as "Miss Adorable" John asserted his "Right to draw upon you for the Kisses as I have given two or three Millions at least. ..." And she wrote of seeing two sweethearts greet each other formally: "Upon my word I believe they were glad to see each other. A tender meeting. I was affected by it. And thought whether Lysander could thus coldly meet his Diana, and whether Diana could with no more Emotion receive Lysander. I dare answer for a different meeting on her part were She under no restraint."[40]

On another occasion when he reproved her for sitting with crossed legs she answered, "I think that a gentleman has no business to concern himself about the Leggs of a Lady."[41]

A dozen years after their marriage she wrote that she had been rereading his letters from Philadelphia

> sometimes with a mixture of paine, sometimes my Heart would bound and palpitate with the pleasing Idea, with the purest affection I have held you to my Bosom till my whole Soul has dissolved in Tenderness and my pen fallen from my Hand.
>
> How often do I reflect with pleasure that I hold in possession a Heart Equally warm with my own, and full as Susceptible of the Tenderest impressions, and Who even now whilst he is reading here, feels all I describe. . . .
>
> Adieu my Dearest Friend, soon, soon return to your most affectionate
>
> > Portia.[42]

Forty-six years after the Warrens' marriage, James, caged up with the gout, wrote his wife, addressing her as usual "My dear Mrs. Warren:"

> My foot grew better the day you left us. I will not say miraculously, but certainly in a manner I can't account for but by supposing it the effects of the prayers of a saint who loves me. . . .
>
> I suppose you are busily engaged in the business of an author of great abilities, discernment, and judgment, yet diffident and therefore hunting for criticism and advice, and correcting proofs with a trembling heart. If you had half the good opinion of yourself that I have of you, you certainly would not feel half the anxiety you do now. I hope the attention and amusements you meet will make your journey agreeable.
>
> Here the weather is fine and all nature in bloom. I long to pluck a rose and gather a plate of strawberries for my little angel. But the distance is too great. I must be content to hope she is happy without the variegated country beauties of this very fine season, which I long to describe but dare not attempt till you send me your poetic mantle. . . .
>
> > Your affectionate husband
> > J. Warren

The next day he added a paragraph—

> Just got from the farm the fragrance of white clover. Vegetation
> of every kind in all glory invites you home. If I had a better foot
> I should have a fine ramble. . . . If we had pearls or rubies and
> diamonds, we would give them to you; we have strawberries and
> cream at your service.
>
> Adieu. For why should I attempt to express the full of my affec-
> tion for you? [43]

North Callahan, the biographer of Henry Knox, represents his
marriage to Lucy as a life-long love affair. In 1792 while he was in
Philadelphia as Secretary of War, Henry wrote to his wife, who was
in Boston, saying that his evenings could not be any cause of jealousy.
"They are stupid indeed. I drive out pretty often, come home, read
the evening paper, then go to a solitary and painful bed—painful from
the reflection that the companion of my soul is at a distance and
that I am deprived of the blessed solace of her arms."[44] The logistics
of the longed-for embrace are a bit puzzling in view of the fact that
Henry then weighed 280 pounds and Lucy 250. They had been
married eighteen years.

Similarly Martha Washington's biographer, Elswyth Thane, and
at least one biographer of her husband (James Flexner) picture a
deep and abiding love. Martha was a far less dynamic person than
Abigail Adams or Mercy Warren, but she conquered her natural
timidity to journey to whatever headquarters her husband occupied.
To a friend at home she admitted, "I confess I shudder every time
I hear the sound of a gun. . . . To me that never see anything of war,
the preparations are very terrible indeed, but I endeavor to keep my
fears to myself as well as I can." Mercy Warren wrote of her that
"The complacency of her manners speaks at once the benevolence
of her heart, candor and gentleness qualify her to soften the hours of
private life, or to sweeten the cares of the hero. . . ." As Flexner says,
"George Washington . . . had his enemies; no evidence exists that
Martha ever made a single one."[45] George's feelings about her are
revealed in his letter of June 23, 1775, from Philadelphia:

My Dearest

As I am within a few minutes of leaving this city, I could not think of departing from it without dropping you a line, especially as I do not know whether it may be in my power to write you again till I get to the camp at Boston. I go fully trusting in that Providence which has been more bountiful to me than I deserve, and in full confidence of a happy meeting with you sometime in the fall. I have no time to add more, as I am surrounded with company to take leave of me. I retain an unalterable affection for you which neither time or distance can change.[46]

NOTES

1. *Adams Family Correspondence*, I, 370.
2. Ibid., I, 382.
3. Ibid., I, 398–99.
4. Ibid., I, 402.
5. Ibid., I, 404.
6. Ibid., I, 420.
7. Ibid., I, 135; II, 38.
8. Katherine Anthony, *First Lady of the Revolution*, New York, 1958, pp. 29–32.
9. *Adams Family Correspondence*, I, 101.
10. Anthony, pp. 85–87.
11. Ibid., p. 94, 95.
12. *Adams Family Correspondence*, I, 246.
13. Elswyth Thane, *Washington's Lady*, New York, 1960, p. 112.
14. Anthony, p. 97.
15. James Thomas Flexner, *George Washington in the American Revolution, 1775–1783*, Boston and Toronto, 1968, pp. 59–60.
16. North Callahan, *Henry Knox: General Washington's General*, New York and Toronto, 1958, pp. 39–59.
17. Ibid., pp. 25–31.
18. Anthony, p. 103.
19. Ibid.
20. *Adams Family Correspondence*, I, 352.
21. Thane, p. 125.
22. Callahan, p. 62.
23. *Adams Family Correspondence*, II, 50.
24. Ibid., I, 182.
25. Ibid., II, 94.
26. Ibid., II, 306.
27. "The Battle of the Kegs."
28. Thane, p. 159.
29. Ibid., p. 158.
30. Ibid., p. 183.
31. Mary A. Beard, ed., *America through Women's Eyes*, New York, 1937, pp. 55–56.

32. *Adams Family Correspondence*, I, 295.
33. Beard, pp. 73–76.
34. Page Smith, *Daughters of the Promised Land*, p. 67.
35. Ellis Paxon Oberholtzer, *Philadelphia: A History of the City and Its People*, Philadelphia, n.d., I, 274–76.
36. Anthony, p. 112.
37. Ibid., pp. 113–14.
38. Ibid., pp. 148–49.
39. Ibid., pp. 202–4, 216.
40. *Adams Family Correspondence*, I, 2, 41.
41. Ibid., I, 47.
42. Ibid., II, 112–13.
43. Anthony, pp. 164–65.
44. Callahan, p. 289.
45. Flexner, pp. 59–60, 282.
46. Ibid., p. 20.

Two

The Republican Court

Sir, your country produces exceedingly fine women.

An English lord to John Adams

The generation which produced *Common Sense*, *The Crisis*, the Declaration of Independence, the Constitution, *The Federalist*, and *The Autobiography of Benjamin Franklin* wrote no novels of remotely comparable quality. For this there were a number of reasons. Freneau lists some of them in *To an Author* (1788). Although he was speaking of poets, the same limitations apply to novelists: the lack of a school of writers, the paucity of critics, the rationalistic and materialistic temper of the age:

> On these bleak climes by Fortune thrown,
> Where rigid Reason rules alone,
> Where lovely Fancy has no sway,
> Nor magic forms about us play,
> Nor nature takes her summer hue,
> Tell me, what has the muse to do?
>
> An age employed in edging steel
> Can no poetic raptures feel;
> Nor solitude's attracting power,
> No leisure of the noonday hour,
> No shaded stream, no quiet grove
> Can this fantastic century move.

In addition the early writers of fiction were under the baleful influence of Richardson and the Gothic novel. In the 1770s novels had become a popular item in Henry Knox's bookstore. They were by English writers but the titles indicate the Richardsonian genre: *Delicate*, *Distress*, *Fatal Step*, *Henrietta*, *Married Victim*, *Rosanna*, and the *Adventures of an Actress*. Knox advertised Brooke's *Fool of Quality* thus: "In this book, the heart is deeply interested; the incidents are wonderful and surprising; a reader of sensibility cannot help paying a tear to many a scene in this agreeable and romantic performance."[1] Knox obviously knew that the feminine readers would be more interested in sentiment than in Brooke's passages on education, social justice, and woman's rights.

In his study *The Sentimental Novel in America, 1789–1860* Herbert Brown states, "Richardson was a household name wherever novels were discussed in the Colonies." After discussing the many American imitations, Brown adds, "The most striking manifestation of Richardson's influence is to be seen in the appalling popularity of the seduction motif with its seemingly limitless possibilities for sentimental and emotional scenes."[2]

Thus what is usually considered the first American novel, William Hill Brown's *The Power of Sympathy* (1789), is a story of seduction, near incest, rape, and suicide. A young man, learning that his sweetheart is really his half-sister, shoots himself, leaving a copy of Goethe's *The Sorrows of Young Werther* on the table beside him. A subplot tells of a scoundrel who seduces his wife's sister, who then kills herself with poison. Two years later Susanna Rowson published *Charlotte Temple*, a novel which eventually went through 160 editions.[3] In it a young English girl is lured to New York on a promise of marriage. Her lover seduces and deserts her. She dies in childbirth. Hannah Foster's *The Coquette* (1797) tells of the seduction of a rebellious, pleasure-loving girl by a glamorous military man, described by Wagenknecht as "a not unskillful pastiche of Lovelace."[4] In the sentimental tradition she also dies. All three novels are full of moral preachments.

It might seem that the heroines are far removed from the clear-eyed virtuous American girls described by foreign travellers, but both *Charlotte Temple* and *The Coquette* are based on contemporary scandals: the first on a tragedy of the Apthorp family of Boston, the second on the case of Elizabeth Whitman, daughter of a Yale trustee. Elizabeth's seducer has been identified in rumor with either Aaron Burr or Pierpont Edwards, the son of the hell-fire preacher, Jonathan Edwards. The grave of the reputed "Charlotte" is in Trinity Churchyard, New York, and Elizabeth's is in Danvers, Massachu-setts.[5]

In his *Travels in North America* Chastellux records meeting two unmarried mothers, neither of whom was ostracized. In fact he wrote, "With them [the Americans] vice is so foreign and so rare that the danger of example is almost nonexistent; so that a mistake of this nature is regarded as would be an accidental illness."[6] However class mores must be taken into consideration: one of these girls was an innkeeper's daughter abandoned by a man she expected to marry; the other was a poverty-stricken girl befriended by the kindly land-lady of an inn. Furthermore the first girl's penitent lover returned and married her.

Obviously because of their likeness to Richardson's heroines none of these girls, as portrayed in *Charlotte Temple* and *The Coquette*, is characteristically American. The first real attempt to represent the American Eve is Charles Brockden Brown's Constantia Dudley in his *Ormond* (1799). Like Brown's other novels, *Ormond* is a confused mixture of plots and subplots, and is filled with unlikely co-incidences, mysterious characters, and melodramatic events. Brown's reputation as a novelist rests to a considerable degree on his early appearance on the American literary scene. But however faulty as a craftsman, Brown is interesting because of his originality. Long before American studies became respectable in academic circles, Brown was praised by a variety of writers, among them Thomas Hood, Godwin, Hazlett, Poe, Cooper, Dana, and Hawthorne. Brown was a serious novelist, very much concerned with philosophical and social questions.

Thus *Ormond* is in part a fictional embodiment of ideas on the rights of women which he had developed three years before in *Alcuin: A Dialogue*. Whether or not this is in debt to Godwin's *Political Justice* (1793) and Mary Wollstonecraft's *Rights of Wom-en*, it grows out of the same intellectual tradition. The dialogue is between a priggish schoolmaster, Alcuin, and the widowed Mrs. Carter, a Philadelphia blue-stocking. As a rule Mrs. Carter takes the more radical positions. She goes beyond Mary Wollstonecraft in arguing for political and economic equality for women. Like Defoe she condemns the kind of education provided for women: one class is trained to be household slaves, the other, upper class instructed in the arts of the coquette. When Alcuin argues that educating men and women together would be injurious to female delicacy, Mrs. Carter answers that separate education which follows divergent paths causes relations between the sexes to become fettered and embarrassed.

Like the feminists of a half century later she inveighs against the Constitution as unjust. A person is denied a voice in the election of his rulers because he is not twenty-one; another because he has not been a resident for two years, or because he cannot show a tax receipt, or because his skin is black, or because she is a woman. Brown is probably the first reformer to link the rights of women and the rights of Blacks, an issue which was to become central in the woman's rights movement after the Civil War.

In *Alcuin* Brown had drawn the outline of the new woman; in *Ormond* he fleshed her out as Constantia Dudley. Constantia's father, finding that she has a good mind, undertakes her education in English literature and Latin; he "unveiled to her the mathematical properties of light and sound, taught her as a metaphysician and anatomist . . . discussed with her the principles and progress of human society."[7]

In a soap-opera sequence Dudley's young partner embezzles money from the firm; Dudley goes blind from cataracts, and becomes an alcoholic. Constantia sells her music and books, does the housework, and takes up needlework to support the family. During the yellow fever epidemic she nurses patients. For three dollars she finds she can buy enough corn meal to feed three people for three months. (Brown is not satirizing her dietary ignorance: after all, physiology textbooks over a hundred years later talked of food values in terms of calories.) Her parents urge her to marry one of her numerous suitors but, "She yielded nothing to caprice or passion. . . . She was no stranger to the pleadings of love, from the lips of others and in her own bosom; but its tumults were brief, and speedily gave place to quiet thoughts and steadfast purposes."

Later on after she is saved from two ruffians who tried to rape her, her rescuer Balfour courts her. However when she discovers "the poverty of his discourse and ideas" she rejects him. In her thoughts she recapitulates the feminist arguments. Despite her meagre income "she was mistress of the product of her own labor." Marriage would annihilate this power. Henceforth she would be bereft even of personal freedom. So far from possessing property, she herself would be the property of another.

In the convolutions of the plot she meets Ormond, who fancies himself an intellectual superman beyond good and evil. It is possible that Brown was trying to show the Godwinian man in the flesh as an inhuman monster. Ormond has a luscious mistress whose 'intellectual deficiencies could not be concealed." His attempts to educate her fail. Constantia muses, "What but the fascination of his senses is it that ties Ormond to Helena? Is this a basis on which a marriage may properly be built?"

Ormond abandons Helena, who commits suicide, leaving her money to Constantia. Although Ormond in Godwinian fashion regards marriage as absurd, he is so attracted by Constantia's unusual intellectual qualities that if he cannot get her as a mistress he will marry her. To get her father out of the way he has him murdered. Then Ormond tries to rape Constantia, who, preferring death to dishonor, threatens to kill herself with a knife. Swearing that he will have her living or dead he moves in, at which point she stabs him.

At this moment her friend Sophia Westwyn comes on the scene. Sophia's testimony helps to exonerate Constantia. The two girls then leave for England.

The ridiculous plot must not obscure Brown's serious intention to portray the new enlightened woman. After all, the story is less violent than *Hamlet*. Constantia has all the virtues except a sense of humor, a defect she shares with her creator. But her virtues are not merely the traditional ones of chastity, compassion, self-sacrifice: they include self-reliance, independence of mind, and a superior intellect. It is significant that instead of the fictional convention of ending with a marriage Brown sends his heroine off to see the world. It would be almost a century before any other American novelist made intellectual attainments a major virtue in any heroine.

As Page Smith describes the popular novels of the nineteenth century, "In many, if not most of these the heroine was fair, chaste, docile, loyal, and uncomplaining. Pitted against her was a dark, voluptuous woman, a figure of sexual potency, full of depraved attractions. . . . The perfect heroine was delicate as a flower, 'fair' accomplished but not vain or ostentatious about her talents, melancholy; much given to weeping, especially over the work of the 'graveyard school of poets.' "[8] This pretty much echoes Herbert Brown's earlier account of the typical nineteenth century heroine. "Her place was in the sick chamber and in the squalid abodes of poverty and suffering. She was the modern Griselda to reclaim erring man by unexampled meekness in the face of the basest injuries."[9]

Obviously, Constantia Dudley has some of these characteristics, but in other respects she differs greatly from the heroines of sentimental novels. For one thing she lacks their intense concern with marriage; for another, because of her father's teaching, she is indifferent about religion. As Herbert Brown points out, "The female novelists also presented a solid front against the illuminati and the advocates of 'the new philosophy' who scoffed at the old-fashioned virtues and proclaimed the new woman."[10]

Certainly the girls and women drawn by the sentimental novelists of the late eighteenth and early nineteenth century had little resemblance to people like Mercy Warren, Abigail Adams, Lucy Knox, Kitty Greene, and Elizabeth Gates. Nor were they like the sophisticated Philadelphia girls who so fascinated the British officers in the glittering social season of 1778 in that city. No novelist then or later ever gave an adequate representation of the wives of the Revolutionary generals, and it was not until the later nineteenth century that novelists portrayed the kind of sophisticated and flirtatious girls who participated in the Mischianza. Both John Richter Jones in *Pemberton* (1872) and S. Weir Mitchell in *Huge Wynne* (1896) have such heroines: Helen Graham and Darthea Peniston. Both girls are Tory sympathizers, both attend the Mischianza. They are both passionate, witty, and daring, and of course end up by marrying American patriots; of the two, Jones's Helen is the more realistically drawn, a girl who enthusiastically kisses a suitor. But like modern historical novelists whose busty beauties jump into bed at the drop of cloak, Jones and Mitchell are conditioned by their eras: Helen and Darthea are essentially Victorian heroines.

The playwright Royall Tyler (1757–1826) was also conditioned by his era but his characters are from his own period. His witty play *The Contrast* (1787) has been revived on college stages, and in 1950 was presented on television. The setting is a fashionable home in New York; the girls in the play are sophisticated and pert. It is true that there are echoes of Sheridan's *School of Scandal* but the characters are more American than British.

Tyler moved in the social world he depicted. Born in Boston of a well-to-do family he got degrees from both Harvard and Yale. He became a major in the Continental Army and served as aide-de-camp to General Benjamin Lincoln during Shays's Rebellion. At twenty-three he was admitted to the bar, and later became a justice of the Vermont Supreme Court. From 1811 to 1814 he was professor of jurisprudence at the University of Vermont. Although he wrote a number of plays, his first, *The Contrast*, was his best.

At one point he was engaged to Abigail Adams II, but John, with his usual pigheadness, opposed the match and ordered that "Nabby" be sent to Boston, then had Abigail bring the girl to London. During her absence the engagement to Tyler was broken off, and she married her father's secretary, Colonel William Smith. He proved to be a spender, a rolling stone, a man with a variety of get-rich-quick schemes. During Tyler's courtship Abigail wrote of Nabby: "Indeed she is not like her Mamma. Had not her Mamma at her age too much sensibility to be prudent."[11]

In Tyler's play there is a similarly dutiful young girl, Maria, whose father has arranged a match with a man she does not love. Unlike John Adams, Maria's father discovers the suitor's unworthiness in time to call off the marriage. One wonders if some of Maria's rather priggish speeches about obeying her father are parodies of Nabby's. But it is not Maria who dominates the play but the witty and cynical Charlotte. Talking to Letitia, Charlotte tells of seeing a group of young fellows in Battery Park: "As I passed them I faultered with one of the most bewitching false steps you ever saw, and then re-covered myself with such a pretty confusion, flirting my hoop to discover a jet black shoe and brilliant buckle. Gad! how my little heart fluttered to hear the confused raptures of—'*Demme, Jack, what a delicate foot!' 'Ha! General, what a well-turned—*' "

Letitia: "Fie! fie! Charlotte (*stopping her mouth*), I protest you are quite a libertine."

Charlotte: "Why, my dear little prude, are we not all such libertines?"[12]

Later on after making a satirical remark about a bride exchanging her dolls for babies, she adds, "Apropos of babies, have you heard what Mrs. Affable's high-flying notions of delicacy have come to?" The entrance of a servant prevents the revelation. On another occasion when Maria says that a man she has just met looked married, Charlotte asks, "How, my dear, did he look sheepish?"

Granted that these girls are not specifically delineated as American types, the setting, the comic servant Jonathan with his Yankee dialect, and the patriotic sentiments of the hero, a Revolutionary veteran, all localize the play. The villain of the piece is a fortune-hunting English cad who plans to add Charlotte to his household as a mistress. At one point Jonathan sings a few stanzas of *Yankee Doodle*, but says he has never been able to remember the whole thing: he knows only a hundred and ninety verses. If the girls are not uniquely American it must be remembered that fashionable ladies in the 1780s had been brought up on English literature. Letitia remarks that Maria's reading of *Sir Charles Grandison, Clarissa Harlowe*, Shenstone, and the *Sentimental Journey* had made her aware of the flimsiness of her suitor's love letters.

The Contrast, which was played in various cities and which has had an enduring attraction, is a useful reminder that audiences recognized other types of girl besides the sentimental heroines of the novelists. It is a point that some social historians would do well to consider.

Royall Tyler caught some of the frivolity of late eighteenth-century high life and Charles Brockden Brown reflected some of its more radical ideas. The latter also gave a vivid account of the yellow fever epidemic which devastated Philadelphia in 1793. His fictional Constantia Dudley's heroic nursing must have been matched by numerous real-life girls during that plague. As has been suggested, the unfortunate heroines of William Hill Brown and Mrs. Rowson owe as much to Richardson as to life. None of these writers nor any other contemporary novelist gave a picture of the remarkable ladies of "The Republican Court."

This was the derisive term which homespun critics applied to Mrs. Washington's social circle—the same critics who labeled her "Lady Washington." Congressman William Maclay from the Pennsylvania frontier as usual dipped his pen in acid to describe the dullness of Washington's dinner parties. The president's formal dinners may have been dull, but the evidence suggests that the social life as a whole was not, if for no other reason than the presence of some remarkable women. Tyler may have been closer to the mark when he wrote in his "Prologue" to *The Contrast*

> Why should our thoughts to distant countries roam,
> When each refinement can be found at home?

Page Smith in his recent history of American women entitles the period of the late eighteenth and early nineteenth centuries as "The Great Repression." He represents it as the beginning of women's loss of status due in large part to capitalist greed. (In his lexicon *capitalist* seems to mean anyone from the grocer to the tycoon.)

Certainly the fashionable ladies of Philadelphia in the 1780s and 90s were not particularly repressed. The Marquis de Chastellux, who visited that city in 1780, described the lady who was to become a great favorite of Washington's—Mrs. Samuel Powell. Her wealthy and sophisticated husband had traveled abroad in such style that he was received by various crowned heads. He had been the last mayor of Philadelphia under the British, and was later to become the first mayor elected under the new charter. He was a member of the American Philosophical Society of Philadelphia and of the Royal Society of London. But it was Eliza Powell who impressed Chastellux:

> Contrary to American custom, she plays the leading role in the family—*la prima figura*, as the Italians say. She received me in a handsome house furnished in the English manner and, what pleased me most, adorned with fine prints and some very good copies of the best Italian paintings, for Mr. Powell has traveled in Europe and has been in Rome and Naples where he acquired a taste for the fine arts. As

for Mrs. Powell, she has traveled, but she has wit and a good memory, speaks well and talks a great deal; she honored me with her
friendship and found me very meritorious because I meritoriously
listened to her. [In the published version Chastellux deleted the last
remarks.] [13]

Elizabeth Willing Powell (1742–1830) was very much the Philadelphia aristocrat. Her father, Charles Willing, was a wealthy merchant; her brother Thomas was the senior partner of Robert Morris;
her niece, Mrs. William Bingham, a celebrated beauty, was the
leader of Philadelphia society; Peggy Shippen was a cousin. Puritanical John Adams, who had dinner with the Powells, called it "a
most sinfull feast."

During the Constitutional Convention the Washingtons lived next
door to the Powells. The two men shared political opinions and an
interest in scientific agriculture. But it was Eliza who most interested
George. On one occasion he noted in his journal that he had drunk
tea with her while Samuel was absent. In the fall of 1787 the
Washingtons entertained the Powells at Mount Vernon.[14]

According to Washington's biographer, James T. Flexner, it was
Eliza's saucy wit which appealed to George. On one occasion she
sent Bushrod Washington, George's nephew, a pair of fur gloves,
saying that because he had not written, she assumed his "Herculean
hands" were cold. When the government moved to Philadelphia
in 1790, the president's house shared a formal garden with the
Powells, the Binghams, and the Morrises. Thus Eliza often had an
opportunity to argue politics eagerly and passionately with the president. Flexner asserts that Washington enjoyed these verbal battles
with a clever and well-read woman.[15]

Among the other women whose company Washington enjoyed
were the three Chew sisters, daughters of Chief Justice Benjamin
Chew. Their city home was near Washington's residency. Their
Germantown home, Cliveden, set in a block-square walled garden,
had been occupied by the British and still bore the scars of Knox's
cannon.* During the yellow fever epidemic, Washington also moved
to Germantown. The president's favorite was Harriet, later married
to Charles Carroll of Carrollton. Always self-conscious and glum

* It still does.

when sitting for his portrait, Washington often took Harriet along to Gilbert Stuart's studio because he said her presence gave him his most agreeable expression.[16]

Abigail Adams, writing to her daughter, gave her impression of the Chew girls at Martha Washington's pre-Christmas reception: "On Friday evening last I went with Charles [her son] to the drawing-room, being the first of my appearance in public. The room became full before I left it, and the circle very brilliant. How could it be otherwise, when the dazzling Mrs. Bingham and her beautiful sisters were there; the Misses Allen, and Misses Chew; in short a constellation of beauties?"[17]

At this stage in her life Abigail Adams was no naive provincial: she had seen receptions at the courts of France, Holland, and England. As the wife of the minister to the Court of St. James she had become acquainted with many of the great ladies of England and dined with lords and ladies.

At the Republican Court, the president always placed her next to Martha, and if any other lady pushed in, he maneuvered her out. For although Washington had no great liking for John Adams, he regarded the vice president and his lady as the second highest ranking couple in the nation. Shortly after the government moved to Philadelphia, Mrs. Adams wrote, "I should spend a very dissipated winter, if I were to accept half the invitations I receive, particularly to routs or tea-and-cards."[18]

Except for theater parties and formal assemblies Martha Washington largely confined her social activities to returning calls and afternoon teas. Nevertheless, the luxurious social life of members of the Republican Court perturbed some persons with more egalitarian tastes, among them Thomas Jefferson. From Paris he sent Mrs. Bingham a rather condescending lecture. After deploring the political ferment there he added:

But our good ladies, I trust, have been too wise to wrinkle their foreheads with politics. They are contented to soothe & calm the minds of their husbands returning ruffled from political debate. They have the good sense to value domestic happiness above all other, and the art to cultivate it beyond all others. There is no part of the earth where so much of this is enjoyed as in America. You will agree with me in this; but you think that the pleasures of Paris more than supply its wants; in other words that a Parisian is happier than an American. You will change your opinion, my dear Madam, and come over to mine in the end. Recollect the women of this capitol, some on foot, some on horses, & some in carriages hunting pleasure in the streets, in routs & assemblies, and forgetting that they have left it behind them in their nurseries; compare them with our countrywomen occupied in the tender and tranquil amusements of domestic life. . . .[19]

It was the sort of preaching which always infuriates an able woman. Obviously Jefferson's egalitarian views did not include the ladies. Mrs. Bingham retorted that French women were superior because they could "interfere with the politics of the country and often give a decided turn to the fate of empires."

Mrs. William Bingham (1764–1801) was the acknowledged queen of the Republican Court. In a romanticized painting of Lady Washington's reception, the artist, Daniel P. Huntington, placed Anne Bingham as the dominant figure at the center of the picture. The figures of Washington, Hamilton, and Jefferson are relegated to the side; John Adams is barely visible; Mrs. Adams and Mrs. Hamilton are almost off the canvas.

As has been noted, Anne Bingham was the daughter of Thomas Willing, senior partner of Robert Morris. At sixteen she married a man who had made his fortune during the Revolution while acting as government purchasing agent in the Indies—then a center of trade with Europe. His biographer, Robert Alberts,[20] largely absolves him of corruption; but in an age less sensitive to conflicts of interest on the part of government officials, Bingham divided his activities between his official duties and the business affairs of the Willing-Morris firm. He also invested in several privateers. In any event, by 1780, when he married Thomas Willing's sixteen-year-old daughter Anne, he was one of the richest men in America.

On the basis of her portrait by Gilbert Stuart, Dixon Wecter is fully justified in saying she had "a face of Fragonard beauty."[21] She also had style, intelligence, and wit. In the gay Philadelphia season of 1782–83 the Bingham house was a favorite of society. The war was over; the city was full of French officers; the Southwark Theatre was reopened; the aristocratic Dancing Assembly resumed, but Tories were now excluded. The French officers especially liked to visit the Binghams. Bingham spoke French tolerably and Anne did delightfully. She was a beautiful and charming hostess who served excellent food; the only flaw was that her husband was too attentive.[22]

In May 1783 Bingham embarked on a business trip to Europe, taking Anne, their sixteen-month-old daughter Ann, and several servants. In December Mrs. Bingham bore a second daughter Maria, but the responsibilities of motherhood did not cramp her social style. The following June she was the principal guest of honor at a supper at the Court of the Hague.[23]

After a stay in Paris, where they saw a good bit of the Adams family, the Binghams went to London. A month later the Adamses followed because John had been appointed minister to the court of St. James. Mrs. Adams wrote to her sister that no English beauty could compare with Mrs. Bingham, Mrs. Platt, and Miss Hamilton—also a Philadelphian: ". . . Mrs. Bingham when taken altogether is the finest woman I ever saw." Soon she was so famous for her beauty that an engraving of her was being sold in the shops. Mrs. Adams's hairdresser asked if she knew the American lady who was so much talked about.[24]

When Mrs. Bingham was presented at court, Mrs. Adams, who accompanied her, wrote to the young John Quincy, "I own I felt not a little proud of her. St. James did not, and could not produce another so fine a woman." Abigail went on to describe a drawing room filled with elegantly dressed ladies pressing close for a glimpse of Anne Bingham, and added " 'You have,' said an English lord to me . . . , 'one of the finest ladies present that I ever saw.' The Emperor's Ambassador whispered to your Pappa, "Sir your country produces exceeding fine women.' "[25]

Mrs. Adams's admiration is all the more remarkable in that her puritanical New England sensibilities were offended by Anne Bingham's use of rouge and enthusiasm for French customs.

Back in Philadelphia William Bingham built the finest mansion in America and filled it with imported marble mantelpieces, furniture, mirrors, and silver. Anne had a bed seven feet square. The three-and-a-half-acre garden was filled with orange, lemon, and citron trees in tubs, and embellished with statuary. There were stables and a greenhouse. When the capital moved to Philadelphia, the Binghams gave elaborate parties and often entertained the Washingtons, who lived nearby. Even dour John Adams, dining there, was pleased to find that he could carry on "something of a political conversation" with Mrs. Bingham; he found she had "more ideas on the subject" than he had expected, "and a correcter judgment."[26]

As a teenage girl Anne Willing had been in and out of the Washington house while the general had his headquarters in Philadelphia. Now as "the uncrowned queen of the Republican court" she was not one of Martha Washington's close friends, but George found her delightful, and occasionally dropped in. She and her husband persuaded Washington to sit for a portrait by Gilbert Stuart to be presented to Bingham's friend Lord Lansdowne, an enthusiast about the United States.[27]

Although William Bingham was overshadowed by his glamorous wife, he was by no means a nonentity. He became probably the richest man in America; he had the finest mansion in Philadelphia plus another on the Schuylkill and a summer home on the Jersey coast; he was a party to the inner councils of the nation, was active in getting the Constitution adopted, and was a senator from Pennsylvania. In the 1790s he speculated hugely and profitably in millions of acres of land, but he also lent and lost money to the impecunious new government. At his death in 1804 his assets were over $3,000,000.

According to twentieth-century theory the Binghams should exemplify the classic pattern of the business-tycoon/bored-wife syndrome. The evidence suggests nothing of the kind. When the Binghams were touring Europe, William wrote letters to his father-in-law praising Anne's amiability and good sense. And when William was on business in New York, Thomas Willing wrote his son-in-law:

> Nancy [Anne] and the little girls are quite well. The former is so nearly crazy at your long absence, that, although she has not yet *walked* in her sleep, yet she started up in bed last night, dreaming of you, I suppose, and knocked her head violently against the wall. She complains of her head yet, and we all laugh heartily at her complaints—so you may believe she is not very bad.[28]

As Thomas's letter suggests, the Willings were not an inhibited family. As has been mentioned, his sister, Mrs. Samuel Powell, impressed Chastellux by her wit and talkativeness. Another sister, Anne's Aunt Mary, noted for her wit, became the second wife of William Byrd III of Westover, a brave soldier but a wastrel and a rake. When he killed himself, she rescued the estate from possible bankruptcy.

Anne's cousin Joshua Francis Fisher deplored the fact that she and her sisters used too much freedom of speech and interlarded their conversation with oaths. Congressman Harrison Otis, who dined with the Binghams and assorted Willings, noted a ribald conversation. Anne's sister Dolly made remarks about the size of her brother-in-law Henry Clymer's stomach and mentioned that the Duke of York was so fat that he had a semicircular piece cut out of his dining table so that he could get at his plate. Mrs. Bingham expressed sympathy for the newly married Duchess. "All this and much facetious matter of the same kind was received with bursts of applause that would have done credit to the national convention especially by Miss Abby [Willing] and Miss Ann who did not disguise their delight nor their bosoms."[29]

The moralists had their innings when in 1799 fifteen-year-old Maria Bingham eloped with Jacques Alexandre, Compte de Tilly. It is ironic that Susanna Rowson had recently dedicated a novel to Mrs. Bingham, for Maria's elopement bore resemblances to that in Mrs. Rowson's *Charlotte Temple*. In the tradition of the sentimental novel there was the gullible heroine betrayed by the handsome and practiced seducer. Tilly at thirty-six was a poet, artist, and witty raconteur; he had been a page to Marie Antoinette, and had escaped France disguised as a coachman. Despite his reputation as a Don Juan, the Binghams enjoyed his company and had him as a dinner guest. Following the script of sentimental fiction Mrs. Bingham, on learning of the elopement, required medical attention and a sedative. From here on the script changed: William Bingham sent out search parties, one of which found Maria and Tilly in bed. She was brought home. Tilly tried a habeas corpus to get her back but eventually salved his heart with a cash settlement of £5000 plus an annuity of

£500. Instead of dying according to convention, Maria obtained a divorce which was got through the legislature by her father. She later married the brother of an English lord.[30]

Possibly their shared trials and tribulations increased the Binghams' affection for each other; in any case Anne bore a son the following year—sixteen years after Maria's birth. Never one to miss a gay evening, Anne went on a sleighing party three months after her confinement. As was then the custom, the party probably took along a fiddler and spent most of the night with stops at inns for suppers and dancing. In any case she caught a chest cold which turned into what was then called galloping consumption. This suggests that she had been suffering undiagnosed tuberculosis. Her husband fitted up a suite on one of his ships and took her to Bermuda where she died in May at the age of thirty-seven.[31]

That summer Bingham took his two daughters to Europe, leaving his infant son with Anne's grief-stricken father, Thomas Willing. From then on Bingham's letters are those of a brokenhearted man. To Visconte de Noailles, his closest friend, he wrote: "The irreparable loss I have sustained casts a gloom over all my pursuits and blunts the edge of every enjoyment of life. Whether time will moderate my feelings is an experiment yet to be tried. It may habituate me to a state of desperation, but it can never obliterate from my mind the recollection of those virtues . . . nor the reflection that they can never be restored." A year after Anne's death, her brother wrote asking when Bingham might return. He answered that his plans were indefinite: "The scenes which constituted my domestic happiness have vanished."[32]

Bingham helped to arrange for the Louisiana Purchase and advanced much of the money for it, but he was a broken man. His daughter Ann wrote his physician friend Sir Charles Blagden, asking if her father might take ten drops of laudanum a day "to quiet his fidgets." In 1809 at the age of fifty-two he died at Bath and was buried in the Bath Abbey. William Bingham could have echoed Shakespeare: after Anne's death there "was nothing left remarkable beneath the visiting moon."

Fifty-seven years after her death, eighty-seven-year-old Samuel Breck, who had known her, wrote in his diary that in her day she was incomparable, and since then no circle in the city had produced her equal.[33]

In the year of Anne's death, Abigail Adams, who had presented her at the Court of St. James, retired to the farm at Braintree following John's defeat for reelection as president. In a letter Abigail said, "I have commenced my operation of dairy woman. . . . Tell Nabby she might see me at five o'clock in the morning skimming my milk."[34]

The America which produced both an Anne Bingham and an Abigail Adams and placed them in the same republican court was indeed a new kind of nation.

NOTES

1. Callahan, *Henry Knox*, p. 30.
2. Herbert Brown, *The Sentimental Novel in America, 1789–1860*, Durham, N.C., 1940, p. 44.
3. Edward Wagenknecht, *Cavalcade of the American Novel*, New York, 1952, p. 4.
4. Ibid., p. 5.
5. Ibid. and *Literary History of the United States*, 1948, I, 178.
6. Quoted in Andrew Sinclair. *The Better Half*, New York, 1965, p. 7.
7. Charles Brockden Brown, *Ormond*, ed. by Ernest Marchand, New York, 1937, p. 28.
8. Page Smith, *Daughters of the Promised Land*, p. 72.
9. Herbert Brown, p. 113.
10. Ibid., p. 108.
11. Janet Whitney, *Abigail Adams*, Boston, 1947, p. 168.
12. Royall Tyler, *The Contrast*, Act I, Scene 1, in Edwin Cody, *Literature of the Early Republic*, New York, 1950, p. 394.
13. Marquis François Jean de Chastellux, *Travels in North America in the Years 1780, 1781, and 1782*, a revised translation by Howard Rice, Jr., Chapel Hill, 1963, I, 302n.
14. Flexner, *George Washington*, II, 315.
15. Ibid., II, 321.
16. Stephen Decatur, Jr., *Private Affairs of George Washington*, Boston, 1933, p. 178.
17. Ibid., p. 177.
18. Ibid., p. 195.
19. *The Works of Thomas Jefferson*, collected and edited by Paul Leicester Ford, New York, 1904, V, 390–91.
20. Robert Alberts, *The Golden Voyage: The Life and Times of William Bingham, 1752–1804*, Boston, 1969.
21. Dixon Wecter, *The Saga of American Society: A Record of Social Aspiration, 1607–1937*, New York, 1937, p. 306.
22. Alberts, pp. 119–20.
23. Ibid., p. 138.
24. Ibid., pp. 151, 153.
25. Ibid., p. 155.

26. Ibid., p. 214.
27. Ibid., p. 290.
28. Ibid., p. 197.
29. Ibid., p. 360.
30. Ibid., pp. 371–79.
31. Ibid., pp. 411–13.
32. Ibid., pp. 426, 416.
33. Ibid., p. 442.
34. Whitney, p. 305.

Three

Her Infinite Variety

To generalize is to be an idiot.
William Blake

Almost all foreign travelers in America during the nineteenth century agreed that the American girl was given greater freedom than the girls of European society. They also tended to agree that the American woman lost this freedom at marriage. Tocqueville wrote, "In America, the independence of woman is inexorably lost in the bonds of matrimony. If an unmarried woman is less constrained there than elsewhere, a wife is subjected to stricter obligations. The former makes her father's house an abode of freedom; the latter lives in the home of her husband as if it were a cloister."[1] Mrs. Trollope stated flatly "Mixed dinner parties of ladies and gentlemen are very rare." She pictured dinners where the men were placed at one end of the table; the ladies at the other. "At regular balls, married ladies are admitted, but seldom take much part in the amusement."[2]

Mrs. Trollope was of course a far less perceptive observer than Tocqueville, and many of her observations on manners raise a question about the kind of social circles to which she gained admittance. Thus she could write: "What we call pic-nics are very rare, and when attempted do not often succeed well. The two sexes can hardly mix for the greater part of a day without great restraint and ennui. . . ."[3] Now if there are any two amusements most often mentioned in diary after diary, they are dancing and picnicking. Both girls and married women record these, and usually say how much they enjoyed them.

A 1971 issue of *American Heritage* carried an article on the nine-teenth-century picnic, showing a variety of contemporary paintings on the subject. One of them, by Thomas Cole in 1844, shows men, women, and children scattered on the grass at the edge of a body of water. A young man is playing a guitar to entertain one group. In a somewhat later painting, again of people of all ages, a girl is playfully putting something into a young man's hair. In 1840 Washington Irving wrote to his sister about picnics: "You would be delighted with these picturesque assemblages on some woodland point putting into Tappan Sea, with gay groups on the grass under the trees, the carriages glistening through the woods; a yacht with flapping sails and fluttering streams anchored about half a mile from shore, and rowboats plying to and from it, filled with lady passengers." In 1842 Dickens described a picnic along the Mississippi.[4]

A more recent commentator on American women, Page Smith, who does not have the excuse of being a foreigner, makes even larger generalizations than Frances Trollope:

> American men accorded their women more deference, lavished more money on them; regarded them with more respect than was accorded to the women of any other country. But they did not particularly like them. They did not enjoy their company, they did not find them interesting or rewarding as people and as women themselves. They valued them as wives and mothers; they sentimentalized over them, they congratulated themselves on their enlightened attitude toward them. *But they did not (and do not) particularly like them.*[5]

This is an example of the only-in-America cliché so beloved by contemporary intellectuals. It disregards such institutions as the purdah, the British men's club, or the Greek all-male tavern. The American male's alleged dislike of women obviously does not apply to men like George Washington, James Warren, Henry Knox, or William Bingham. Even John Adams, who seldom liked anyone very much, seems to have made an exception of Mercy Warren and of course of Abigail.

The language and context of Smith's indictment suggest that he was considering chiefly the middle- and upper-class American engaged in business or politics—men who had money to spend on their wives. Undoubtedly there have been men in all societies who disliked women. Chaucer's Wife of Bath claimed that it was impossible that any clerk would speak well of wives. She supported her views on men and women with evidence from experience which she declared had more authority than the works of scholars.

It is a good method. Instead of countering one large generalization with another, this chapter and the following ones will present in some detail what women said about themselves and their marriages, and what their husbands said.

The dark ages for women postulated by Page Smith are happily invisible in the letters of Margaret Bayard Smith[6] (1778–1844) who was a central figure in Washington life for forty years, beginning in 1800. She knew almost everyone of importance including Jefferson, the Madisons, the Clays, the Randolphs, the Crawfords, and Andrew Jackson. She wrote for *Godey's*, the *Southern Literary Messenger*, and *Peter Parley's Annual*; she published two books: *A Winter in Washington* and *What is Gentility?*

She was born in Philadelphia, the daughter of Colonel John Bayard, a member of the Continental Congress, a Revolutionary soldier, and later speaker of the Pennsylvania Assembly. In 1800 she married her second cousin Samuel Harrison Smith, whom Jefferson had asked to come to Washington to edit *The National Intelligencer*. Later Madison appointed him as the first commissioner of revenue; in 1814 he was an *ad interim* secretary of the treasury; from 1809 to 1819 president of the Bank of Washington, and later president of the Washington branch of the Bank of the United States.

The marriage had been a love match. She did not hesitate to leave friends and "the kindest of fathers" to enter a land of strangers because at her side was "a husband so beloved." Here again, as with Mercy Warren and Abigail Adams, was what might be called the American pattern: the close relationship between father and daughter followed by love in marriage. Three years later Margaret on a visit to her sister in New York, was writing to her husband, "Tomorrow week, I expect dearest husband to be again in your arms."[7]

In an earlier letter she had written to her sister about a merry evening in company when "Captain T" joined with his wife and daughters in song.[8] She wished her sister could have been there to dance, especially with General Van Courtland. Obviously Mrs.

Trollope's picture of American women and men segregating themselves at parties did not apply to Margaret Smith's circle.

She met Jefferson when an unknown caller turned up looking for
her husband. This proved to be the man denounced as "the violent
democrat, the vulgar demagogue, the bold atheist and profligate
man."[9] She found him utterly charming. During the time when
Jefferson's election hung in the balance in the House of Representatives, she suffered through sleepless nights. The country seemed on
the verge of civil war. Then in March she wrote her sister that
whereas changes in government in every age "have most generally
been epochs of confusion, villany and bloodshed, in this our happy
country take place without any species of distraction or disorder."
At a president's dinner she was, at twenty-three, seated next to
Jefferson and enjoyed his conversation. Shortly afterward, describing a party, she echoed Jefferson's first inaugural address, "Thus
you see that we are here at least all Republicans and all Federalists."[10]
Jefferson may not have approved of women discussing politics, but
for forty years Margaret Smith filled her letters with informed political discussion.

She also wrote of the lighter side of the Washington scene. At a
reception "There was a lady, too, who offered us great diversion. I
titled her, Madame Eve, and called her dress a fig leaf." At a later
occasion the wife of a foreign diplomat caused a mob of boys to
crowd around her carriage because she was "an almost naked woman." In an Empire dress which had "scarcely any waist to it and no
sleeves; her back, her bosom, part of her waist and her arms were
uncovered and the rest of her form visible."[11] Several ladies told her
to put on more clothes.

Much of the social life was on an informal level. In the mornings
there was constant visiting, and in the evening one or more members
of Congress dropped in on the Smiths. At a tea given by Jefferson's
daughter, Martha Randolph, Mrs. Smith found her hostess seated
beside her father on a sofa "with all her lovely children [she
eventually had twelve] playing around them. With what delight
did I contemplate this good parent, and while I sat looking at him
playing with these infants, one standing on the sopha with its arms
round his neck, the other two youngest on his knees, playing with

him, I could scarcely realize that he was one of the most celebrated men now living, both as a Politician and Philosopher."[12]

Jefferson had indeed tried to be a good parent. When his wife died, his daughter Martha was only ten. At Monticello she became his closest companion and when she attended school in Philadelphia her father wrote her copious letters of advice on her education. While he was minister to France he put her in a convent school, until she announced her intention to become a nun. After he took her out of school, she met and became engaged to Thomas Randolph, who was visiting in Paris. The wedding took place at Monticello. According to modern theory Jefferson had been almost too authoritarian and protective. Margaret Smith, who of course had never heard of an Electra complex, stated, "Never have I known of a union between any two beings so perfect as that which almost identified this father and daughter."

Mrs. Smith describes a visit from the Madisons and the Thorntons. They sat on benches under the trees, swung in the hammock, and strolled about. Mrs. Smith took them to the milk house to show some of the sixty pounds of butter she herself had made.[13]

Because of her intense admiration for Jefferson, Margaret Smith was at first not enthusiastic about the succession of Madison. However, like everyone else, she loved Dolley, whose kindness was legendary. It was not long before Margaret came to admire James also. When the Smiths visited Montpelier, the Madison home, Dolley said there were twenty-three in the house, but wished that Margaret had brought her own children. She took Margaret upstairs to rest after the trip and lay on the bed with her where they were served with wine, ice, punch, and pineapples. In the evening the visiting women put their children to bed while the men sat on the piazza.

However, in that era women were not segregated. On another occasion after putting her own children to bed Mrs. Smith came down to play chess with the men. The House of Representatives was the "lounging place for both sexes." Once Mrs. Smith joined the female crowd who thronged the Supreme Court room—a place where she thought "women have no business." But "On every public occasion a launch, an oration, an inauguration, in the court, in the representative hall, as well as the drawing room, they [the women] are treated with mark'd dictinction." On one occasion she went to hear Clay speak. Afterward he came out to the lobby and sat on the steps with her. During Webster's speech in reply to Hayne, the senators gave up their seats to the ladies.[14]

Not all the women were interested in politics or social affairs. Mrs. Clay preferred sewing for her six children, but could be persuaded to play the piano while others danced.

Margaret Smith liked to dance and often mentioned doing so until late hours. But she commented "I know of no pleasure equal to that derived from the conversation of men of genius." In 1828 she wrote to her son about an argument she had had with Robert Owen on the effect of environment. Owen, who had founded New Harmony and other cooperative communities, preached the doctrine that man's character is wholly dependent on environment.

After a visit to the Madisons, Margaret described Dolley at sixty: "She certainly has always been, and still is one of the happiest of human beings. . . . Time seems to favour her as much as fortune. She looks young and says she feels so." At dinner James kept up a stream of talk about history and personalities until ten. He told of Franklin and Washington, and of the making of the Constitution. Margaret thought that many of his anecdotes were very droll, and every sentence was worth recording. "It was living history."

During the visit Dolley took young Anna Smith by the hand and said, "Come, let us run a race . . . Madison and I often run races here, when the weather does not allow us to walk."[15] James was then seventy-seven.

When Harriet Martineau visited the United States she called on Mrs. Smith. President Jackson, who was always courtly with women, gave a dinner for the famous bluestocking. At a presidential levee Miss Martineau noted that "All was quiet and orderly; and there was an air of gaiety which rather surprised me."[16]

Mrs. Smith tried to explain some of Miss Martineau's ideas to various women but most of them were interested only in seeing a celebrity. At first the men laughed at this deaf woman who wrote books on the unfeminine subject of economics, but soon became "her most devoted admirers and frequent callers. Mr. Webster, Mr. Clay, Mr. Calhoun, Preston, Judge Story and many others often visit her and when she goes to the Senate or Court Room, they show still more personal evidences of regard."[17]

Margaret Bayard Smith's letters covering forty years give a far different picture of the position of women in the early republic than that given by the novels of the period or by a recent historian like Page Smith. It has been necessary to quote her at length to avoid the dangers of slanted generalization or sentimentalized paraphrase. Like Mercy Warren and Abigail Adams, Margaret Smith was an intellectual who felt at ease with the leading men of her time. Her intellectual interests appear not only in her enjoyment of conversations with brilliant men, but in her constant references to solid reading. She was delighted to have access to the congressional library. What gives her an especially American flavor is that this bluestocking was also mother, child's nurse, housekeeper, dairymaid, and loving wife. At fifty-four she was writing about her anxiety during a plague for "dear husband."

Obviously her account does not support Page Smith's large generalization that "the vast majority of American marriages, at least in the larger cities of the East and Middle West in the nineteenth century were minor disasters."[18] In 1805 Dolley, kept at home by an infected knee, wrote frequent, sometimes daily letters to James, who was in Philadelphia: "A few hours have passed since you left me, my beloved, and I find nothing can relieve the oppression of my mind but speaking to you, in this the only way," read one. The next day she wrote that the watchman's cry had waked her at one o'clock, "and from that moment I found myself unable to sleep, from anxiety for thee, my dearest husband." A day later: "This clear, cold morning will favor your journey, and enliven the feelings of my darling. . . ."[19] Over twenty years later when the ailing Madison, as rector of the University of Virginia, had to make one of his trips to Charlottesville, she wrote:

> Monday, 9 o'clock. My Beloved: I trust in God that you are well again, as your letters assure me that you are. How bitterly I regret not going with you! Yours of "Friday midday" did not reach me till last evening. I felt so full of fear that you might relapse that I hastened to pack a few clothes and give orders for the carriage to be ready and the post waited for. This morning, happily the mes-

senger has returned with your letter of yesterday, which relieves
my heart and leads me to hope you will be at home on Wednesday
night with your own affectionate nurse. . . .[20]

It would be a mistake to represent life in Washington as typical of
that elsewhere in America. A national capital, while drawing to
itself people from all over a country, develops a milieu of its own.
Especially before New York became the commercial capital of the
nation, Washington society was probably more sophisticated and
luxurious than any other American city except Philadelphia and
possibly Charleston. Most women in the early republic were faced
with more primitive conditions. As will appear, a number of women
who became prominent later in the century grew up on farms where
they shared the drudgery of housework, milking, washing, baking,
and carrying water and firewood.

The lot of the pioneer was even harder. In 1810 twenty-year-
old Margaret Van Horn Dwight made a late autumn journey from
New Haven, Connecticut, to Warren, Ohio. She traveled by wagon
with a parsimonious deacon and his family. Margaret's father, who
died when she was six, was the brother of Yale president Timothy
Dwight; she was the granddaughter of Jonathan Edwards. After her
father's death, a grandmother brought her up. On her grandmother's
death in 1807 she lived with an aunt whose son, Theodore Dwight
Woolsey, was to become another president of Yale.[21] The journey
to the home of cousins in Ohio suggests that Margaret was shunted
off by both her remarried mother and an aunt who had a nine-
year-old son.

The journey was rugged, the inns filthy, the food coarse. Margaret
commented, "I have learned Elizabeth to eat raw pork and drink
whisky—don't you think I shall do for a new country?"[22]

Crossing the Pennsylvania mountains they stopped at an especially
dirty inn where there was much drunkenness and rough talk. As
Margaret waited at her bedroom door for a candle, a drunken
wagoner put his arm around her neck and said something she was
too frightened to hear. In another inn when she had lain down after
taking off her dress and boots, "one of the wretches came into the
room & lay down by me on the outside of the bed." She clung to her

unperturbed landlady until the man left, saying "he intended no harm, & only wish'd to become acquainted with me. . . ."[23]

To lighten the load on the wagon she often walked as much as eight miles a day, even in stormy weather. Although she had almost worn out her boots the deacon said it would not hurt any of them to walk nine miles every day of their lives. ". . . if I am caught with a deacon of any name again, I shall deserve to suffer," she wrote in her journal.[24]

As the remark suggests, Margaret Dwight, unlike nineteenth-century fictional heroines, had an ironic scense of humor. At one tavern: "I found the people belong'd to a very ancient and noble family—they were first & second cousins to his *Satanic Majesty*—I could but wonder that he should suffer them to lead so laborious a life, for they are among his most faithful friends and subjects. . . . The man is only related by marriage to his lordship."[25]

She had her own views on marriage: "If I were going to be married I would give my *intended*, a gentle emetic, or some such thing to see how he would bear being sick a little—for I could not coax a husband as I would a child. . . ." Later on she added "After giving an emetic I would take a long journey with my *intended*, to try his patience—mine is try'd sorely now—my frock is wet & dirty a quarter of a yard high."[26]

Obviously this was a girl with few romantic illusions. A year after she got to Warren, she married William Bell, by whom she had thirteen children. Their home in Pittsburgh became a center of hospitality, for Margaret was an active and very vivacious hostess.

In the Jacksonian era Harriet Martineau with her wide-ranging eye gave vignettes of a variety of American women from those in Washington society to the mill girls of Waltham and Lowell, Massachusetts, and Patterson, New Jersey. In Lowell the cotton mills had 5,000 employees, 3,800 of whom were women. She thought there had been much silent poverty before the factories came. The girls at Patterson were well dressed with hair styled after the latest New York fashions. The New England girls lived in corporation houses whose standards of cleanliness, food, and propriety were supervised by the mill owners. Sometimes girls brought their mothers to keep house in a dwelling bought with their earnings. Girls were able to save two or three dollars a week to clear mortgages on their father's farms or send a brother to college, or for their own doweries. Miss Martineau saw "a whole street of houses built with the earnings of the girls; some with piazzas, and green venetian blinds; all neat and sufficiently spacious." The corporation gave a building for a lyceum, in which the workers put a good library. Many of the girls had good private libraries.[27]

Lucy Larcom (1824–1893), whose mother kept one of the Lowell boardinghouses, entered the mills at thirteen. In her reminisences of 1889 she said that the Lowell girls were typical of the New England girls of the day. As she summed it up, "The girls there were just such girls as are knocking at the doors of young women's colleges today. They had to work with their hands, but they could not hinder the working of their minds also. Their mental activity was overflowing at every possible outlet." Many of them were working half the year to attend academies and seminaries the other half. Mary Lyon, the founder of Mount Holyoke Seminary, was a heroine to the mill girls.[28]

Her own record of authors read includes Jeremy Taylor, Shakespeare, Milton, Pope, Cotton Mather, Wordsworth, and Coleridge. Her older sister Emelie went in for things like *Watts on the Improvement of the Mind*, Locke, and Young. Some of the mill girls subscribed to *Blackwood's*, and the *Westminster* and *Edinburgh Reviews*. A friend got Lucy to study German with a native professor who had organized a class of mill girls. Visiting celebrities like John Quincy Adams, Edward Everett, Whittier, and Emerson lectured at Lowell.[29]

As Lucy remembered the mills, there was a relaxed atmosphere. The girls filled the windows with house plants; they frolicked among the spinning frames, played games, and told stories. This was possible because their work was the changing of bobbins every three quarters of an hour. For girls from remote farms the social life of the mill was delightful. One girl told of a home where snow kept the family from seeing a neighbor for weeks. The hours of work were long but girls took days off to go off on the stage for a visit to relatives.[30]

Next to the stylish appearance of the girls the thing which most impressed foreign visitors was the *Lowell Offering*, the first magazine to be entirely written by women. Both Dickens and Harriet Martineau praised it for its high quality.[31] Lucy Larcom and her sister both wrote for it.

Summing up her experience of nine years in the mill she wrote, "I regard it as one of the privileges of my truth that I was permitted to grow up among those active, interesting girls, whose lives were not mere echoes of other lives, but had principle and purpose distinctly their own."[32]

In sermons they constantly heard about the need of teachers in the West. Thus when an agent came looking for recruits, many of the Lowell girls went, including Lucy Larcom. The pioneering was rugged: she taught in a log schoolhouse with the nearest cabin a mile away. There was not a tree in sight. She interrupted her teaching to attend Monticello Seminary, then taught for ten more years in various seminaries.

During those years she began to publish in magazines. James Russell Lowell accepted a poem of hers for the *Atlantic*. In 1865 she became editor of *Our Young Folks* until 1872 when *St. Nicholas* took it over. In 1875 she published *An Idyl of Work*, a long narrative poem on the Lowell mill girls.[33]

Contrasted with the active lives of the mill girls and the hardships of the migrants to the West there was the enervating life of the ubiquitous boardinghouse. In Harriet Martineau's opinion this was one of the worst influences on American women. Because of the scarcity of domestic servants and because couples married early before they could afford a home, many young people started married life in a boarding house. They often tended to continue this effortless life after they had children. As Miss Martineau described the scene after the men left for work in the morning, "There the ladies sit for hours doing nothing but gossiping with one another, with any gentleman of the house who may happen to have no business, and with visitors."[34] Mrs. Trollope painted a similar picture. Many of the ladies told her that it was "the perfection of comfort to have nothing to fix for oneself." The men came home for midday dinner, eaten in silence; then the wives walked along to the office and went shopping.[35] Mrs. Martineau attributed the frequency of heavy drinking among women of station and education to "the vacuity of mind of many women."

It is possible that travelers like Miss Martineau, Mrs. Trollope, and David Macrae exaggerated the place of the boardinghouse in American society for the same reason that modern tourists tend to judge a country by its hotels. A traveler would probably get into more boardinghouses than private homes. Henry James called the "maison Upham," where he boarded in Cambridge, an American version of the Maison Vanquer in Balzac's *Père Goriot*. Like the boardinghouse presided over by the Autocrat of the Breakfast Table, Miss Upham's was populated chiefly by unmarried people of various ages. It is significant that none of the scores of diaries and biographies examined in the course of this study records married life in a boardinghouse. Of course women with feckless husbands like Bronson Alcott took in boarders, but that is not the same thing as the idle life described by Miss Martineau and Mrs. Trollope.

In the South, women suffered from a patriarchal society where men took black mistresses and regarded their wives as ornaments. "I have seen, with heart sorrow," Miss Martineau wrote, "the kind politeness, the gallantry, so insufficient to the loving heart, with which the wives of the south are treated by their husbands."[36]

These observations are in accord with Anne Firor Scott's findings in her excellent study, *The Southern Lady*. Women, along with children and slaves, were expected to recognize their proper and subordinate place and to be obedient to the head of the family. . . . It was no accident that the most articulate spokesmen for slavery were also eloquent exponents of the subordinate role of women."[37] Therefore, "From earliest childhood girls were trained to the ideals of perfection and submission." Boarding schools put less emphasis on mind than on manners.

This role was sugar coated with some of the most syrupy prose on record. Using phrases from the *Southern Literary Messenger*—language which she says can be matched in speeches, poems, and other journals—Mrs. Scott describes the idealized Southern woman:

> This marvelous creation was described as a submissive wife whose reason for being was to love, honor, obey, and occasionally amuse

her husband, to bring up his children and manage his household. Physically weak, and "formed for the less laborious occupations," she was endowed with the capacity to "create a magic spell" over any man in her vicinity. She was timid and modest, beautiful and graceful. "The most fascinating being in creation . . . the delight and charm of every circle she moves in." [38]

But once married this soft creature was expected to guide her husband in the paths of piety and morality. Nineteenth-century men tended to put morality in the wife's name, and nowhere was this more true than in the South. The Southern lady was by definition modest and chaste. Yet as the incomparable Southern diarist, Mary Chesnut, recorded,

> . . . what do you say to this? A magnate who runs a hideous black harem, with its consequences under the same roof with his lovely white wife, and his beautiful and accomplished daughters? . . . Fancy such a man finding his daughter reading "Don Juan." "You with that immoral book!" And he orders her out of his sight. [39]

Elsewhere she wrote:

> Like the patriarchs of old our men live all in one house with their wives and their concubines; and the mulattoes one sees in every family resemble the white children. Any lady is ready to tell you who is the father of all the mulatto children in everybody's household but her own. [40]

Mrs. Scott speaks of the shock of the sudden transition from belle to plantation wife. No matter how wealthy the establishment was, the mistress had to oversee spinning, weaving, sewing, gardening, poultry raising, the preparation of food, and the care of the sick. Fine ladies supervised hog butchering. [41]

As Mrs. Scott shows, other Southern ladies besides Mrs. Chesnut were restive in the role assigned to them. Before the Civil War, widows often successfully ran large plantations, and after the able-bodied men went off to war, it became almost the rule for a woman to manage the slaves and the planting, harvesting, and marketing of the crops. Like her sisters in the North, she often served in military hospitals. And unlike the more fortunate Yankee women, many of those in the South had to pack up goods and families to flee from approaching armies.

After Appomattox they picked up the pieces of a ruined economy. In Alabama alone there were eighty thousand widows. In state after state there were many more women than men, and a considerable number of the men were war cripples. As Mrs. Scott says, "the war came, and as wars do, it speeded social change and opened Pandora's box."[42]

NOTES

1. Tocqueville, *Democracy in America*, p. 235.
2. Frances Trollope, *Domestic Manners of the Americans*, ed. by Donald Smalley, New York, 1949, p. 299.
3. Ibid., pp. 298–99.
4. "Picnics Long Ago," *American Heritage*, June 1971, pp. 42–45.
5. Page Smith, *Daughters of the Promised Land*, p. 72.
6. Margaret Bayard Smith, *The First Forty Years of Washington Society*, ed. by Gaillard Hunt, New York, 1906.
7. Ibid., pp. 1, 41.
8. Ibid., p. 18.
9. Ibid., p. 7.
10. Ibid., p. 31.
11. Ibid., pp. 19, 47.
12. Ibid., p. 50.
13. Ibid., p. 52.
14. Ibid., pp. 97, 145–46, 310.
15. Ibid., pp. 235–37.
16. Harriet Martineau, *Society in America*, New York, 1937, II, 219.
17. Margaret Bayard Smith, p. 268.
18. Page Smith, p. 132.
19. Katherine Anthony, *Dolly Madison*, New York, 1949, p. 169.
20. Ibid., p. 307.
21. *A Journey to Ohio in 1810, As Recorded in the Journal of Margaret Van Horn Dwight*, ed. by Max Farrand, New Haven, 1912, pp. v–vi.
22. Ibid., p. 37.
23. Ibid., p. 40.
24. Ibid., p. 61.
25. Ibid., p. 60.
26. Ibid., pp. 23, 36.
27. Martineau, II, 54–58, and Lucy Larcom, *A New England Girlhood*, New York, 1961 (originally 1889), pp. 222–23.
28. Larcom, p. 223.
29. Ibid., pp. 241, 253–54.
30. Ibid., pp. 154, 181–86.
31. Ibid., pp. 222–23.
32. Ibid., p. 196.
33. Daniel Dulany Addison, *Lucy Larcom: Life, Letters, and Diary*, Boston and New York, 1895, pp. 157, 179.

34. Martineau, II, 247.
35. Francis Trollope, pp. 283–85.
36. Martineau, II, 125.
37. Anne Firor Scott, *The Southern Lady: From Pedestal to Politics*, Chicago, 1970, p. 17.
38. Ibid., p. 4.
39. Mary Boykin Chesnut, *A Diary from Dixie*, ed. by Ben Ames Williams, Cambridge, 1949, p. 122.
40. Ibid., p. 21.
41. Scott, p. 31.
42. Ibid., p. 92.

Four

Girls and Goddesses

I grant I never saw a goddess go
My mistress when she walks treads on the ground.
Shakespeare, Sonnet 130

The preceding chapter suggests the immense variety of American women waiting for the writers of fiction. Instead, the sentimental novelists represented their heroines as delicate flowers, emotional rather than intellectual, given to fainting and to moral and religious preachments, and, of course, chaste in thought and deed. As William Wasserstrom says, "Womanliness came to mean sexlessness."[1] In his study of the sentimental novel between 1789 and 1860 Herbert Brown says of the typical heroine, "Her place was in the sick chamber and the squalid abodes of poverty and suffering. She was the modern Griselda to reclaim erring man by unexampled meekness in the face of the basest inequities."[2]

A popular song of 1843 sums it up:

Oh don't you remember sweet Alice, Ben Bolt,
Sweet Alice whose hair was so brown,
Who wept with delight when you gave her a smile,
And trembled with fear at your frown?

These qualities were incompatible with physical activity and a sense of humor. But it was not only the sentimental novelists who gave this kind of picture: the women portrayed by major novelists from Cooper to Howells and James are remarkable for their sedentary nature and their deadly solemnity. Courting customs are represented as having the stylized formality of a minuet. It is doubtful if the conversations were ever heard on land or sea.

Cooper's forest maidens necessarily engage in some physical activity, but Celia Howard in *The Pilot* (1823) is seen as "a female figure clad in virgin white . . . reclining on the end of a distant couch. A small hand which seemed to blush at its own naked beauties, supported her head, imbedded in the volumes of her hair like the fairest alabastor set in the deepest ivory." Fashionable girls like Eve Effingham and Grace Courtland in *Home As Found* (1838) spend their time in drawing rooms engaged in mouthing some of Cooper's most pedantic opinions.

Hawthorne's Hester Prynne does walk about the village on errands of mercy; he emphasizes her skill with the needle, but she is never shown doing the kind of hard work then required of a lone woman: scrubbing clothes, digging a garden, chopping wood. *The Marble Faun* is a good example of the selectivity used by nineteenth-century writers in their depiction of women. Hilda is represented as an American artist with her own studio in Rome. To that extent she resembles the sculptor Harriet Hosmer, a characteristically American type. But there the resemblance ends. Hilda, physically and emotionally, is drawn from Sophia Hawthorne, the least dynamic of the Peabody sisters. Like Sophia, Hilda is not a creative artist but a skilled copyist of paintings. She is compared to "a flower that finds a chink for itself and a little earth to grow in"; her fellow artists call her Hilda the Dove. She has a friend or two in Rome but no companions except a flock of doves.

All this is very different from a real-life artist Hawthorne knew in Rome. Born in Watertown, Massachusetts, Harriet Hosmer (1830–1908) was brought up by a widowed father who had lost three other children. To insure Harriet against the fate of her mother, who had died of tuberculosis, her physician father gave her an outdoor life. She had a horse, a gun, a boat, and freedom to roam. After attending Mrs. Sedgwick's school in Lenox, she studied drawing and modeling in Boston, then enrolled in the medical department of the University of St. Louis to study anatomy. On a trip down the Mississippi she smoked a peace pipe with some Indians, and on a wager climbed a mountain which has been since known as Mt. Hosmer.

In Rome she became a great friend of the Brownings. From St. Louis she received commissions to do a statue of Beatrice Cenci and a huge bronze of Thomas Hart Benton. Her Zenobia was shown in the London exhibition of 1862. The Prince of Wales, later Edward VII, bought a copy of the Puck which he had seen in her studio. After doing a statue of the former Queen of Naples she became a friend of the queen's sister, who was Empress of Austria.

In Rome she scandalized the natives by riding astride her horse.[3] However, instead of depicting this very American girl, Hawthorne chose to give us a sentimental dove.

Henry James's women rarely seem to walk farther than the terrace. Isabel Archer is first shown seated in an old library. "She had never opened the bolted door nor removed the green paper (renewed by other hands) from its sidelights; she had never assured herself that the vulgar street lay beyond." At the English estate, Gardencourt, she and her cousin Ralph Touchett "strolled about the grounds . . . and in the long afternoons . . . they took a boat on the river . . . or drove over the country in a low, capacious, thick-wheeled phaeton. . . ."[4]

Daisy Miller says that her mother never walks ten steps; Daisy herself first appears strolling in the hotel garden in Geneva. "She was dressed in white muslin, with a hundred frills and flounces, and knots of pale-colored ribbon. She was bare-headed; but she balanced in her hand a large parasol, with a deep border of embroidery."[5] Not exactly a hiking costume.

When Catherine Sloper of *Washington Square* is in Europe with her father, James mentions that they are good walkers, but she is most often pictured seated in the house on Washington Square. After her final farewell to her suitor, "Catherine meanwhile, in the parlor, picking up her morsel of fancy-work, had seated herself with it again—for life, as it were."

A real-life contemporary of these girls, Julia Newberry of Chicago, daughter of a very rich man, enjoyed rowing, croquet, dancing, and bowling. On one occasion she beat her brother with a score of 132, although he turned the tables in another game by bowling 203. Before she became ill with what may have been tuberculosis, she could play croquet for four hours at a stretch. Her wit and humor will be recorded in a later chapter.

James liked to pose his women against such backgrounds as Gardencourt, the salons of Claire de Cintre and Mme. de Vionnet, or at Gloriani's party in a walled garden.

Howells's women chose less glamorous settings. Penelope Lapham frequently visited the circulating library and attended many church lectures; her sister Irene "spent her abundant leisure in shopping for herself and her mother. . . . They all three took long naps every day, and sat hours together minutely discussing what they saw out of the window." In the summer they went to mountain and seaside resorts where "multitudes of girls, lovely, accomplished, exquisitely dressed" sat around "humbly glad of the presence of any sort of young man." Howells was of course censorious of the idleness of the Lapham girls, but he accepted in all seriousness the view of women's physical and mental weakness. Irene, who gets a headache from a long walk on the beach, says, "What a fool I was to take that walk."[6]

In the semi-autobiographical novel *Their Wedding Journey* the Marches, no longer young, spend their honeymoon at Niagara Falls. At the Falls the Marches cross a small suspension bridge from Goat Island. Mrs. March is so terrified that she sinks down at the root of a tree and says she can never cross back. Her husband finally shames her into doing so. Twelve years later the Marches return to Niagara. Now "her nerves were most sensitive and electrical; her apprehensions had multiplied quite beyond the dangers that beset her."[7]

In *Indian Summer* Coleville, aged forty-one, is wandering about Florence where he had studied architecture as a young man and been jilted by a girl. He meets Mrs. Bowen, an American widow with a thirteen-year-old daughter, Effie, and a ward, Imogene Graham. Mrs. Bowen has brought up Effie according to European standards: "For her daughter there were to be no buggy rides, or concerts, or dances, or lingering at the gate with her youthful escort home from the ball."[8] Little Effie's only exercise seems to be strolling about with her gloved hand in Coleville's. When he suggests that she join him in skipping stones over the water, she refuses lest it dirty her gloves. And Coleville himself refuses to let twenty-year-old Imogene skip stones because it would be unladylike.

Coleville considers himself too old to dance, but against Mrs.

Bowen's orders against dancing at a festival Imogene gets him out on the floor a couple of times. She persuades herself that she is in love with him. Had Imogene been able to meet some young men and get some outdoor exercise she might not have got herself engaged to the old-maidish Coleville.

Mrs. Bowen and Imogene are completely lacking in even a rudimentary sense of humor; otherwise the plot would have evaporated. In *The Rise of Silas Lapham* Penelope is said to have brought back amusing accounts of the church meetings she attended, but no Howells woman ever made a recorded witty remark. For that matter, with the exception of Miss Gostrey in *The Ambassadors*, few if any of Henry James's women have a sense of humor. Unlike the real girls of the time, a nineteenth-century fictional heroine almost never makes a wisecrack.

A notable exception to the hothouse atmosphere is Louisa May Alcott's *Little Women* (1868). Although it somewhat merits its author's description, "moral pap for children," it presents a group of healthy girls who shovel snow, throw snowballs, row a boat, play croquet, and enjoy dancing. Jo, the tomboy, likes boys' games, work, and manners. She resents her expected role of staying home to knit "like a poky old woman" while her father is in the Union army. "I am dying to go and fight with papa."

It is significant that the story is highly autobiographical. In her journal Louisa had written, "I've often longed to see a war, and now I have my wish. I long to be a man. . . ." Like her heroines she was physically active. At twenty-six she noted: "Took care of L. W. who was ill. Walked from C to B one day, twenty miles, in five hours, and went to a party in the evening. Not very tired. Well done for a vegetable production." She rode horseback, laid carpets; in one day she did a big wash alone, baked, swept the house, picked hops, got dinner, and wrote a chapter of *Moods*. Not surprisingly she noted, "I feel very mortal today." In November 1862 she recorded, "Thirty years old. Decided to go to Washington as a nurse if I could find a place. Help needed, and I love nursing, and I *must* let out my pent-up energy in some new way."[9]

Such activities did not preclude those engaged in for fun. As a girl Harriet Beecher (1811–96), who helped her father carry wood, also joined him and her brothers on fishing trips; with other young people she went on houseboat excursions, picnics, and hayrides. To her friend, Mary Dutton, she wrote about the pre-breakfast horseback rides prescribed by her bossy sister Catharine.[10]

Riding a horse either for travel or for fun is mentioned by girls in scores of diaries. Early in the century, fifteen-year-old Mary Ann Bacon, a student at the excellent school kept by Sarah Pierce in Litchfield, Connecticut, noted that she left Roxbury at eight in the morning, rode until ten, then again from noon until two. Apparently her father rode with her. That afternoon she attended school.[11] Elizabeth Cady (1815–1902) decided to learn Greek and horseback riding. When she jumped her horse over a fence or a ditch, she longed to have her father say, "Well, a girl is as good as a boy, after all."[12]

Even the Alcott girls, who had to help their mother support the family, took up riding. Louisa made riding habits for herself and May: "had some fine rides. Both [horses] needed exercise, and this was good for us."[13]

In the South the nature of plantation life and generally poor roads necessitated the ability to ride. Kate Stone (1841–1907), whose widowed mother managed an estate of 1,260 acres and 150 slaves, is a case in point. Interspersed with accounts of running a sewing machine to make dresses and hem towels was her recording of following the hounds for a mile or so—"a delightful dash" or "we had a gay gallop home" or "Had a charming canter home, notwithstanding rough roads and a misty rain." Even while the family were refugees from the war, her sister Emily fell backward off a horse while racing Kate. She was up in an instant and pledged all of the witnesses to silence lest her mother should forbid riding.[14]

City girls, of course, had a greater temptation for physical inactivity. In 1836 in her immensely popular *Letters to Young Ladies* Mrs. L. H. Sigourney said that city life, affluence, and habits of refinement had produced an enervating effect. She advocated daily exercise in the open air: walking, horseback riding, and sea bathing.[15]

Writing of a visit to Philadelphia in 1830, Frances Trollope described the life of a typical lady of fashion who lived in a handsome house, and who had a fine carriage with a coachman:

She rises, and her first hour is spent in the scrupulously nice arrangement of her dress; she descends to her parlour neat, stiff, and silent; her breakfast is brought in by her free black footman; she eats her fried ham and her salt fish, and drinks her coffee in silence while her husband reads his newspaper. . . . Her carriage is ordered at eleven: till that hour she is employed in the pastry-room her snow-white apron protecting her mouse-coloured silk. Twenty minutes before her carriage should appear, she retires to her chamber, as she calls it, shakes, and folds up her still snow-white apron, smooths her rich dress, and with nice care, sets on her elegant bonnet, and all the handsome *et caetera*; then walks down stairs, just at the moment that her free black coachman announces to her free black footman that the carriage waits. She steps into it, and gives the word "Drive to the Dorcas society."

There the ladies sew and discuss missions and clergymen until three. At home after a glance over the dinner table she sits down, work in hand to await her spouse. "He comes, shakes hands with her, spits and dines. The conversation is not much and ten minutes suffices for the dinner; fruit and toddy, the newspaper and the workbag succeed." [16]

The wealth of catty detail suggests that Mrs. Trollope had some talent as a writer of fiction. For instance one wonders if an elegant Philadelphia gentleman spat on entering the house, or if a dinner served with the cut glass and fine silver (mentioned by Mrs. Trollope) was eaten in ten minutes, especially considering the lavish menus of the period. It is hard to believe that the society whose witty and sophisticated ladies of four decades earlier had impressed European aristocrats had become so deadly dull.

As it happens there is a voluminous diary of an upper-class Philadelphia lady covering the years from 1848 to 1853—that of Adele Biddle—which casts doubt upon the accuracy of Mrs. Trollope's picture.[17] Adele's father was Nicholas Biddle, president of the Bank of the United States from 1822 until 1836, when Jackson revoked its charter. He had died in 1844, but the family continued to be in the forefront of Philadelphia aristocracy. Adele Biddle's account gives a picture of the society in which she moved.

She was twenty when she began the diary, and as she recorded two years later, "I was thinking today how very small part of one's life is put down in a diary when the individual life, the feeling is left out." Admittedly the diary if chiefly a record of the daily activities of a rather serious-minded young woman. Perhaps half the entries concern her reading and her comments upon it. She read some poetry, a few novels, sermons and religious works such as Butler's *Analogy*, books of travel, and a great deal of history and biography. She mentioned Irving's *Mahomet and His Successors*, Macauley's *History of England*, Sparks's *Washington*, Franklin's *Autobiography*, Chesterfield's *Letters*, and several books on Napoleon, one of them apparently in French. Among the novelists she read were Scott, Dickens, and Madame de Staël. A book called *Self Formation* gave her "infinite pleasure, and Hobart's sermons "always especially please me." Even the poetry she chose was likely to be serious: Milton and Wordsworth's *Excursion*. Like many another reader she thought she should admire Wordsworth but found it difficult to do so. She heard Emerson lecture but disagreed with his statement that one should read only books that one liked.

On a typical day she would get up early, knit, read, and take a long walk—as much as six and a half miles. Even in mid-January she walked from the Delaware to the Schuylkill, a distance of about two and a half miles each way. She occasionally attended riding school, and she and another girl sometimes hired horses—once for a ride out to the Falls of the Schuylkill about eight miles from her home. Sometimes she and her mother went bowling at a nearby alley. For a time Adele enthusiastically took up spinning, spending all day at the wheel.

She knew enough music to transcribe a half dozen waltzes and polkas for a friend, and she took up the study of harmony. Although she enjoyed dancing she apparently did not spend many evenings doing so. She liked plays and concerts—saw Charlotte Cushman play the part of Queen Catherine, attended a number of Fanny Kemble's Shakespeare readings, and heard Jenny Lind sing. With another girl she visited the exhibitions at the Academy of the Fine Arts.

In the summer she went with her mother to Cape May for the sea bathing. They went into the water even when the surf was so rough it knocked down her mother and brother. Once she hired a horse to ride to Cold Spring but the animal proved to be afraid of the sound of the waves. One evening Adele played waltzes for an impromptu hop.

The life pictured in the diary is not glamorous or luxurious, but it certainly is not a sedentary one. Apparently the widowed Mrs. Biddle did not keep a carriage, for Adele took some youngsters to Fairmount Park in an omnibus, and rode one on other occasions. She taught a Sunday School class and sometimes had a few of the pupils in her own home. When her mother had a serious illness Adele took the nursing shift from midnight to four in the morning.

One gets the impression of affectionate family relationships. Brothers and sisters went together to hear Mrs. Kemble read Shakespeare. Some of them took up a fad of cold baths in the morning under the pump. Adele and her sister were nearly run over by their older brother, Edward, who was running around the lawn to get warm after a cold plunge; the tone of the diary entry about the incident is one of amusement. Another time, her brother Craig inveigled her into a shooting gallery where she was at first terrified but later tried her hand with a gun. When a brother graduated from Yale, Adele made the long journey to New Haven and sat through sixteen orations. Visits to Andalusia, the beautiful Greek revival mansion on the Delaware, always made Adele sad because they brought back memories of her happy childhood with her father. On one occasion at her mother's request Adele read aloud one of her father's speeches.

Like Adele Biddle's, the diary of Anna Yarnall,[18] of a wealthy Philadelphia Quaker family, is filled with accounts of her reading. Born in 1844, she began her diary at the age of twelve and continued it for nearly thirty years. It is not an account of a glamorous life, but especially during her adolescence Anna gives a picture of the day-to-day activities of a girl in the 1850s and 1860s. Like Adele Biddle's diary this one is filled with accounts of very solid reading. When she was twelve her father gave her a history of England for her birthday. That same year she listed over fifty books she had read, some of them obviously moralistic tales, but others including *She Stoops to Conquer, The Good Natured Man, Two Years Before the Mast, Uncle Tom's Cabin, The Alhambra* and *The Conquest of Granada*, and various superficial historical accounts. Later she moved on to the *Iliad*, Shakespeare, Lamb, Scott, Carlyle, Bulwer-Lytton, Ruskin, Dickens, and Motley. Her father was amused to find her taking up Plato. A Quaker, he had hidden away *The Fortunes of Sir Nigel*, but Anna found it and read it secretly. Even after she finished school she continued to study Latin and took up Greek.

Certainly the diaries of a great variety of nineteenth-century girls contradict Mrs. Trollope's statement that in America there was a "very slight acquaintance with the best models of composition. . . . What they class as modern literature seems to include little beyond the English publications of the day. . . . As for 'the wits of Queen Anne's day,' they are laid *en masse* upon a shelf, in some score of very old fashioned houses, together with Sherlock and Taylor, as too antiquated. . . ."[19] As it happens both Adele Biddle and Anna Yarnall read Taylor and Addison.

Just as Adele Biddle's extensive reading did not prevent a considerable amount of physical activity, Anna Yarnall's school and reading never kept her from attending riding school every afternoon. She learned to handle vicious horses, and continued riding during her young adulthood. With other young people she went on hikes and picnics; she frequently played croquet. At an afternoon party when she was sixteen, two of the girls "laid a most remarkable trap to be kissed: which succeeded to admiration."

These Quaker schoolgirls were obviously rather different from Mrs. Trollope's boarding-school miss who came into the reception room to meeet a girl friend, but "finding a young man with her, put her hands before her eyes, and ran out of the room again screaming 'A man! a man! a man!' " She told of another young lady meeting a fourteen-year-old boy on the stairs, who became so agitated that "panting and sobbing" would not pass until the boy moved off the stairs.[20]

Mrs. Trollope's shy misses were prototypes—one could not suppose that they became mothers—of the girls in Howells's novels. For instance when Silas Lapham, while showing his unfinished mansion to young Cory, points out what is to be the girls' bedroom, both girls blush at what Howells obviously regarded as Lapham's crudity. In *The Lady of the Aroostook* (1879), Lydia Blood finds herself the only woman aboard a ship bound for Europe. She plays shuffleboard and ringtoss with two young men, Dunham and Staniford. The latter, a dabbler in the arts and literature, never expects to marry. However, he is increasingly attracted to Lydia. On one occasion as they are walking on deck he holds her hand and then kisses it. One might suppose that a small-town girl who had attended local dances had been kissed before—and not on the hand—but Lydia is a Howells girl. Therefore she does not come to breakfast the next morning, and at dinner she is pale and heavy-eyed, and has no appetite. When she glances at Staniford, she blushes. "Staniford knew he was to blame for the headache and the blush."

Nineteenth-century diaries give a very different picture. A young law student in Litchfield, Connecticut, wrote in 1820 about some of the girls at the nearby Pierce school. Of Mary Parks: "have seldom seen a girl look so kissable." A Miss Mary Ann "thought she was near being swallowed at the kissing bout which has been held in L—," and "They say Helen was all but kissed to death at the Landons—The wonder would be if she were not." These girls did not resemble Sweet Alice of the song. When it fell to the lot of Sam Sheldon to carve he held up a rib of pork and remarked "that was such a thing as women was made of. Yea, says Polly Hopkins and (in both cases) it was taken out of much such a creature."[21]

Boys took girls for walks, escorted them to college debates and lectures, and congregated at young ladies' homes to chat, eat apples and cakes, and gather around the piano to sing. In the 1830s Jacob Motte, a Harvard student, went over to Boston one morning, took a girl to the frog pond, bought her some ice cream, and went with her on a shopping errand. At President Quincy's he met "an uncommonly fine girl" with whom he "spent such delicious moments in conversation" that he let everyone go home first. He spent a pleasant evening listening to still another girl play the piano, but soon met one even more charming. "Oh ye gods! she was irresistible. . . . Oh, such eyes! she had teeth too, and such teeth! ye gods, was the like ever seen?" He walked this vision home.[22]

At Amherst in the 1840s William Hammond conducted one of the most complicated series of flirtations on record.[23] One October day he walked home with Mary Warner, called on Jennie Gridley, but declined to make calls with her; saw Sabra Howe at a window and dropped in. Jennie turned up, and finding him "very much at home on the arm of a sofa . . . looked most unutterable things." Later in the day he ran into Mary Adams in the bookstore and walked her home, where he spent an hour or two. He cut prayers to call on Miss Henry.

Going over to Mount Holyoke for a blind date with Ellen Holman, he feared he might meet Miss Lyon and "the assistant dragoness." Instead he was ushered into the parlor where within an hour he and the young lady were "*Willy* and *Nelly*." She took him on a tour of the seminary, where he met "any number of plain young ladies" and caught "sly peeps into their little boxes of sleeping rooms" and said "beautiful" at every eligible window. Obviously unlike Howells's Latham girls, Nelly did not blush at the mention of a girl's bedroom.

At one boardinghouse another day he played backgammon with his landlady's daughter; then after moving to Mrs. Dwight's, taught chess to Fannie Dwight. When he called on Jennie Gridley he found her a bit cool because he had not appeared earlier. Jennie, just back from boarding school, he found "rather *improved* for the worse with new *airs*, etc." However before long he and Jennie were kissing good-by in the hall. As he recorded the experience, "It was not the voluptuous kiss of love, or the *lip*-touching, *tip*-touching of a prude, but the pure kiss of friendship, the *beau ideal* of kissing without alloy."

Even at puritanical Oberlin boys and girls went sleighing and buggy riding. A girl telling of a drive to Elyria reported that the boys raced carriages, the crowd had a big supper and played blindman's buff, and on the way home her escort let her drive so that he could sit close to her. Her considered opinion was, "I do not wish *truly* and honestly to have another *kiss* from Perkins K. Clarke to the longest day I live."[24]

A Yale student contemporaneous with William Hammond met a girl who claimed to have read Shakespeare and the *Essays of Elia*. As this particularly literate being kissed him good-by, she slipped into his hand a note giving her name, which he evidently did not know, and containing a quotation from the *Psalm of Life*. As this should have warned him, he met disillusion when he showed her

Niagara Falls. Her comment was, "I declare, it beats the bugs."[25]

In 1861 John Henry Smith (1843–1913), a student at Madison College, now Colgate, visited his home in Newark, New Jersey: "I went to the Sewing Circle of the North Baptist Church, had a good time there, went over the river with Miss Hutchins 3 couples of us remained there till 1 ½ in the morning. Came up with Lizzie Green. I don't know how many kisses I had that evening, was almost smothered with the sweet things."[26] Two days later he and another boy "escourted" two girls to a Mrs. Norwood's where they played cards and ate chestnuts. "Miss Albert gave me a sweet kiss before I was aware of the fact; went home with my lady. She too gave me a farewell salute and bad me call on my return."

In the light of all this, Lydia Blood's trauma at a kiss on the hand and Colville's from a kiss by his fiancee seem particularly idiotic. The only kiss in *The Portrait of a Lady*—perhaps the only one in a James novel—is also a traumatic experience. When Casper Goodwood takes Isabel in his arms:

> His kiss was like white lightning, a flash that spread, and spread again, and stayed; and it was extraordinarily as if, while she took it, she felt each thing in his hard manhood that had least pleased her, each aggressive fact of his face, his figure, his presence, justified of its intense identity and made one with the act of possession. She had heard of those wrecked and under water following a train of images before they sink. But when darkness returned she was free. She never looked about her; she only darted from the spot.

Of course all girls did not kiss on casual acquaintance. Mary Haines Harker, a young Quaker from Philadelphia, held off for nearly three months after meeting Jack Slaughter, the man she fell in love with in 1853. However they did a lot of concentrated spooning. She met him late in May during a trip to Virginia, her reward for graduating with high marks from St. Mary's Hall in Burlington, New Jersey. On June 1 and 2 she danced until three in the morning. Jack sent her a copy of Hood's poems. On the seventeenth her horse ran away and Jack saved her life at the edge of a precipice. He sent her a rosebud bouquet and she gave him her violets. At a dance on the twenty-second they went into the library and then out for a walk. "Oh! never was moonlight so sweet as this."

Two days later she was reprimanded for again staying out late with him. However "Frannie stayed up all night talking to Mr. Otey. Oh Fran!"

In August Jack visited her parents, apparently to ask for her hand, and bringing Mrs. Browning's poems. "I—I—I kissed him for the first time. So I couldn't die first." In December they were married.[27]

In the North young men frequently took girls out skating or sleighing. The engravings and lithographs of the period show about as many girls as men on frozen ponds and rivers. Young Hammond took a particular charmer out in a hired sleigh. Admiring her profile, he upset the sleigh and came down "with a mingled mass of red cloak and disheveled curls." The horse ran away and someone else took Mary home.[28]

Sleighing and skating are some of the amusements mentioned in the diary of Caroline Cowles Richards,[29] who grew up in Canandaigua, New York. Her mother had died when Caroline was seven so she, her two older brothers, and her four-year-old sister were brought up by their maternal grandparents, Mr. and Mrs. Thomas Beals. Beals, a banker, seems to have been a doting grandfather. For instance when they were children he built them a teeter-totter in the yard; he took them sleighing in his cutter; he loved to stand and watch them as they set off to Sunday School; and when they were older, he took them downtown to show them through the new bank.

His wife, a very pious woman, was rather strict. "I never knew anyone who liked to go to church as much as Grandmother does," wrote fourteen-year-old Caroline. "She says she would rather be a doorkeeper in the house of our God than dwell in the tents of wickedness. They don't have women doorkeepers, and I know she would not dwell a minute in a tent."[30]

Grandmother's strictness made little impression on Caroline's younger sister, Anna. When the latter asked for a topic for a composition, Mrs. Beals suggested "A Contented Mind." Anna replied that she had never had one and didn't know what it meant. Given religious music to play she practiced "Mary to the Saviour's Tomb" until she could play it as fast as a waltz. On receiving a malachite from her grandfather, Anna remarked "she always thought Malachite was one of the prophets." When Grandmother learned that Anna had skipped school with some other girls, she said she hoped she would never get such a report again. "Anna said she would not if she could possibly help it." Grandfather chipped in with advice on being careful of what they did because they were making history. "Anna says she shall try not to have hers as dry as some that she had to learn at school to-day."[31]

As might be expected of such high-spirited misses, they sneaked off on a forbidden sleigh ride. Fourteen-year-old Caroline noted, "I had no idea that sleigh-rides could make one feel so bad." They were found out and promised not to do it again. A party of the girls climbed to the top of the new courthouse under construction.* One of them, Abbie Clark, who always had "some quotation at her tongue's end," climbed up on a beam and recited Alexander Selkirk's soliloquy beginning, "I am the monarch of all I survey." At a picnic this same girl picked her way out to a rock in the middle of a brook and declaimed Roderick Dhu's bombast:

> Come one, come all, this rock shall fly
> From its firm base, as soon as I.

Then the stone tipped over and Abbie had to wade ashore.[32]

With the coming of the Civil War, the girls took flowers to the trains loaded with departing soldiers who in turn cut off buttons to give as souvenirs. But Caroline was wise enough to reflect "we hear the martial music and see the flags flying and see the recruiting tents on the square and meet men in uniform at every turn and see the train loads of the boys in blue going to the front, but it will not seem so grand if we hear they are dead on the battlefield far from home.[33]

Like their sisters North and South the girls went daily to the courthouse to sew and roll bandages. In 1863 the girls of the sewing society sent a letter to General McClellan expressing admiration and confidence. As Caroline's name headed the roster she got a personal answer from the General.[34] (By that time she had a soldier sweetheart in the Union army.)

The diary gives far less about her courtship than about Lincoln's

---

* In fiction the Lapham girls become scornful when their father suggests that they sit on a trestle in the new house.

second inaugural address and later assassination. However in July 1866 she was married at twenty-two. On her wedding day her eighty-seven-year-old widowed grandmother "bless her" watched from the window as the couple drove away.

The sentimental novels of the period—for instance *Tempest and Sunshine* (1854) by Mary Jane Holmes—always contrasted a sober-minded heroine with a light-minded sister or rival. Of course the irreverent girl always lost out. However in real life the irreverent Anna was valedictorian of her small graduating class and eventually married.

In their diaries various girls mentioned sermons they liked, or recorded religious sentiments, but only rarely is a diary filled with pious musings. Sometimes, like Anna Richards, a young minx made fun of moralistic teachings. When Miss Pierce told her pupil, Mary Goodwin, that she saw inbred sin on her back, the girl made a drawing of the lady with inbred sin on *her* back. One day when the same girl laughed at prayers, Miss Pierce said, "Mary Goodwin, Mary Goodwin, you will be cast into outer darkness where there is weeping and gnashing of teeth." To which Mary commented, "Then I suppose those who have no teeth will have to gum it."[35]

By contrast, nineteenth-century novels represent girls as evangelical angels. In *Tempest and Sunshine* (1854), the dying Julia asks forgiveness of the sister she has wronged. To which Fanny answers, "As I hope for pardon in heaven, so do I forgive you for the great wrong you have done me." When Julia says she can never find heaven, "Earnestly then did Fanny speak of a Savior's love, which receives all, pardons all, who come to him." While she speaks, Dr. Lacy comes into the room and says, "Teach me, too, the way of life, for I fear I have never walked in it."[36]

In Maria Susanna Cummings's *The Lamplighter*, published the same year, Emily says:

> Speak not of my blindness as a misfortune . . . I have long ceased to think of it as such. It is only through the darkness of the night that we discover the lights of heaven, and only when we shut out from earth that we enter the gates of Paradise. With eyes to see the wonderful working of nature and nature's God, I nevertheless closed them to the evidences of almighty love that were around me

on every side. While enjoying the beautiful and glorious gifts that were showered on my pathway, I forgot to thank and praise the Giver....[37]

There is of course more of this. In a similar fashion Harriet Beecher Stowe, as Alice Crozier demonstrates,[38] represents a number of her heroines as angelic figures. Of Little Eva:

> an airy and innocent playfulness seemed to flicker like a shadow of summer leaves over her childish face. . . . Always dressed in white, she seemed to move like a shadow through all sorts of places, without contracting spot or stain . . . that visionary golden head, with its deep blue eyes, fleeted along.

> [To Uncle Tom] she seemed something almost divine; and whenever her golden head and deep blue eyes peered out upon him from behind some dusky cotton-bale, or looked down upon him over some ridge of packages, he half believed that he saw one of the angels stepped out of the New Testament.

In Mrs. Stowe's *The Minister's Wooing* (1859), Mary Scudder lectures Aaron Burr on his betrayal of Mme. de Frontignac's love:

> Mr. Burr, you remember the rich man with flocks and herds, but nothing would do him but he must have the one little ewe lamb which was all his poor neighbor had. Thou art that man! You have stolen all the love she had to give,—all that she had to make a happy home; and you can never give her anything in return, without endangering her purity and her soul . . . and if you die, as I fear you have lived, unreconciled to the God of your fathers, it will be in her heart to offer up her very soul for you, and pray that God will impute all your sins to her, and give you heaven. Oh, I know this because I have felt it in my own heart.

Unlikely as it seems about Aaron Burr:

> The diviner part of him was weeping, and the cold, proud demon was struggling to regain its lost ascendency.

When Mary read from the Bible to Virginie de Frontignac, "her face grew solemnly transparent as of an angel." Of the dying Mara, heroine of *Orr's Island* (1862), Mrs. Stowe wrote of "the holy innocents who come into our households to smile with the smile of angels . . . whose life was like Christ's in that they were made, not for themselves, but to become bread to us."

In Hawthorne's *The Marble Faun* (1860), the sculptor, Kenyon, muses about Hilda in Rome: "She had trodden lightly over the crumble old crimes; she had taken her way amid the grime and corruption which Paganism had left there, and a perverted Christianity had made more noisome; walking saintlike through it all, with white, innocent feet."[39]

As Hawthorne did with Hilda, James as late as 1902 used the dove to characterize Milly Theal. *The Wings of the Dove* is much too solid a novel to be classified as merely sentimental fiction, but as in that tradition the saintly heroine produced a kind of moral regeneration in Merton Densher.

Like the very gentle perfect knight of the middle ages and the noble savage of the eighteenth century, the saintly heroine came to be accepted as fact. Thus in *Letters to Young Ladies*, Mrs. Sigourney wrote, "Does not the influence of woman rest upon every member of her household like the dew upon the tender herb, or the sunbeam silently educating the young flower?"[40]

When the novelistic heroine was not reclaiming sinners, she was involved in a dreary misunderstanding about who was in love with whom. This theme which made up half or more of the plot of a typical novel is remarkably absent from the love affairs recorded in diaries. Even Howells, who fancied himself as a realist, devoted a large part of *The Rise of Silas Lapham* to the absurd notion developed by Mrs. Lapham and her moronic daughter that Tom Corey is in love with Irene.

It is a relief to turn from these sentimental waxwork figures to the realistic portraits in Fanny Fern's (Mrs. Sara Willis Parton) *Folly as It Flies* (1868), a series of essays based on her popular newspaper columns. In a section "Some Varieties of Women" she lists the slattern, the over-zealous housekeeper, the butterfly woman, the library woman, "who walks around a baby as if it were a rattlesnake," and the female viper—"your cat—your hyena. All claws, nails, and tongue." Then there is

the rabbit woman. She has four chins and twelve babies. She has two dresses—a loose calico wrapper for home wear, and a black silk for meetin'. She eats tremendously, and never goes out; she calls her husband "Pa." She is quite content to roll leisurely from her rocking-chair in the nursery to the dining-room table, and thence back again, year in and year out. She knows nothing that is passing in the outside world, nor cares. She never touches a book or a newspaper. . . . She has a voice like an auctioneer, and prefers cabbage to any vegetable extant.[41]

Fanny Fern was equally realistic about the drudgery of the farm wife, the seamstress working on $200 gowns for $3.50 a week, and the girl leaving a tenement to slave in a factory where she gets a half hour at lunch to eat bread and butter or an apple: "we all know that human strength and human nature have limits, and the dreadful pressure of temptations and present ease, upon the discouragement, poverty, and friendlessness of the working girls. New York must be gratifying to the devil."[42]

As for the "coming woman,"

She will not of necessity sour into a pink-nosed old maid, or throw herself at any rickety old shell of humanity. No, the future man will have to step lively; this wife is not to be had for the whistling. . . . Thick-soled boots and skating are coming in, and "nerves," novels and sentiment . . . are going out. . . . the coming woman shall be no cold, angular, flat-chested, narrow-shouldered, sharp-visaged Betsy, but she shall be a bright-eyed, full-chested, broad-shouldered, large-souled intellectual being. . . .[43]

When Fanny Fern hears a woman saying she would not give a fig for a vote, "I feel pity that in this glorious year of our Lord 1869, she should still prefer going back to the dark ages."[44] Her ideal women are a lot closer to the ones who wrote diaries and memoirs than to most nineteenth-century heroines of fiction.

She was equally sharp tongued about men. The patience of Job was a proverb that needed revamping. "Like all the rest of his sex . . . he could be heroic only for a little while at a time. He began bravely; but ended as most of them do under annoyance, by cursing and swearing. Patient as Job! Did Job ever try, when he was hungry, to eat shad with a frisky baby on his lap?"[45]

In one of her novels she gave an unflattering portrait of her brother Nathaniel Parker Willis. Not that she was a man-hater: she married for the third time after being widowed and divorced. She thought that there was no woman who would not prefer to be married, and that beneath the smooth ice of the self-sufficient woman there smouldered a volcano. It is difficult to escape the confusion that, as contrasted with nineteenth-century heroines, the real girls and women were earthier, more physically active, much better read, and far wittier—in other words more interesting as human beings.

NOTES

1. Wasserstrom, *Heiress of All the Ages*, p. 24.
2. Herbert Brown, *The Sentimental Novel in America, 1789–1860*, p. 113.
3. Ernest Earnest, *Expatriates and Patriots*, Durham, 1968, p. 171.
4. Henry James, *The Portrait of a Lady* (New York Edition), New York, 1908, I, 30; I, 88–89.
5. Henry James, *Daisy Miller, Pandora, The Patagonia and Other Tales* (New York Edition), New York, 1909, p. 8.
6. William Dean Howells, *The Rise of Silas Lapham*, introduced by David Mead, New York, 1964, pp. 25, 84.
7. William Dean Howells, *Their Wedding Journey*, ed. by John K. Reeves, Bloomington, Ind., 1968, p. 181.
8. William Dean Howells, *Indian Summer* (Everyman), New York, 1951, p. 15.
9. Edna D. Cheney, *Louisa May Alcott: Her Life, Letters and Journals*, Boston, 1895, pp. 127, 104, 169, 140.
10. Johanna Johnston, *Runaway to Heaven: The Story of Harriet Beecher Stowe*, New York, 1963, pp. 5, 45, 64.
11. Emily Noyes Vanderpoel, *Chronicles of a Pioneer School, Being the History of Miss Sarah Pierce and Her Litchfield School*, ed. by Elizabeth C. Burney Bird, Cambridge, 1903, p. 69.
12. *Elizabeth Cady Stanton, As Revealed in Her Letters, Diary and Reminiscences*, ed. by Theodore Stanton and Harriet Stanton Blatch, New York, 1922, p. 24.
13. Cheney, p. 120.
14. *Brokenburn: The Journal of Kate Stone, 1861–1868*, ed. by John Q. Anderson, Baton Rouge, 1955, pp. 63, 65, 80, 303.
15. Lydia H. Sigourney, *Letters to Young Ladies*, Fifth Edition, New York, 1839, pp. 93–94.
16. Frances Trollope, pp. 281–82.
17. All the excerpts are from Adele Biddle's manuscript diary, 1848–53, owned by the Historical Society of Pennsylvania.
18. Anna Yarnall, unpublished diary, 1856–85, in the Quaker Collection, Haverford College.
19. Frances Trollope, pp. 312–13.
20. Ibid., pp. 136–37.
21. "George Younglove Cutler—His Journal," Pierce School, pp. 207, 202.
22. *Charleston Goes to Harvard: The Diary of Jacob Rhett Motte, a Harvard Student of 1831*, ed. by Arthur H. Cole, Cambridge, 1940, pp. 23–24, 66, 77.
23. *Remembrance of Amherst: An Undergraduate's Diary, 1846–1848*, ed. by George F. Whicher, New York, 1946, pp. 25, 55, 76, 109, 186.

24. Robert Samuel Fletcher, *A History of Oberlin College from Its Foundation through the Civil War*, Oberlin, 1943, II, 424.

25. *Yale Literary Magazine*, No. 9 (August 1844).

26. John Henry Smith, unpublished diary, owned by Professor Gordon Smith of Temple University.

27. "Journal of a Quaker Maid, from the Diary of Mary Haines Harker, May–December, 1853," *Virginia Quarterly Review*, II (January 1935), 61–81.

28. *Remembrance of Amherst*, pp. 220–23.

29. Caroline Cowles Richards, *Village Life in America,1852–1872*, New York, 1912.

30. Ibid., p. 53.

31. Ibid., pp. 35, 38, 73, 129.

32. Ibid., pp. 68–69, 110.

33. Ibid., p. 140.

34. Ibid., pp. 158–59.

35. Vanderpoel, p. 290.

36. Mary Jane Holmes, *Tempest and Sunshine* (bound with Maria Susanna Cummings's *The Lamplighter*), ed. by Donald A. Koch, New York, 1968, p. 168.

37. Cummings, *The Lamplighter*, p. 533.

38. Alice Crozier, *The Novels of Harriet Beecher Stowe*, New York, 1969, pp. 123, 134, 136–41.

39. *The Complete Novels and Selected Tales of Nathaniel Hawthorne*, ed. by Norman Holmes Pearson (Modern Library), New York, 1937, p. 828.

40. Sigourney, p. 12.

41. Fanny Fern, *Folly as It Flies*, New York, 1868, pp. 288–89.

42. Ibid., p. 229.

43. Ibid., p. 265.

44. Ibid., p. 66.

45. Ibid., p. 53.

Five

The Door Openers

My daughters have as good minds as my sons, and I see no
reason why they should not be taught to use them in the
same way.

Samuel Blackwell

The unique features of American life made the demands for
woman's rights and education inevitable. The women, and many
men, very early recognized that the opening sentence of the Declaration of Independence might logically be applied to women also.
A nation which had thrown off the rule of kings and nobles could
not easily justify an autocratic family structure. But although ideological arguments were exchanged for over a hundred years, the real
forces were social and economic. Of the two, the economic pressure
is the most obvious. Middle-class women early participated in or ran
business affairs. It is small wonder that they demanded some control
over the money they earned. It made no sense that it should become
the property of husbands to dispose of as they pleased, even to the
exclusion of widows' rights. Blackstone's dictum that marriage meant
civil death for a woman was clearly unjust in the context of American life. A heritage from a landholding aristocracy, it was as out-
moded as primogeniture and entail.

But despite Marxian theory it is possible that economic forces are
less influential than social mores. These are of course influenced by
economics, but also by religion, geography, and folkways. As Henry Adams pointed out, the vast expenditures on twelfth-century
churches and cathedrals are not to be explained by economics. It is
significant that Quaker religious theory and practice produced some
of the leading proponents of woman's rights. Of this more later.

A less obvious force was the upbringing of American children.

At first glance this might seem a product of the isolation of rural families, but that is not where the phenomenon developed. If anything, the farm tended to perpetuate the patriarchal order; certainly the plantation did. The characteristic pattern developed in well-educated middle-class families. Unlike the British home where young children were relegated to the nursery and ate their meals with a nannie, American youngsters shared in family life and sat at the table with adults. Brothers and sisters were not segregated at an early age in separate boarding schools.

With a mixture of awe and disapproval, Anthony Trollope described American children an an age when he said he had not got beyond a silver spoon and was under the care of a nursemaid:

> One will often see five or six seated at the long dinner table of the hotel, breakfasting and dining with their elders, and going through the ceremony will all the gravity, and more than all the decorum of their grandfathers . . . in the States the adult infant lisps to the waiter for everything at the table, handles his fish with epicurean delicacy, is choice in the selection of his pickles, is very particular that his beefsteak shall be hot, and is instant in his demand for fresh ice in his water.[1]

A few years later the British traveler David Macrae reported that a New England mother of eleven children told him that hers had been brought to the table at seven months, and at the age of thirteen months "could handle their forks as neatly as she could." Not only were children permitted a share of everything on the table, "they begin at a preternaturally early age to take an interest in general affairs." A small boy of eight asked him, "What do you think, sir, of the present state of the country?" In Brooklyn a little boy upbraided his father for having supported Andrew Johnson. A girl "not much higher than my knee with whom I was playing a game on the carpet" asked him what he thought the effect of the acquisition of Alaska would have on Great Britain.[2] He admitted that such remarks were exceptional but said that American children as a general rule struck him as more polite, more considerate, and more orderly than those of Britain. American youngsters "need to be dealt with in a different way. You must treat them as persons who have a will of their own, and a right to exercise it. You must appeal to their reason and good sense—not merely to your own authority."[3]

The new pattern started very early in America. In 1724 James Logan, Penn's deputy in Pennsylvania and owner of a famous library, wrote to a friend in England about his nine-year-old daughter Sarah: "Sally, besides her needle, has been learning French, and this last week has been busy in the dairy at the plantation, in which she delights as well as spinning; but is this moment at the table with me . . . reading the 34th Psalm in Hebrew, the letters of which she learned very perfectly in less than two hours time, an experiment I made of her capacity only for my diversion. . . ."[4] Although Logan did not plan to educate his daughter in any language other than French, it is obvious that little Sally was not immured in a nursery. In fact her father, then mayor of Philadelphia, was baby-sitting while his wife was out.

Logan noted that the younger sister, Hannah, at three had learned to spell out her primer. At twenty-four Hannah was so beautiful, poised, and charming that a visitor from Virginia, lost in admiration, forgot how hot the tea was and burnt his mouth several times. Her successful suitor, John Smith, a young lawyer, filled his diary with references to her intelligent and "melting" conversation. On one occasion he discovered her fishing in the Schuylkill and spent a delightful afternoon with her. Hannah Logan is a preview of the American woman to follow: a girl whose intellectual development was encouraged by a father, a girl who could combine domestic employment, outdoor recreation, intellectual interests, social poise, and "melting" conversation.

Hannah Logan was not a pioneer in the woman's rights movement, but as Quaker she was part of a society which more than any other gave women a position of equality. As will appear, Quaker women were among the first to break the taboo against women on the platform. But, as has been suggested, Hannah's relationship with a learned father helped to enable her to impress her future husband with her intelligent and informed conversation.

As William Wasserstrom points out, a considerable number of the women reformers of the nineteenth century had close relationships with fathers who tutored them. This is obviously related to a familial pattern in which children sat with parents at meals and listened to adult conversation in the living room. It was not only fathers and daughters who were close: the American pattern brought girls into association with their brothers and greatly influenced the relationship of husbands and wives, mothers and sons.

It will be remembered that as a girl Mercy Warren was allowed to listen to her father's political discussions with friends; that her brother, James Otis, helped her with her intellectual development and discussed politics with her; that both her husband and son encouraged her to write. The close association of other husbands and wives of the Revolutionary generation has already been discussed.

The peculiarly American family pattern appears in Margaret Bayard Smith's account of the first forty years of Washington society—for instance, her description of Jefferson seated on a sofa surrounded by his Randolph grandchildren. At breakfast at Monticello all the Randolph children ate at the family table.[5] When William Crawford was running for President in 1824, Mrs. Smith found him at home on election eve surrounded by his family. Little Susan had her arms around his neck and the small boy sat on his knee. After his defeat he wanted to be with his children: "they do not fatigue me."[6]

This American pattern is visible in the lives of four important nineteenth-century women: Emma Willard and Catharine Beecher in education; Sarah Josepha Hale in journalism; and Elizabeth Blackwell in medicine. Although they lived in different cities and were not formally associated, they aided and abetted each other. All of them had brothers who were both companions and tutors. All of them tended to maintain close family ties with parents and siblings. Two of the women married and raised families.

The influence of mothers on many of the outstanding women is difficult to assess. For one thing, the biographers, even of their own sex, have little to say on the subject. It is obviously easier to trace the sources of a person's intellectual development than the unrecorded influences on character and emotional life. Before 1830 or 1840, when most women had little education, they obviously could not contribute much to the intellectual development of their daughters. It was women like Catharine Beecher, Mary Lyon, Sarah Hale, and Elizabeth Blackwell, and an increasing provision for secondary and higher education for women, which helped to change all this. It is also possible that the women who became pioneers in the struggle for rights, education, and the suffrage were, consciously or not, rejecting the life style of their mothers in paternalistic families. The advantages enjoyed by fathers and brothers became the things to strive for and emulate. Rejection of the subservient feminine role did not necessarily mean a rejection of the mother as a person. Thus although the biographer of Lucretia Mott mentions that her mother, Mrs. Coffin, kept a store for a time in addition to managing a large family, the only reference to Lucretia's feelings is her remark at the time of Mrs. Coffin's death: "She was companionable in every way. Her grandchiln [*sic*] as well as her childn delighted in her society."

Like the Coffin family, that of Emma Willard (née Hart) seems to have shared tasks and intellectual tastes. Emma was the sixteenth child of Samuel Hart, who had been a captain in the Revolution. Denied a college education because of the death of his father, he ran a farm near Berlin, Connecticut. When Samuel's first wife died, he married a woman ten years younger who became the mother of Emma.[7] As in all farm families of the time everybody worked: men in the fields, women cooking, making soap, spinning and weaving. But some kinds of work were made into social occasions: maple syrup boiling, quilting bees, corn huskings, barn raisings. Emma was fond of Thanksgiving family gatherings, despite the work of baking pumpkin pies, the cleaning and roasting of turkeys, and all the other preparations for a feast.

But in addition to the endless tasks, the Harts found time for books. Often either the father or mother read aloud from Chaucer, Milton, or Shakespeare. Captain Hart borrowed books from friends or the town library. A liberal in politics, he discussed the subject with his family. As Emma remembered him, "He was fifty years my senior, yet he would often call me when at the age of fourteen from household duties by my mother's side to enjoy with him some passage of an author which pleased him, or read over some essay which he had amused himself in writing."[8]

At first the district schools admitted girls only in the summer when the boys were in the fields, but gradually girls were allowed to stay on during the winter. In New England, secondary schools tended to become coeducational. When the Worthington Academy opened, Emma and her sister went there for two years. The master, Thomas Miner, was a Yale graduate. In later life Emma said that probably no school in the country at that time gave better instruction to girls.

At seventeen she started teaching. Then she got an offer to reopen a female academy in Middlebury, Connecticut, which had closed because of the illness of its headmistress. In this undertaking Emma Hart had the help of Dr. John Willard, a leading citizen of Middlebury. In 1809, two years after taking over the school, she married him. She was twenty-two; he fifty.

As was not then unusual, a man of that age had lost a wife or two—in his case, two. No doubt one of the reasons for the slow development of divorce legislation was that in the natural course of events so many people lost a spouse. Widowers tended to marry younger women, who in turn became relatively young widows. Women who survived childbearing, then as now, usually outlived their husbands.

One of the difficulties of a second or third wife is the problem of stepchildren. In the Hart family this seems not to have been serious, but Emma had trouble with the Willard children. A year after marriage she had a child of her own. However, she found time to continue her studies. Her husband encouraged her interest in medical books, and a nephew joined her in the study of Paley and Locke. But her favorite reading was Scott.[9]

When a robbery in her husband's bank left him without funds, she opened a boarding school with seventy pupils. Her biographer says she taught twelve hours a day. This probably means that she was on the job that long, doing both teaching and supervisory work. Even in that era pupils were not in class twelve hours a day or anywhere near that long.

Throughout most of the nineteenth century the great problem of women's education was lack of public support. Towns, cities, and state legislatures appropriated funds for boys' schools and colleges, but only grudgingly for the education of girls. Quaker schools and many of the New England academies were coeducational, but publicly supported schools beyond the elementary level were slow to provide for girls. As a result the education of women at the secondary and junior college level was largely undertaken by female seminaries.

These institutions became, with some justice, the target of widespread criticism. After 1830 scarcely an editor in the country could keep off the subject. A long satiric poem in *Harper's* for September 1858 described the school of Madam Cancan with "her morals infernal, her manners elysian."[10] The usual charge against the female seminary was that it stressed accomplishments at the expense of intellectual training. This was often true and nowhere more so that in the South. In her study of the Southern woman, Anne Firor Scott states that the girls of that region were expected to be trained chiefly in correct behavior to become decorative and obedient wives in a patriarchal society.[11]

Whatever its faults, the female seminary reflected the society which created it. It was financially weak because Americans would not appropriate public funds for women's education; it stressed accomplishments because that is what parents wanted, especially parents who were themselves socially unsure. Margaret Bayard Smith's novel *What is Gentility?* shows a newly rich Irish-American couple whose daughter thinks gentility is having fine clothes and a $500 piano or better still an $800 harp.[12] When such girls were sent to a seminary, they tended to stay only a few months. In a fifteen-year period, out of 1,600 pupils who entered the schools run by Zilpha Grant, only 156 completed the three-year course. The seminaries run by Emma Willard, Mary Lyon and Catharine Beecher—all superior schools—had similar difficulties.

Mrs. Willard moved her school to Waterford, New York, at the suggestion of Governor De Witt Clinton, who had been impressed by her "Plan for Improving Female Education." Dr. Willard went with her to present the plan to the New Work legislature. Her proposal was for a large state-aided seminary under the direction of a board of trustees. The plan combined religious, moral, intellectual, domestic, and ornamental instruction, including such courses as psychology and natural science. There should be good paintings to stimulate artistic interest. President Monroe and former presidents

Adams and Jefferson wrote letters of recommendation; Governor Clinton urged the plan upon the legislature. The bill passed the state senate but failed in the house.[13]

Then in 1821 Troy, New York, with a population of only five thousand, raised money to start an academy, and invited Mrs. Willard to run it. It began with ninety pupils, some from states as far away as Vermont, Georgia, and Ohio. At the time probably no girls' school in the country offered such a complete course of study.[14] Three years later Catharine Beecher opened a somewhat less ambitious school at Hartford, but it was not until 1837 that Mary Lyon raised enough money to open Mount Holyoke Seminary.

None of these schools pretended to be a college. In fact Mrs. Willard declared that the "absurdity of sending ladies to college" must "strike everyone."[15]

There is a question of semantics here: *college* then meant an institution devoted chiefly to the teaching of Greek and Latin, with some mathematics, a smattering of science, and a senior course called moral philosophy. The better seminaries, like those of Emma Willard, Catharine Beecher, and Mary Lyon, were essentially what would later be called junior colleges or normal schools.

As late as 1851 Catharine Beecher complained that the better seminaries too closely copied the curricula of men's colleges. She demanded more preparation of woman for "her distinctive profession as housekeeper, mother, nurse, and chief educator of infancy and childhood."[16]

These women had a point; in the traditional colleges students did not become acquainted with English literature in the classroom or college library, but rather in their own literary societies. If they wanted to study French or German, they did so at their own expense.

Both Emma Willard and Catharine Beecher were concerned with the training of teachers, chiefly for elementary schools. No college course then offered was relevant to this purpose. Mary Lyon's concern was the training of Christian missionaries. Even so, an English woman, after visiting Mrs. Willard's school, warned that it was educating girls too highly; they would not want to marry. Mrs. Willard replied that she had never experienced that difficulty: young men sought the girls "so resolutely for wives" that she could not keep them as teachers.[17] Later her own son married one of the students. Catharine Beecher, who had opened a school in Cincinnati when her father had moved there to direct the Lane theological seminary, reported that the West needed thirty thousand teachers plus another ten thousand a year.[18]

Like Emma Willard, the Beecher girls had grown up in close association with an able father, and like Sarah Hale and Elizabeth Blackwell, with congenial and helpful brothers. Catharine had been engaged to a young professor who died in a shipwreck, leaving his library to her. Perhaps more of a propagandist and promoter than an educator, she founded seminaries in Hartford, Cincinnati, and Milwaukee. She also took a leading part in the development of physical education for women. All three of these pioneer educators: Emma Willard, Catharine Beecher, and Mary Lyon developed systems of physical education for their pupils.[19] Both Sarah Hale and Elizabeth Blackwell preached the need for exercise and a more sensible form of dress than the current fashion of tight lacing.

Emma studied with Professor Amos Eaton when Governor Clinton imported him from Williams College to give scientific lectures to the legislature—an innovation which unfortunately has not been copied. As Eaton was sympathetic to women's education, Mrs. Willard was able to get him to teach at the seminary until women were trained to take over. He published a scientific textbook especially for the seminary and dedicated it to Mrs. Willard.[20]

Other honors came: Lafayette visited the seminary in 1824 and again in 1825. He invited Mrs. Willard to visit him in France. When the Erie Canal was opened, Governor Clinton invited her and her pupils for a boat trip to the "nine locks." She collaborated on a geography and wrote a textbook on American history, both of which were so successful that she became financially independent.

Thus when Dr. Willard died in 1825, she was able to turn over the management of the school to her widowed sister, Almira. In 1830 she sailed for Europe with her son John, who at twenty had resigned from West Point and entered a college in Hartford. In France, Lafayette called on her and took her to the opera. She was presented at court. In both France and England she visited many schools. She was astounded at the superiority of female education in America. In a school in Liverpool she found American textbooks in use, including her own. But she thought that English men talked down to women and were afraid that they might get to know too much.[21]

When she got back to Troy, she found that Almira had run the school well but was preparing to remarry. Elizabeth Cady, who was then a pupil, later remembered the joy with which Mrs. Willard was welcomed back.

She introduced physiology into the curriculum, but because of prudish criticism, the pictures of the human body were pasted over. Unlike men's colleges of the time with their emphasis on gerund grinding, the Troy seminary developed interrelated studies in the history, geography, and literature of a given period. Along with the more usual French and German, both Spanish and Italian were offered. In men's colleges the only respectable history was ancient. At Troy the girls studied the American Revolution and were required to draw from memory maps showing its progress year by year. They were expected to give analyses of the Declaration and the Constitution. And of course there was instruction in composition, elocution, drawing, singing and gymnastics—all of which were extracurricular in men's colleges.

Because the female seminaries were less bound by ossified tradition, they were able to experiment with new subjects and methods. With all their faults and limited means the seminaries probably gave women a more practical and modern education than the old-line colleges provided for men.

It is small wonder that in 1833 Sarah Hale gave publicity to Mrs. Willard's school in her *American Ladies' Magazine*. The period was the beginning of great forward strides in the education of women. Oberlin, the first coeducational college, opened in 1833, Wheaton Seminary in 1834, Mount Holyoke Female Seminary in 1837, the Georgia Female College in Macon, 1839. During the 1840s and 1850s women's colleges sprang up in Ohio, Illinois, Tennessee, Pennsylvania, and New York. In many instances the term *college* represented the kind of wishful thinking which today leads an upgraded teachers college to call itself a university. The first women's college with anything approaching an adequate endowment was Vassar in 1865.

Mrs. Willard was shrewd enough to keep title to the seminary for herself and her son when in 1838 she married Dr. Christopher Yates. She left him after nine months and got a divorce in 1843. Fortunately her son and daughter-in-law, a former pupil, were willing and able to take over the management of the school. As Emma wrote to a niece, "Mrs. John Willard, with five children, performs well the duties of principal of this school."[22]

In later life Mrs. Willard traveled extensively, conducting teachers' institutes and acting as a consultant. Her national influence on women's education may have been greater than that of Catharine Beecher but there was glory enough for both.

Part of their success was due to their national prominence. As a member of the flamboyant Beecher family, Catharine needed no publicity agent, but Emma Willard probably owed much to the championship of Sarah Josepha Hale (1788–1879), who edited two women's magazines with a national circulation. As editor of *Godey's Lady's Book* for forty years, this able woman had a tremendous influence on the lives of American women. She also wrote novels and raised a family of four children. In the *Lady's Book* she campaigned for child welfare, sanitation, the training of nurses, organized charity, the education of women, and equal economic and property rights for women. She published Poe's stories when he could not find a market elsewhere.

As one of her biographers points out, Mrs. Hale was "singularly blessed in her dealings and relations with men. Her father, brother, husband, sons were all gentlemen as was Mr. Godey."[23] She got along well with all these men, but the two who most influenced her were her brother, Horatio, and her husband, David. Her father, Captain Gordon Buel, who served in the Revolution under Horatio Gates, was first a farmer, then a tavern keeper. However, there were books in her childhood home: *Pilgrim's Progress*, Milton, Addison, Pope, Johnson, Cowper, and Burns. Her mother helped with her early education, but for some odd reason Sarah traced her first awareness of women's interests to her reading of Mrs. Radcliffe's *The Mysteries of Udolpho.* Pope became her model of style.[24] While her brother was at Dartmouth, she tried to keep up with his studies in Paley, Locke, and Edwards, and in grammar, rhetoric, composition, and geography. "To my brother Horatio," she wrote, "I owe what knowledge I have of Latin, of the higher branches of philosophy. He often regretted that I could not like himself, have the privilege of a college education."[25] When he was at home, he and Sarah kept regular hours of instruction.

After teaching school until she was twenty-five, she married a young lawyer, David Hale. Together they began a systematic program of study and reading for two hours each day. In their nine years of marriage they had five children. When her third child was on the way, she was threatened with consumption. Her husband told her she was not going to die, and leaving the two children with uncles, took her on a six weeks trip through the mountains. This and an unlikely regimen called a grape cure restored her health.[26]

It was David who died of pneumonia, two weeks before the birth of their fifth child. According to one biographer, his death was the great tragedy of her life. Sarah herself said that their life together had been a period of unbroken happiness.[27]

She tried a millinery business which failed, then published a book of poems. In 1827 she published *Northwood*, the first novel to deal with the problem of slavery. It was successful enough to be published in England. However, it is not an *Uncle Tom's Cabin*: the characters are wooden; the plot involves embezzlement and forged letters; it has the necessary happy ending. The most interesting parts are those dealing with a benevolent South Carolinian whose slaves love him, but who detests slavery and feels trapped by the "peculiar circumstances." He marries an empty-headed Northern beauty who screams when she sees a house filled with Negroes.* A New England squire answers the criticism of an Englishman by saying that the English forced slavery on America.

Mrs. Hale, like many of the liberals of her time, believed the solution was Negro colonization outside the United States. She thought that even if the slaves were freed, they would remain bonds-

---

* Because *Negro* was the term in use throughout all the discussions of the time, I have used it rather than *Black*.

men in America, and that the races could not live together in harmony.

The importance of the work is that, like Charles Brockden Brown's *Ormond* and Cooper's later novels of social criticism, it is concerned with ideas. Unfortunately none of these writers developed a technique adequate to their purposes. Even more strange, and especially so for Sarah Hale, none of them created a memorable portrait of an American woman.

The novels brought her an offer in 1828 to edit the *Ladies' Magazine* in Boston. Years later she stated the principle which she had followed for nearly fifty years: "My first object in assuming my new position was to promote the education of my own sex." Thus even before she went to Boston she arranged for the publication in the first number of the magazine an article on this subject. For the *Ladies* she wrote nearly half of the verse, fiction, and articles. The nonfiction was the most important part of the magazine: articles on rearing children, on the legal condition of women, book reviews.[28]

Louis Godey, who had founded his *Lady's Book* in 1830, acquired Mrs. Hale as editor six years later. Eventually the two magazines were merged. When Mrs. Hale took over, the circulation of *Godey's* was about 10,000; by 1850 it was 62,500, and during the peak year of 1864 was 1,512,000.[29] Even some groups of soldiers subscribed to it—possibly for pictures to pin up. Originally forty-eight pages in size, it grew to about a hundred.

Today it is chiefly remembered as a fashion magazine, but it carried stories, poems, book reviews, reading lists, and serious articles. Apparently it was Godey who kept it from publishing articles on politics and theology. He emphasized fashions to a greater degree than did Mrs. Hale.[30] It was partly due to the women's magazines that American women of the middle and working classes astonished foreign visitors by the stylishness of their clothes. Harriet Martineau remarked on the good clothes and modish hairdos of the mill girls of Patterson.[31] Lucy Larcom, who worked in the Lowell mills, said that the girls subscribed to *Graham's Magazine* and the *Lady's Book*. In a bookstore in Oregon James Bryce saw the wife of a railroader buying a fashion magazine. He noted that there was a demand for such journals among the wage-earning class. As a result "the women in these little towns were following the Parisian fashions very closely, and were in fact ahead of the majority of English ladies belonging to the professional and mercantile classes."[32] By the time Lord Bryce wrote, *Godey's* had disappeared, but it had long since set a pattern and created a demand for the fashion magazines which followed it.

The fiction in *Godey's*, however, instead of establishing a trend, followed the formulas of the sentimental tradition. The villain always got his desserts and any violation of the moral laws was punished. A rare exception to the sentimental writers of stories was, of course, Poe. Before he began to write for *Godey's*, Mrs. Hale had already favorably reviewed his poetry and his *Tales of the Grotesque and Arabesque*. From 1844 through 1846, *Godey's* was probably Poe's chief source of income.[33] Among other things it published *The Cask of Amontillado*, his fine essay on Hawthorne, and a series, *The Literati of New York City*. In his own department Godey prophesied, "We are much mistaken if these papers of Mr. Poe do not raise some commotion in the literary emporium."[34] He was not mistaken. Mrs. Hale took the ensuing uproar in her stride, saying it was her job to publish Poe's opinions *not our own.*"[35]

Among a host of forgotten contributors to the magazine some names stand out: Irving, Bryant, Longfellow, Lowell, Whittier, Emerson, and Holmes. William Gilmore Simms was a frequent contributor of prose and verse.[36] Perhaps equally important were Mrs. Hale's book reviews. Any reviewer of many books must deal with a lot of trash, but Mrs. Hale was perceptive enough to praise Melville's *Typee*, *Omoo*, and *Mardi*—those stories of the South Seas which so greatly shocked a missionary-minded society.[37] She thought *Mardi* valuable for its information on Polynesian life and customs. (It is worth noting that her son became an anthropologist.)

Although the stories in *Godey's* were in the sentimental tradition, Mrs. Hale wrote an attack on the "silly morals" which flooded the magazines and book stalls. She rebuked her own sex for their part in writing such stuff. Certainly her lists of recommended books were solid enough: Butler's *Analogy*, Irving's *Life of Columbus*, Bancroft's *History of the United States*, Cooper's *Naval History*, Marshall's *Life of Washington*, Sparks's series of American biographies. In 1847 she added Plutarch, Homer, Herodotus, Xenophon, Thucydides, Aeschylus. In June that year she included Emerson and Prescott. In August she listed philosophers, and in September a group of famous women writers including Mmes Guyon and de Staël, Jane Austen, and Maria Edgeworth.

That this sort of thing was not an idle gesture is shown by numerous nineteenth-century diaries: women were doing an astonishing amount of serious reading. In the absence of adequate opportunities for formal education the women set about educating themselves. Lucy Larcom's account of her own reading and that of other Lowell mill girls has already been recorded.

Their combination of domestic virtues, manual labor, and educational aspiration was exactly that reflected in *Godey's*. Sarah Hale published the educational views of Emma Willard and articles on the value of the sewing machine; she gave advice on child rearing and cooking; she promoted good reading and outdoor exercise; she attacked unhealthful tenements and tight lacing. But her most constant crusade was for women's education. When Matthew Vassar was about to start the first great college for women, Mrs. Hale condemned the use of the term *female* in the name of the institution. Vassar dropped it and wrote her "Your long cherished wishes are realized." She demanded women faculty members. When the college opened, there were twenty-two women and eight men on the faculty. Although she and Matthew Vassar never met, they exchanged friendly letters and he asked her for advice.[38]

Even more controversial were Mrs. Hale's views on medical education for women. In 1836, Mrs. Sigourney in her popular *Letters to Young Ladies*,[39] while arguing that women should be able to earn their own living in case of need, warned "I would not counsel you to invade the province of the physician. In our state of society, it would be preposterous and arrogant." The experiences of pioneering women physicians suggest that most ladies agreed with Mrs. Sigourney. Mrs. Hale thought otherwise and said so. She championed the cause of Elizabeth Blackwell, who became the first American woman to get a medical degree. After being turned down by medical school after school she was finally accepted by Geneva Medical College, Geneva, N.Y. With the resistance to social change for which the medical profession is notorious, the *Boston Medical and Surgical*

Journal wrote: "It is to be regretted that Miss Blackwell has been induced to depart from the appropriate sphere of her sex and led to aspire to honors and duties which by the order of nature and the common consent of the world devolve upon men."[40]

A year after Miss Blackwell's admission to Geneva, Oliver Wendell Holmes, a friend of Sarah Hale's, persuaded the Harvard medical faculty to admit Harriet K. Hunt. However, the students passed a resolution saying in part, "Resolved that we object to having the company of any female forced upon us, who is disposed to unsex herself and to sacrifice her modesty by appearing with men in the medical lecture room."[41]

Like Emma Willard and Sarah Hale, Elizabeth Blackwell (1821–1910) came from a home in which girls were encouraged to develop their minds. Elizabeth's father, Samuel, said, "My daughters have as good minds as my sons, and I see no reason why they should not be taught to use them in the same way. As to what use they will put them in later life, that will be for them to decide." Samuel Blackwell, a liberal and a dissenter, had come to America in 1833 after the failure of his sugar refinery in England. His liberal views are indicated by the fact that he named an American-born son George Washington Blackwell. And although sugar production depended on slavery, Blackwell was an anti-slavery man who brought home William Lloyd Garrison as a guest. And as Elizabeth's biographer remarks, unlike most English children of the time, the nine Blackwell boys and girls were not shoved off to the nursery when company arrived.[42]

The young people shared a passion for books, and stinted on necessities to give each other such things as the poems of Goldsmith and Coleridge, Bacon's essays, Taylor's *Holy Living*, novels by Scott, and *The Pickwick Papers*.[43]

When Samuel was attacked by pro-slavery mobs, he moved the family to Long Island. His offense had been support of Prudence Crandall, a young Quaker teacher in Canterbury, Connecticut, who had outraged the community by accepting a Negro girl into her school. When Mrs. Crandall started a school for Negro girls, she was arrested for vagrancy and convicted. After she appealed the case, it was dropped. The older Blackwell sisters, Anna and Marianne, then organized a small school for Negro children. Elizabeth was brought in to help.[44]

After another move to what is now Jersey City, Elizabeth was sent to school in New York and also tutored in music and French. After a visit to a Columbia commencement she wrote, "How I long to go to college. The Greek oration called up a multitude of thoughts and the melancholy reflection that the enchanting paths of literature were not for me to walk in."[45] Harriet Beecher encouraged her in her educational aspirations. Elizabeth taught for a time in a school run by Dr. Samuel Dickinson in North Carolina. When the school closed, the Dickinsons took her to Charleston, where Dr. Dickinson encouraged her to study Greek. He let her use his medical library.

In her reading she discovered that in the Middle Ages there were women professors and that a whole department for female diseases was entirely handed over to women. At the University of Bologna, Anna Manzolini succeeded her husband as professor of anatomy.

When Elizabeth began to think of a medical career for herself, Sarah Hale suggested that she practice after a year of study. However Elizabeth insisted on getting the full course—then two years—and at last succeeded in getting into the medical department of Geneva College. In 1849 she got her medical degree and was accepted as a nurse at the vast Blockley almshouse hospital in Philadelphia, which even then had two thousand patients. As a woman she was not permitted to become an intern. She wrote her thesis on "ship fever," a form of typhus brought in by Irish immigrants. Her recommendations were for cleanliness, ventilation, and exercise—in other words preventative medicine.[46]

At the same time Sarah Hale was helping to start the Women's Medical College of Philadelphia—the first of its kind. Today Philadelphia boasts of this as one of its "firsts," but no one mentions that at the first graduation only two clergymen from the whole city would sit on the platform. The Philadelphia County Medical Society asked:

> Will woman gain by ceasing to blush while discussing every topic as it comes up with philosophic coolness, and man be improved in the delicate reserve with which he is accustomed to address women in the sickroom? The bounds of modesty, once passed in the pro-

fessional intercourse, will the additional freedom of speech and manner thus acquired impart grace and dignity to woman in her new character? . . . God never intended women to be doctors.[47]

With equal philosophic coolness, Dr. Charles Meigs of the University of Pennsylvania Medical School wrote an article for the *Lady's Book*, March 1852, in which he praised the delicacy of women who preferred to suffer rather than have their maladies fully explored. "I say it is an evidence of a fine morality in our society."[48] This was the same Dr. Meigs who opposed the use of ether in childbirth and who denied the theory of asepsis, saying he preferred to attribute the many deaths "to accident or providence."[49] Mrs. Hale turned the tables on Meigs by using his statements about the modesty of women patients as an argument for women as physicians.

She espoused the cause of ether despite the attacks of the clergy who saw it as thwarting the will of God that man and especially woman should suffer. However, then as now, the physicians, unlike the clergy, had a powerful craft union. Women could challenge it at their peril.

Thus in 1858 the Board of Censors of the Philadelphia County Medical Society recommended that "members of the regular profession . . . withold from the faculties and graduates of the female colleges, all countenance and support and that they cannot, consistently with sound medical ethics, consult or hold professional intercourse with their professors or alumnae." The faculty members thus ostracized were with few exceptions male physicians, some of them prominent. The ban was not withdrawn until 1871.[50]

Inspired no doubt by their elders' version of "sound medical ethics," several hundred male students gathered to stone and spit tobacco juice on the thirty women from the female college who had been granted admission to the teaching clinics of the Pennsylvania Hospital. A week later the profession gave the young gentlemen moral support. At a meeting at the University of Pennsylvania a formal resolution was drawn up and signed by the medical faculties of Penn and Jefferson, plus the staffs of various hospitals and other members of the profession. Among other things the doctors protested the "admixture of the sexes at clinical instruction in medicine and surgery, and do respectfully lay these views before the Board of Managers of the hospitals in Philadelphia."[51]

It is only fair to say that the handful of Quaker physicians who favored medical education for women remained loyal to the college. Perhaps the leading fighter against the action of the Philadelphia County Medical Society was Dr. Hiram Corson of the Montgomery County Medical Association, but in Lancaster County Dr. John Levergood and Dr. Joseph Brinton also supported the women's cause.

But it was primarily a women's battle; they were the ones who got stoned and spat upon. The most reasoned and eloquent answer to the Philadelphia County group was that in 1869 by Ann Preston, an early graduate who had become the first woman dean of the Women's Medical College.* Far too long to quote here, it ends "we must protest, in the sacred name of our common humanity, against the injustice which places difficulties in our way, not because we are ignorant or pretentious or incompetent or unmindful of the code of medical or Christian ethics, but because we are women."[52]

The historian of the Women's Medical College has much to say about Elizabeth Blackwell's example as an influence on the founders, some of whom knew her. Ann Preston, beginning the study of medicine, went to New York in a snowstorm to consult Dr. Blackwell, who although struggling to establish a practice, had already become widely known.[53]

Elizabeth went to Paris for postgraduate work, but could enter only the Maternité, a school for midwives. In 1850 she was admitted as a student at St. Bartholomew's Hospital in London. While there she met Florence Nightingale who, incidentally, disapproved of women physicians. Miss Nightingale characterized Elizabeth Blackwell as "inferior to a third-rate apothecary of thirty years ago."[54]

---

* In her graduation thesis in 1851 Ann Preston developed a theory of psychosomatic medicine, e.g., "There is not a disorder from a scratch on the toe to an inflammation of the brain that may not be modified by mental emotion" (Alsop, *History of the Women's Medical College*, p. 32). A year earlier Hawthorne, in *The Scarlet Letter*, had written, "Wherever there is a heart and an intellect, the diseases of the physical frame are tinged with the peculiarities of these." It is just possible that Ann Preson found Hawthorne a wiser instructor than contemporary advocates of purges and bloodletting.

In the hospital Elizabeth picked up an infection which cost her an eye.

Her sister Emily also decided to study medicine. With the help of Horace Greeley, a believer in the equality of the sexes, she was admitted for study at the Bellevue Hospital in New York. The following year she was accepted by the Rush Medical College in Chicago. The Medical Society of Illinois promptly censured the college for admitting a woman. As a result Emily was dropped as a student before she could finish her last year. Greeley published in the *Tribune* a scathing denunciation of the action. However, the Western Reserve Medical College accepted her as the lone woman in the class. When she graduated she had done such remarkable work that she was given a paper of special commendation signed by every member of the faculty.[55]

The doors were slowly opening for women doctors. In Rochester and Syracuse, New York, groups of physicians organized coeducational medical schools. In England, Elizabeth Garnet, a disciple of Dr. Blackwell's, founded the first women's hospital; much later the two helped to found the first women's medical school in England.[56] In America, Elizabeth and Emily Blackwell established the New York Infirmary for Women and Children in 1857. Its medical school eventually became affiliated with Cornell University.

For years Sarah Hale had campaigned for nurses' training schools. Such institutions had developed in Europe as early as 1836. In their New York Infirmary the Blackwell women instituted the first training school for nurses in America.[57] It was not until 1873 that the Bellevue Hospital in New York, the Massachusetts General Hospital in Boston, and the Connecticut Training School in New Haven undertook the training of women nurses.[58] In 1862 Elizabeth Blackwell sent fifty nurses to serve with the Union Army.

Elizabeth Blackwell never married; however, in her late twenties she wrote to her sister Hannah saying she approved of the divine institution of marriage and would get married as soon as she got a chance. Apparently she never got that chance. Nor did she share the nineteenth-century disapproval of sex. In a lecture on the education of girls, she advocated sex education and said: "Physical passion is not in itself an evil; on the contrary, it is an essential part of our nature. It is an endowment which, like every other human faculty, has the power of high growth. *For good or evil, sex takes a first place as a motive power in human education"* (italics mine).[59] That was four years before the birth of Sigmund Freud.

Like Catharine Beecher and Sarah Hale, Elizabeth Blackwell had congenial brothers who were sympathetic to her pioneering activities. In fact, two of the Blackwell men married crusaders for woman's rights and were themselves active in the movement. Henry Blackwell persuaded a reluctant Lucy Stone to be his wife, but only after together they had drawn up a long protest against current marriage laws. Samuel married Antoinette Brown, the first American woman to be ordained as a minister, and a leader in the woman's suffrage movement.

Elizabeth herself seems to have taken little interest in woman's suffrage; her concern was for educational and professional opportunity. This was also true of Emma Willard and Sarah Hale; Catharine Beecher was outspokenly opposed to votes for women. It is possible that the familial pattern which helped to give these women a sense of their own worth and abilities also made political rights seem less important. Militants like Elizabeth Cady Stanton and Lucy Stone had felt put upon as young girls; they had relatively unsympathetic fathers. Like some of today's more intransigent supporters of woman's liberation, the early advocates of women's suffrage sometimes displayed a hostility to men. On the other hand, women like those discussed in this chapter had fathers and brothers who not only encouraged them but hiked, fished, and studied with them.

The popular novelist and pioneer in promoting kindergartens, Kate Douglas Wiggin, née Smith (1856–1923), described a similar background. Starting a diary at the age of ten, she recorded a variety of housekeeping chores and extensive reading, but also outdoor activities like coasting and snowballing. One day after lessons in geography and Latin she prepared supper, then danced with her father while her mother played the piano. Then Kate played while her parents danced. In the Maine village where they lived, she recalled that the adult conversations which the children heard were "good substantial stuff." A visitor back from France and Italy had done translations of French novels. Kate's father and uncle likened the lady to Madame de Staël and George Sand.

Learning that Dickens was to give a reading at Portland sixteen miles away, Kate, at the age of twelve, was allowed to go by herself to hear him. On the train when she discovered Dickens sitting alone, she plopped down beside him. He was startled to discover that the little girl had read all but two of his books, and *David Copperfield* six times.[60]

Mrs. Wiggin was married twice, but she devoted much less of her autobiography to her marriages than to her pioneer work in establishing a free kindergarten in San Francisco and with her sister in founding the California Kindergarten Training School.

Very possibly these women were sensible in making education and professional opportunities their primary goals. The right to vote did not come until the next century, and oddly enough the percentage of women earning professional degrees has declined ever since.[61] By contrast the nineteenth-century efforts to train women as teachers succeeded dramatically. According to Sarah Hale, not one publicly employed teacher in 1828 was a woman. By 1862 there were 7,381 in Illinois as compared to 7,713 men. In New York State the figures were more dramatic: 18,915 women and 7,585 men.[62] In the era that Page Smith calls the Great Repression his own figures for 1886 show that in institutions "of more or less higher education" there were 35,976 women and 78,185 men.[63] Although some of the women's colleges were no doubt glorified seminaries, it should be noted that in 1880, 51.3 percent of college women were in coeducational institutions; by 1890 the percentage was 65.5.[64] More girls than boys were in high school because the boys tended to drop out to get jobs.

Emma Willard, Catharine Beecher, Sarah Hale, and Elizabeth Blackwell were pioneers in a tremendous revolution.

NOTES

1. Anthony Trollope, *North America*, ed. by Donald Smalley and Bradford Allen Booth, New York, 1951 (originally published 1862), pp. 26–27.
2. David Macrae, *The Americans at Home*, pp. 44–47.
3. Ibid., p. 48.
4. *Hannah Logan's Courtship*, ed. by Albert Cook Myers, Philadelphia, 1904, p. 8.

5. Margaret Bayard Smith, *The First Forty Years of Washington Society*, p. 70.
6. Ibid., pp. 179, 188.
7. Alma Lutz, *Emma Willard, Pioneer Educator of American Women*, Boston, 1964, p. 2.
8. Ibid., p. 7.
9. Ibid., pp. 18–21.
10. Ernest Earnest, *Academic Procession: An Informal History of the American College, 1636–1953*, New York, 1953, p. 170.
11. Scott, *The Southern Lady*, p. 7.
12. Margaret Bayard Smith, *What Is Gentility?*, Washington, 1828, p. 45.
13. Lutz, pp. 28–32.
14. Ibid., pp. 39–40.
15. Earnest, *Academic Procession*, p. 175.
16. Ibid., p. 193.
17. Lutz, p. 58.
18. Ibid., p. 87.
19. Earnest, *Academic Procession*, p. 177.
20. Lutz, p. 55.
21. Ibid., pp. 78–83.
22. Ibid., p. 110.
23. Isabelle Webb Entrikin, *Sarah Josepha Hale and Godey's Lady's Book*, Philadelphia, 1946, p. 70.
24. Ibid., pp. 2, 4.
25. Ruth E. Finley, *The Lady of Godey's: Sarah Josepha Hale*, Philadelphia, 1931, p. 29.
26. Ibid.
27. Ibid., p. 36.
28. Entrikin, pp. 18–21.
29. Ibid., p. 121.
30. Ibid., p. 123.
31. Martineau, *Society in America*, II, 56.
32. James Bryce, *The American Commonwealth*, London and New York, 1889, pp. 595–96.
33. Entrikin, pp. 23, 66.
34. Ibid., p. 88.
35. Finley, p. 247.
36. Ibid., pp. 256–57.
37. Entrikin, pp. 91, 96–97.
38. Finley, pp. 206, 211–19.
39. Sigourney, *Letters to Young Ladies*, p. 90.
40. Dorothy Clark Wilson, *Lone Woman: The Story of Elizabeth Blackwell, the First Woman Doctor*, Boston, 1970, p. 188.
41. Ibid., p. 290.
42. Ibid., pp. 27, 29.
43. Ibid., p. 68.
44. Ibid., pp. 55–56.
45. Ibid., p. 67.
46. Ibid., pp. 165–166, 174.
47. Ibid., p. 283.
48. Finley, p. 103.
49. Ernest Earnest, *S. Weir Mitchell, Novelist and Physician*, Philadelphia, 1950, pp. 3, 245n.

50. Gulielma Fell Alsop, *History of the Women's Medical College, Philadelphia, Pennsylvania*, Philadelphia, 1950, pp. 61, 58.
51. Ibid., p. 56.
52. Ibid., p. 71.
53. Ibid., p. 30.
54. Wilson, p. 369.
55. Ibid., pp. 292–93, 306–8.
56. Ibid., pp. 189, 363.
57. Ibid., p. 339.
58. Finley, p. 109.
59. Wilson, p. 286.
60. Kate Douglas Wiggin, *My Garden of Memory*, Cambridge, 1923, pp. 16–21, 41–42.
61. Page Smith, p. 295.
62. Finley, p. 234.
63. Page Smith, p. 296.
64. Earnest, *Academic Procession*, p. 197.

Six

The Crusaders

We would have every arbitrary barrier thrown down. We
would have every path laid open to Woman as freely as
to Man.

Margaret Fuller

There is always a danger of forcing social phenomena into
some kind of pattern. The foregoing chapters present some evidence
which supports William Wasserstrom's theory of the close relationship between outstanding women and their fathers. A more accurate
generalization would include the influence of brothers and husbands.
Sarah Hale and Elizabeth Blackwell are cases in point. So too are
some of the women to be discussed in the present chapter, but others
were in revolt against their fathers or were even hostile to men.

The only safe generalization is to say that nineteenth-century
women reformers came from a wide variety of social and family
backgrounds. If there is any common experience it is that of a
society which gave American women greater freedom than that
enjoyed by their contemporaries elsewhere. It was a society at once
deeply religious and abounding in unorthodox theories. A Calvinistic
sexual puritanism coexisted with the doctrines and practice of free
love. It was a restless society in which people moved from place to
place and from one social stratum to another. Scarcely any of the
outstanding women stayed put.

It would be difficult to imagine the career of Lucretia Mott (1793–
1880) in a social context other than that of the United States. Her
father, Thomas Coffin, Jr., was a whaler; her mother kept a small
grocery store in Nantucket. In winter the seven children dressed
by candlelight and did the chores before leaving for school. After
school Lucretia took her turn at minding the store; she also learned

the manifold household skills of the time. In later years, despite her active public life, she had the reputation for being a fine cook. On one occasion she mentioned doing a big wash, moving the parlor furniture, and preparing a meal for forty adults and some children. By that time she had servants in the house.[1]

In 1804 after the loss of his ship, Thomas Coffin moved the family to Boston, where he prospered in business. Lucretia was sent first to a public school, then to a Friends' Academy in southeastern New York. As a reward for excellence she was made an assistant teacher. Shortly before her graduation at seventeen, the family moved to Philadelphia. So too did James Mott, Jr., an instructor at her school. She married him in 1811. After the birth of two children she returned to school teaching until her third child was born. She eventually had five.

As the Society of Friends permitted women to speak in public, Lucretia began preaching in 1818. At twenty-eight she was officially recognized by the Society as having "a gift for the ministry." Between 1830 and 1840 she was successively clerk of the Women's Yearly Meeting, treasurer, and representative from Abington to the Philadelphia Yearly Meeting. Whittier, than editor of the *Pennsylvania Freeman*, was a frequent visitor at the Mott home. She helped to organize the Philadelphia Anti-Slavery Society and later the National Anti-Slavery Convention of American Women.[2]

When Prudence Crandall was run out of Canterbury, Connecticut, for accepting Negro girls in her school, Lucretia Mott tried to help her set up a Negro school in Philadelphia. However they encountered so much opposition from "a few of our *prudent* abolitionists," as Mrs. Mott described them, that Mrs. Crandall and her husband went back to Connecticut.[3] Philadelphia, despite the Quaker influence, was perhaps the most pro-slavery city in the North. Wealthy Philadelphians had investments in the South; merchants and manufacturers did a thriving business in importing plantation products and exporting manufactured goods. Then, as now, lower-class whites were hostile to blacks who competed for jobs.

In this atmosphere the opening in 1838 of Pennsylvania Hall, a handsome $40,000 building to be used for abolitionist meetings, stirred up the mob. On the day the building was dedicated, a brick was thrown through the window. Two days later a meeting of the Anti-Slavery Convention of American Women brought a concerted attack. While Angelina Grimké and Abby Kelly were speaking in the hall, a shower of stones hit the windows. The next day, despite the hostile crowd outside, Lucretia Mott spoke.[4] That night the mob burned the hall, then started for the Mott house, where a meeting was in progress. A friend of the Motts by a ruse led the crowd off in another direction.

In 1840 Mrs. Mott was sent to England as a delegate to the British and Foreign Anti-Slavery Society. James Mott went with her. In London the women, among them Elizabeth Cady Stanton, Lady Byron, Mrs. Amelia Opie, and Anna B. Jameson, were banned from the main floor and forced to sit in the balcony. Because Mrs. Mott belonged to a Hicksite meeting, the Orthodox Quakers shunned her. On her return home James wrote a book denouncing this social injustice and blind prejudice caused by the hidebound dogma of religious sects. Mrs. Mott's biographer contrasts its grave tone with his wife's sometimes sarcastic wit.[5]

On the subject of slavery, the Motts saw eye to eye. James, in his prosperous mercantile business in Philadelphia, had eliminated the import of all cotton goods, and restricted his business to wool. When he became a member of the Free Produce Society, the Motts used substitutes for slave-produced sugar in their children's candy. The young people amused themselves by composing anti-slavery couplets to accompany the "free sweets." Mott became a member of the all-male Free Produce Society of Philadelphia, an action endorsed by his wife.[6]

As so often happened, people active in one reform movement branched out into others. Lucretia Mott went about the country speaking to Non-Resistance organizations, Free Produce meetings, the Anti-Sabbath Convention, and of course anti-slavery societies. Women quickly saw the logical connection between freedom for Negroes and rights for women. As Mrs. Mott remarked, "Negroes, idiots and women were in legal documents classed together." She once stated, "I grew up so thoroughly imbued with women's rights, that it was the most important question of my life from a very early day." For forty years she kept on her center table a copy of Mary

Wollstonecraft's *Vindication of the Rights of Women.* However, the event which triggered her activism was probably her experience in London. The segregation of the women delegates was especially galling. This was also the beginning of her long association with Elizabeth Cady Stanton, twenty-two years her junior.[7]

Like many other people Elizabeth Stanton was charmed by Lucretia Mott. Lord Morpeth, who met Mrs. Mott at the anti-slavery convention, said, "She would grace the court of St. James."[8] His sister, the Duchess of Sutherland, named a daughter Rachel Lucretia after her. Because the Motts belonged to the American Anti-Slavery Society and the Stantons to the rival American and Foreign Anti-Slavery Society, Elizabeth had been warned against Mrs. Mott as an infidel and "as very dangerous person." After their meeting the two women became warm friends.[9]

Elizabeth Cady Stanton (1815–1902) came from a more cultured family than did Mrs. Mott and was more of an intellectual. The remarkable longevity of many of the crusaders and their activity into old age suggests a superior physical as well as mental endowment. Mrs. Stanton even exceeded Mrs. Mott in bearing children—seven as compared to five.

Elizabeth's father, Daniel Cady of Johnstown, New York, was a lawyer, judge, and member of Congress. Her rather stern parents brought her up in the hell-fire tradition. Late in life she wrote, "I can truly say, after an experience of seventy years, that all the cares and anxieties, the trials and disappointments of my whole life, are light, when balanced with my sufferings in childhood and youth from the theological dogmas which I sincerely believed . . . and the gloom connected with everything associated with the name of religion. . . ." Even as children she and her sister resented the fact that their Negro servant, Peter, a devout Episcopalian, had to sit in a segregated part of the church. The children insisted on sitting with him.[10]

When her brother, a graduate of Union College, died, and the eleven-year-old girl climbed up on her father's knee to comfort him, Daniel Cady sighed and said, "Oh, my daughter, I wish you were a boy." Throwing her arms about his neck she answered, "I will try to be all my brother was." In her *Reminiscences* she pictured this as a turning point in her life. She visited their pastor, the Reverend Simon Hosack, and asked which he liked best—boys or girls. When he said girls, she told him she wanted to learn Greek and horseback riding. She made excellent progress in both. When her teacher praised her or when she took a fence or a ditch on horseback, she longed to hear her father say, "Well, a girl is as good as a boy, after all." But he never did.[11]

At the Johnstown Academy, where an older boy won the first prize in Greek, she won the second. When she showed it to her father he again said, "Ah, you should have been a boy." At the academy boys and girls shared games and study, but when the boys went off to college, Elizabeth's "vexation and mortification knew no bounds."[12] It was a plaint which echoes throughout the diaries and memoirs of able women before college doors were opened to their sex.

At the age of fifteen Elizabeth was sent to Emma Willard's Seminary in Troy. Although she enjoyed the school she found that girls shut away from boys developed an excessive interest in them and also talked about sex in a way that boys and girls did not when they associated freely. Thus she came to believe in the superior value of coeducation.[13]

In her father's law office Elizabeth Cady heard the complaints of women whose property had become that of husbands or of sons. In this community with feudal ideas of women and property, a man might leave his entire estate to a son with the provision that he provide for his mother. Thus a widow often became a dependent in a home where a daughter-in-law perhaps resented her presence. When Elizabeth protested the injustice of this, her father took down the law books to show her the statutes which applied. The law students she knew amused themselves by reading to her the worst laws they could find and passages from English literature such as the remark of Milton's Eve, "God thy law, thou mine." Her father apparently had some sympathy for her views, for he told her that when she was grown up she must go to Albany and tell the legislators of the suffering she had seen in his office, and try to persuade them to pass new laws. But when she later did just that, she found him entirely opposed to her public career.[14]

After leaving school she had the most pleasant years of her girl-hood. Her sister Tryphenia married Edward Bayard, who brought gaiety into the lives of Elizabeth and her sisters. Edward discoursed on philosophy, history, law, and poetry; he read aloud from Scott, Bulwer, Cooper, and Dickens; he organized dancing and games. With him the girls went sleighing in winter and took long horseback rides in summer.[15] Elizabeth fell in love with her brother-in-law.

He and Tryphenia moved to Seneca Falls but there were family visits back and forth to Johnstown. Often he accompanied Elizabeth and her sister Madge to New York for visits to their married sister Harriet. For Edward had fallen in love with Elizabeth and told her he knew she loved him. On moonlit walks along the Battery he tried to persuade her to run away with him. Torn between her love and her conscience she went back to Johnstown.[16]

Fortunately she had a refuge, the home of her mother's nephew, Gerrit Smith. Smith was a friend of the Oneida Indians, ran a station on the Underground Railway, and entertained scholars, judges, bishops, and statesmen. Here Elizabeth met the anti-slavery orator Henry B. Stanton, ten years her senior, and a kind of hero to her. They went riding together during what she called "those glorious days of October." He proposed, and possibly on the rebound from Bayard, she accepted. When her father opposed her marriage to an abolitionist and a radical, she broke the engagement, but when Henry wrote saying he was a delegate to the World's Antislavery Convention in London and asking her to go along as his wife, she gave in.[17] Marriage to a man she liked and respected was a way out of an im-possible situation with Bayard, and the London meeting was enticing. The evidence suggests that the marriage developed into a happy one.

Before sailing she played tag on deck with her brother-in-law, Daniel Eaton. A fellow passenger, James G. Birney, anti-slavery nominee for president, complained that it was unladylike for her to be hoisted up to the masthead or in the presence of strangers to call her husband "Henry." At the London meeting where the ladies were segregated, she complained that they had to listen to "masculine platitudes on women's sphere." The clergy "seemed to have God and his angels especially in their care and keeping."[18]

The Stantons toured England and then went to France. Like Lucretia Mott, who detested the Puritan Sabbath, Elizabeth Stanton enjoyed the gaiety of a Sunday in France. Despite her Calvinistic fear of being struck by lightning she engaged in some of the festivities. The French were very different from the English who were "as silent as if they had been born deaf and dumb . . . afraid to speak to each other for fear of recognizing one out of one's class."[19]

After ten months abroad the Stantons returned to Johnstown, where Henry studied law with Elizabeth's father. She devoted her time to reading law, history, and political economy; and to participating in temperance and anti-slavery work. She also taught a Sunday School class of Negro children. When her first child was born, she read everything she could find on babies, but agreed with Theodore and Angelina Weld that such books were bad. She refused to swaddle her child or use the soothing syrups containing opium which were then in vogue. She insisted on testing the child's bath water with a thermometer, and on open air and sunshine.[20]

Thus by defying nineteenth-century theories of child care, she was able to rear six of her children to adulthood despite one son's experiment of launching a baby in a homemade life preserver, and another's shooting himself in the hand. Apparently the Stanton children inherited their mother's daring.

In 1843 Henry was admitted to the bar and moved to Boston. There Mrs. Stanton met Theodore Parker, Whittier, Frederick Douglass, Emerson, Lowell, and Hawthorne. The Stantons were often in Garrison's home—always "a haven of rest" to Elizabeth. She did not get much rest at home: she helped the laundress do the wash; she spent much time preserving, pickling, and experimenting with new dishes. Like Mrs. Mott, she enjoyed housekeeping. Some of her happiest memories were of sitting on the upper piazza with her children, reading and enjoying the view.[21]

In 1847 the Stantons moved to Seneca Falls, New York. Here Elizabeth learned something of lower-class life: she helped to calm drunken Irish husbands who were beating their wives; she remarked on "the mountains of sorrow and suffering endured in unwelcome motherhood in the abodes of ignorance, and vice. . . ." With poor servants and numerous children of her own, she was attracted to Fourier's idea of a phalanstery with a cooperative, community household.[22]

The year before this, Margaret Fuller, who had been a member of the Fourieristic colony at Brook Farm, published *Woman in the Nineteenth Century*, which dealt with some of the same evils which Mrs. Stanton was becoming aware of. However, Mrs. Stanton could hardly share Mrs. Fuller's view that "The idea of Woman must be represented by a virgin" because a married woman belonged to her husband.[23] Margaret Fuller eventually changed her mind, for in Italy she bore a son, possibly out of wedlock. Along with Mary Wollstonecraft's *Vindication of the Rights of Women*, Margaret Fuller's *Woman in the Nineteenth Century* became one of the textbooks of the crusader.

Sarah Margaret Fuller (1810–50) was one of the nineteenth-century women tutored by their fathers. Timothy Fuller, a lawyer well read in French and English literature, tried to make his daughter heir to all he knew. At six she began the study of Latin, later of French, Italian, and German. Within three months after taking up the last she was reading it with ease. She planned to write a life of Goethe. Her dream of study in Europe was postponed for several years because of the death of her father, an event which forced her to support herself by teaching and holding transcendental "conversations" with groups of women.[24]

Her *Woman in the Nineteenth Century* (1845), although a pioneering work, is marred by her preoccupation with literature and history. In trying to demonstrate the abilities of women she cited a mixed lot of historical, fictional, and mythological figures. For modern taste the book is flawed by sentimentality, as in her description of the feminine side as "the side of love, of beauty, of holiness."[25] Had she not gone abroad and become involved in a love affair and the Italian Risorgimento, she might have become one of the American crusaders. However, her tendency was for transcendental rhetoric as opposed to the political realism of people like Lucretia Mott, Elizabeth Cady Stanton, and Susan B. Anthony.

While Mrs. Mott was attending the yearly Quaker meeting in Waterloo, New York, Mrs. Stanton came over from nearby Seneca

Falls for a visit. In their conversations they developed the idea of a Woman's Rights Convention.* They got permission to use the Wesleyan Chapel in Seneca Falls. Thus this obscure community became famous in the history of the struggle for woman's rights. The notices for the two-day meeting came out only five days before it opened on July 19, 1848. Seneca Falls became the watershed of the cause: before it, there had been only lonely voices; afterward, the movement became an organized force.

In setting up the meeting, Mrs. Mott and Mrs. Stanton had the help of Lucretia Mott's sister, Martha Wright, and two Waterloo Quakers: Mary Ann McClintock and Jane Hunt. Among the men who joined in the meeting were James Mott, Richard P. Hunt, Thomas McClintock, the ex-slave Frederick Douglass, and his Negro associate in publishing the *North Star*, William S. Nell. The links to the anti-slavery movement are obvious, not only because of the Motts and the Negro spokesmen, but because McClintock was a leader in the Free Produce movement.[26]

Because women were inexperienced in conducting a meeting, James Mott was chosen as chairman. Eleven resolutions were adopted, calling for better education of women, opportunities in law and medicine, the breaking down of barriers in industrial occupations, and the repeal of laws restricting women's property rights and the guardianship of children. The most controversial resolution was that calling for the right to vote. It carried by a slim margin, but a hundred people signed it and Frederick Douglass campaigned for it in the *North Star*.[27]

The clergy and the press as a whole launched a violent attack on the resolutions. In a largely fundamentalist society, the ladies found that Saint Paul was their worst enemy. Preachers loved to cite his dictum: "Let your women keep silent in the churches; for it is not permitted unto them to speak; but *they are commanded* to be under obedience, as also saith the law. And if they will learn anything, let them ask their husbands at home: for it is a shame for women to speak in the church." At the Rochester convention two weeks after the Seneca Falls meeting Mrs. Mott remarked that,

* In London in 1840 they had agreed to hold such a convention on their return to America (*History of Woman Suffrage*, I, 61, 68).

"Many of the opposers of Woman's rights who bid us obey the bachelor St. Paul themselves reject his counsel—he advised them not to marry."[28]

After the meetings at Seneca Falls and Rochester Mrs. Stanton began to lecture and write articles for the press. In 1851 she met Susan B. Anthony, who became her most intimate friend for the next forty-five years. In some ways it was an unlikely friendship. Despite their shared goals the two women were rather different in temperament: Elizabeth tolerant and humorous, Susan prudish and often harsh.

Like so many of the crusading women, Susan B. Anthony (1820–1906) was born a Quaker. Her well-to-do father, a cotton manufacturer, tried to get hold of material which had not been produced by slave labor. Her mother Hannah had been a Quaker preacher. Daniel Anthony was a man of independent mind: he refused to sell liquor in his company store or to permit anyone except Quaker preachers to smoke or drink in his home. Despite the criticism of neighbors he encouraged his daughters to be self-supporting, and permitted young people—but not his own children—to dance in his home. For this he was read out of meeting.[29]

Susan learned to read and write at the age of three. When the family moved from Adams, Massachusetts, to Battensville, New York, she attended the district school, then went for a year to a boarding school near Philadelphia. She became a teacher, and from 1846 to 1849 was head of the Female Department of Canajoharie Academy.

In the *DAB* sketch of her life, Harris Elwood Starr describes her early letters as prudish: she rebuked her uncle for drinking ale; she deplored President Van Buren's attendance at the theater and revelings in the tents of luxury and use of "all debasing wine"—could a man who practiced such abominable vices be "suffered to sit at the head of our government"? In later years she became less puritanical but, despite various suitors, she resolved never to marry. According to Mrs. Stanton, she believed there should be secular orders similar to Catholic sisterhoods, and devoted to public service.[30]

Nineteenth-century woman's rights crusaders tended to begin their activities in abolition or temperance organizations. As might be expected of one with Miss Anthony's views on ale and wine, she started in the temperance movement, acting as a delegate to a meeting in 1852 of the Sons of Temperance in Albany. As so often happened, masculine chauvinism caused the ladies to set up organizations of their own. When Miss Anthony tried to speak at the Albany meeting, she was advised that "sisters were not invited to speak but to listen and learn."[31] This must have been especially galling to a woman brought up in the Quaker tradition of women speakers. She and others promptly organized the Women's State Temperance Society of New York. But the continued opposition to women activists convinced her that only equal rights was the answer.

Symbolic costume is frequently one of the marks of a revolutionary movement—in this case the rather hideous Turkish trousers designed by Elizabeth Smith Miller and promoted by Amelia Bloomer, for whom they were named. Elizabeth Stanton, Susan B. Anthony, and Lucy Stone found the costume much more comfortable than the crinolines then in vogue, but abandoned it because it distracted attention from what they had to say. Years later Mrs. Stanton noted that Diana's costume worn by Ellen Tree in *Ion* would have been more artistic and convenient.[32] In giving up bloomers Miss Anthony made the shrewd observation that "to be successful a person must attempt but one reform."[33]

Like most of her sister crusaders she neglected her own advice. Along with her campaign for equal rights for women she conducted one for abolition with the slogan "No Union with Slaveholders." These were the same causes preached by the Grimké sisters, especially by Angelina.

Sarah Grimké (1792–1873) and Angelina (1805–79) were two of the outstanding women in an era of remarkable women. Born into an aristocratic slave-owning family in South Carolina they became two of the most challenging abolitionists in the nation. Their father, John Grimké, had joined Franklin and Pinkney in London to petition the king against closing the port of Boston; he had been a captain in the Revolution, had been Speaker of the South Carolina House of Representatives, and after 1779 a judge. The girls were sent to a seminary but Sarah also studied her brother Thomas's lessons in mathematics, geography, natural science, history, and Greek. Although Judge Grimké spent much time with his six children, he disapproved of Sarah's desire to study Latin. Mrs. Grimké thought the idea preposterous.[34] When Sarah was twelve, Thomas went to Yale. Like many another girl of the time she regretted that she could not get a good education; her ambition was to become a lawyer.

Instead she was taught the skills of plantation ladies: to spin and weave cloth for slaves' clothing, to pick and shell corn, even to pick cotton. Her favorite pastime was a daily horseback ride. Every Sunday afternoon the Grimké girls taught Bible classes to Negro children. Despite a law in South Carolina making anyone teaching a Negro to read liable for a fine of a hundred pounds, Sarah taught a slave girl to read. For this she was lectured by her father. However, her diary of the time shows an absorption in the gay life of a Southern belle.[35]

What seems to have turned Sarah and later Angelina Grimké against slavery was their knowledge of the brutal punishments which must have been common. Sarah, hearing an exclamation of horror from a coachman, saw a human head on a pole—a punishment for a runaway slave. A mulatto woman who repeatedly ran away was given a brutal whipping and fitted with a pronged iron collar, in which condition she sat sewing with her mistress. So that she could be easily identified all her front teeth had been pulled. At school Angelina fainted on seeing a small boy who could hardly walk because his back and legs were scarred and scabby with recent whip marks. Later she saw slaves sent to the workhouse to be beaten by a treadmill contraption. Fifteen minutes with it would cripple a slave for days.[36] Families with house servants thus disabled would borrow others to serve at dinner parties. Such grim tales gave the sisters material for their later anti-slavery speeches.

In 1819 Sarah accompanied her ailing father to Philadelphia, where he went for treatment by the famous Dr. Philip Syng Physick. Sent to Long Branch for the sea air, John Grimké died there. In Philadelphia Sarah had stayed with a Quaker family, then had returned South with a group of Friends. Soon afterwards she went back to Philadelphia to become a Quaker preacher. When a widower proposed to her, she found it hard to give him up but decided she could not accept "earthly love."[37]

At twenty-four Angelina also went to Philadelphia and became a Quaker. She enjoyed the freedom of going to market without having to summon a coachman. At first the sisters were not interested in politics, but Angelina held meetings for the inmates of the Arch Street Prison. Their brother Thomas, who had become interested in abolition, died of cholera. Angelina later remarked, "I sometimes feel frightened to think how long I was standing idle in the market-place."[38]

However when she became active, she made up for lost time. In 1836 the sisters went to New York where they took a training course under Theodore Weld. At meetings where both women spoke, Angelina was the main attraction. Like Weld they pled for an end to racial prejudice in the North. Weld had eaten and slept in Negro homes and attended their weddings and funerals. Angelina tried to get black women to participate in anti-slavery work; she said white women were inefficient because of aristocratic feelings.

As delegates to the Anti-Slavery Convention in New York in 1837, the sisters were associated with Lucretia Mott, Lydia Child, and other leaders. The women were learning how to run an organization: they set up executive committees in Boston, New York, and Philadelphia. Angelina sent a message saying, "Tell Mr. Weld . . . that when the women got together they found they had *minds* of their own and could transact their business without his direction." The portent in clear: women's organizations for abolition were drawn into the woman's rights movement. Angelina makes this clear in an article she prepared for the convention. After deploring the refusal of northerners to associate with Negroes or admit them to institutions of learning or even zoos, she went on: "Women ought to feel a peculiar sympathy in the colored man's wrongs, for, like him, she has been accused of mental inferiority, and denied the privilege of a liberal education."[39]

In her *Appeal to the Christian Women of the Southern States*, she refuted the Biblical arguments for slavery, and urged women to free their slaves, pay wages, and educate the freed slaves. The pamphlet was publicly burned by the Charleston postmaster, and the Charleston police warned Mrs. Grimké that if her daughter visited the city, she would be arrested and jailed. Even the Quakers opposed the sisters' anti-slavery activity. When she was rebuked by an elder, Sarah gave up the Quaker ministry.[40]

Although Angelina tended to outshine her older sister it was Sarah who first took up the cause of woman's rights. She talked about the plight of women and children who were paid far less than the men in the mills and factories of Lynn and Danvers. Then she published *Letters on the Equality of the Sexes*. Meanwhile Angelina was bringing out her *Letters to Catharine Beecher*, Miss Beecher having come out against women's attempts to organize abolition societies, and against petitions to Congress by women. In her view, the subordination of women to men was "a benificent and immutable Divine law."[41] Angelina defended the right of petition as the only political right enjoyed by women. She went on to argue that they should have a voice in the laws by which they were governed, to sit in general assemblies or in the presidential chair of the United States. Sarah was preaching equal pay for equal work.

All this was ten years before the Seneca Falls Convention and seven before Margaret Fuller's *Woman in the Nineteenth Century*. However, the Grimké sisters were not only ten years ahead of their time but a hundred years. Whereas most abolitionists ignored wage slavery and concentrated their fire on the South, the Grimkés attacked both southern slavery and northern economic exploitation; they pointed out that "Northern prejudice against color is grinding the colored man to the dust in our free states. . . ." Despite their radical views the sisters attracted large audiences. Angelina was a charismatic person: women walked miles to hear her. In Lowell, Massachusetts, 1,500 people crowded into City Hall to hear Angelina and hundreds were turned away. In a period of twenty-three weeks the sisters spoke at least eighty-eight meetings in sixty-seven New England towns; they faced over 40,500 people.[42]

Angelina charmed not only audiences but also Theodore Weld. He told her that she had his whole heart but feared that she was so strict a Quaker that she would consider anyone outside her denomination as a heathen. She wrote, "I feel my Theodore that we are two halves of one whole, a twain one, two bodies animated by one soul, and that the Lord has given us to each other.[43] The wording suggests that she had been reading Plato or John Donne, or perhaps she was merely rediscovering the immemorial experience of lovers. Despite Mrs. Grimké's distaste for Weld's views, she consented to the marriage. Among the guests were William Lloyd Garrison, the abolitionists who had left Lane Seminary, Henry Stanton, Henry C. Wright, and a number of Negroes: Sarah Douglas* and her mother, and some former house slaves of the Grimkés. Six whites and six blacks acted as groomsmen and bridesmaids. Both a black and a white minister offered prayers.[44]

The next day, May 15, 1838, the sisters took part in the anti-slavery convention at Pennsylvania Hall in Philadelphia—the occasion when Angelina was stoned. The Society of Friends disowned Angelina for marrying out of meeting,[45] and Sarah for attending the wedding.

During the next six years Angelina bore three children and had one miscarriage. Theodore pulled out of the anti-slavery movement and started a school in which both Angelina and Sarah taught. In addition the two sisters, reared in a wealthy home with servants, did all the cooking, washing, cleaning, and mending for twenty students. In 1853 the Welds joined the Raritan Bay Union, an offshoot of the North American Phalanx at Red Bank, New Jersey. Theodore Weld directed the school, a pioneering institution where young women worked out in the gymnasium, rowed boats, and learned swimming and high diving.[46] Emerson and Greeley lectured at the Raritan school and Thoreau read his essay on walking.

The Grimké sisters took little or no part in the controversies that in the seventies fragmented the woman's rights movement. Instead they were involved in the pioneering educational programs at Dio Lewis's school. Lewis introduced courses in anatomy and physiology; he emphasized physical training, amusements, and loose-fitting clothing. In her teaching at the school Angelina was not satisfied to depend on textbooks: she read major writers "so as to be a live teacher and lift the pupils' minds above the glitter of war and conquest."[47] It took American colleges seventy or eighty years to catch up with her ideas.

Nor was she daunted by the discovery that she had a black nephew

* Sarah Douglas (1806–82) started a Negro school in Philadelphia and was active in the anti-slavery movement.

lecturing at Lincoln University in Pennsylvania. He was one of her brother's three sons by a slave woman. The Welds and Sarah Grimké contributed to the younger boys' expenses at Lincoln. Angelina attended a commencement and invited them to her home. One of them, Henry, entered Harvard Law School and got his degree in 1874; another, Archibald, became the outstanding Negro leader between the death of Frederick Douglass and the rise of Booker T. Washington. He credited his aunts with making him "a liberal in religion, a radical in politics and on the race question." The third brother, Frank, became the pastor of a Presbyterian church in Washington for fifty years, and a trustee of Howard University.[48]

Less famous than Lucretia Mott, Elizabeth Cady Stanton, and Susan B. Anthony—all of whom are immortalized in marble in Washington—the Grimké sisters, especially Angelina, are two of the most remarkable women in the annals of abolition and woman's rights. They not only preached their doctrines but lived them. Apparently they avoided the intransigence of Susan B. Anthony and Lucy Stone.

Before the Civil War there were some small gains for woman's rights. In 1859 Lucy Stone was the only suffragist to reply to Sam Wood's request for suggestions about laws pertaining to women which might be included in the constitution for Kansas. That state became one of the first to give mothers equal guardianship over their children. In New York, a joint session of the legislature in 1860, after listening to Mrs. Stanton, amended the women's property law to give women the right to their own earnings and equal guardianship of their children. Two years later during the war the law was repealed.

It is ironic that the Civil War, which brought so many women out of the kitchen and nursery, set back the woman's rights movement for many years. The war and reconstruction brought emancipation and Negro franchise to the fore at the expense of woman's rights and suffrage. Mrs. Stanton and Miss Anthony stuck to Garrison's position of "No compromise with Slaveholders. Immediate and Unconditional Emancipation." To Susan, Mrs. Stanton complained that "You Garrisonians are such a crochety set, that when other men see cause for rejoicing, you howl the more grievously." However she admitted that she was "one of you."[49] Both women opposed the nomination of Lincoln because the Republican platform went no further than opposition to the extension of slavery into new territories. The National Loyal League of Women, arguing that freedom for slaves was the only way to win the war, collected 300,000 names on petitions for emancipation.[50]

In true Garrisonian style Susan spoke of "the bloated self-conceit of traitors and rebels, who in their barbarous warfare, their cruelty to our dead and dying, and prisoners of war, had violated all and every law of civilized nations. No, no, there can be no reconstruction on the old basis, but by the humiliation of the North. . . ." She went on to use such phrases as "arrogant usurpers of the South," "Hydra monster," "gory lips."[51]

Lucy Stone, another strong abolitionist, supported a stern policy of reconstruction and was pleased when Andrew Johnson was impeached.

It was the intransigence of the crusaders for abolition and woman's rights which split the suffrage movement in the 1870s. It is characteristic of radical movements to fragment: the leaders are by definition nonconformists—a stance which militates against compromise and cooperation. Even the biographers of the woman's rights leaders tend to become partisans. Thus it becomes difficult to distinguish the issues from the personalities involved. Henry James in *The Bostonians* was unjust in reducing the woman's rights movement to motivations which later generations would call Freudian. Nevertheless it is difficult to avoid Freudian explanations of some of the controversies.

Obviously it would be impossible in the present study to give a detailed account of a movement which has been the subject of whole books or of persons whose individual biographies fill a large shelf. Therefore the details of the controversies will be subordinated to the purposes of this book: to show the variety and vitality of American women between 1776 and 1914.

The major reason why the women's movement split into two factions was that one group was primarily concerned with the enfranchisement of the Negro; the other demanded that women also be given the suffrage. Former male advocates of woman's rights like Charles Sumner, Frederick Douglass, William Lloyd Garrison, Theodore Tilton, Thomas Wentworth Higginson, and Wendell Phillips cooled off. "This is the NEGRO's HOUR" became a catch phrase of the time which described their position.[52]

There were also personal and regional rivalries: the Boston group tended to draw apart from others in the abolition and rights movements. A number of the people involved in these causes were uncompromising partisans to the point of fanaticism, for instance Sumner, Phillips, Garrison, Susan B. Anthony, and Lucy Stone. Elizabeth Stanton's views on divorce alienated many of the woman's rights people. For a time both Mrs. Stanton and Miss Anthony were associated with rather dubious characters.

In their campaign for woman's suffrage in Kansas in 1867 they were financed by George Francis Train, a wealthy eccentric who was rumored to be a Copperhead and to have made derogatory remarks about Negroes. He also put up money to start a weekly paper called *Revolution*. Then Train left for Dublin, where he was jailed as a Fenian agitator.[53] Miss Anthony tried to carry on *Revolution* and eventually assumed its debts. In 1870, two years after its founding, the Boston group started a rival paper, the *Woman's Journal*. Its editor, Mary Livermore, had as associates Lucy Stone, Julia Ward Howe, William L. Harrison, T. W. Higginson, and Henry Blackwell. Susan B. Anthony was obliged to sell *Revolution*, which soon went out of existence.

The founding of the *Journal* was largely the result of a split in the suffrage movement which had taken place the year before. In 1869 Mrs. Stanton and Miss Anthony left the Equal Rights Association to organize the National Woman Suffrage Association. A few months later "Lucy Stone and Co.," as Susan referred to her rivals, founded the American Woman Suffrage Association. In 1870 Theodore Tilton called a meeting of representatives from both groups to try to bring about a merger and Mrs. Mott, aged seventy-seven, came to New York to work for reconciliation. In an effort to promote harmony both Mrs. Stanton and Miss Anthony withdrew as candidates for office in the new Union Woman Suffrage Association. Theodore Tilton was elected president. However the American group would make no concessions and rather resented Tilton's efforts for a merger. The name "Union" was dropped and the National continued operation with Stanton and Anthony at its head.[54] For the next twenty years the movement was weakened by the division of its forces.

Lucy Stone (1818–1893), who, with her husband Henry Blackwell, was one of the leaders of the American Association, seems to have been an even more thorny person than Susan B. Anthony. In view of their uncompromising personalities and their penchant for harsh rhetoric it was probable that a split was inevitable. Also at various times Susan Anthony had strong emotional attachments to Elizabeth Stanton, Lucy Stone, and Antoinette Brown.[55] There is some evidence that she resented the marriages of Lucy and Antoinette to the Blackwell brothers.

Lucy Stone's resentment about women's lot began early. As the eighth of nine children living on a farm in Massachusetts, she pitched in to help her overworked mother. At twelve she got up before dawn to do the washing for ten or twelve people; then walked a mile to school, coming home at noon to take in the wash. She regarded her father as a harsh man: "There was only one will in our home and that was my father's."[56] When she begged for more schooling so that she could teach, her father reluctantly gave in, but took her note for the tuition. It took her years to pay it off.

Lucy Stone sat in the balcony when the Congregational Ministerial Conference adopted the Pastoral Letter directed especially against the Grimké sisters, and denouncing females who bore an "obtrusive and ostentatious part in measures of Reform."[57]

After short periods at two academies Lucy earned enough money to enter Mount Holyoke in 1839. Like Lucy Larcom she apparently regarded Mary Lyon as a liberator of women. Then in 1843 at the age of twenty-five she entered Oberlin. There she met Antoinette Brown, seven years her junior, who was preparing to enter the ministry. Lucy and the other women refused to submit graduation essays because they were not permitted to read them on the platform as the men did.

In 1848 Lucy Stone began her career as a lecturer on abolition and woman's rights. In this activity she came to know William Lloyd Garrison and Wendell Phillips, who became her long-time associates.

Mrs. Stanton described her as a speaker: "Her sweet voice and simple girlish manner made her first appearance on the platform irresistible."[58] It was Miss Stone's eloquence which helped to bring Susan Anthony into the woman's rights movement. Taking the well-traveled route from abolition to woman's rights, Lucy Stone and Antoinette Brown attended the first National Woman's Rights Convention at Worcester, Massachusetts in 1850. Both were unmarried at the time, and Susan Anthony saw them like herself as dedicated spinsters. Three years later she wrote to Antoinette Brown, "My heart aches to love somebody that shall be all its own . . . [but] I shall not be married ever. I have not yet seen the person whom I have the slightest wish to marry. . . ."[59]

At that time neither had Lucy Stone. However, Henry Blackwell, seven years her junior, had met her in his hardware store in 1850. Three years later when he came East to attend anti-slavery meetings, he told his brother he wanted to see her "as I decidedly prefer her to any lady I ever met."[60] Armed with a letter of introduction, he found her whitewashing a ceiling. She refused his help but did let him peel some potatoes. He sent her a volume of Plato.

However it took more than potatoes and Plato to win Lucy. Henry argued that Angelina and Theodore Weld had kept their individualities in marriage; he took her driving at Niagara Falls on what he called "that sacred night"; he spoke at a Woman's Rights Convention in Cleveland, where she also spoke. In December of 1854 she admitted that she loved him but would not marry because of unjust laws.[61] The following May, after drawing up a long protest against present laws, they were married by T. W. Higginson. At first Lucy accepted the name of Blackwell, but then discarded it in favor of her maiden name—perhaps the act for which she is most often remembered.

Apparently abolition and woman's rights were conducive to romance: the Motts, the Stantons, the Welds, then the Henry Blackwells and in 1856 Antoinette Brown and Samuel Blackwell—in each case the husband and wife were fellow workers. However the marriages created tensions between the Blackwell wives and Susan Anthony. It requires no great psychological insight to see Freudian implications in Susan's reaction when in 1857 Lucy had a baby:

"neither of us have *time*–for such personal matters." Later she wrote Antoinette Blackwell, "Now Nettie, not another baby is my peremptory command."[62] Nettie did not take the advice: she eventually had six.

Susan's estrangement from Anna Dickinson also suggests sexual jealousy. They probably met in New York in 1862 when Anna spoke on abolition and woman's rights. Shortly after their meeting Susan wrote: "I want to see you very much indeed, to hold your hand in mine, to hear your voice, in a word, I want you. . . ." During the next few years Susan, according to her biographer, beseiged Anna with letters, using such phrases as "Darling Anna Dick" and "Chicky Dicky."[63]

Anna Dickinson (1842–1932), the most beautiful of all the crusaders, was young enough to be Susan's daughter. She was born in Philadelphia of Quaker parents whose home was a station on the underground railway. When she was two, her father died after making an anti-slavery speech. Her mother supported five children by teaching and keeping boarders, but a philanthropic trust paid for good schools: Friends Select and Westtown. Anna became a copyist for a publishing house and various law firms, then taught briefly.[64]

At seventeen she came into prominence when she made a speech at a meeting of the Pennsylvania Anti-Slavery Society held at Kennet Square. In it she argued that there was a higher law than the Constitution and complained that the Republican platform merely opposed the extension of slavery. In 1861 Lucretia Mott and Hannah Longshore helped to arrange for her to speak in New York on "The Rights and Wrongs of Women." She spoke in favor of women physicians and argued that if it did not debase a woman to stand in line to pay taxes why should it debase her to stand in line to vote. As to women lawyers, did not male lawyers browbeat female witnesses? In a report on the two-hour address the *Evening Bulletin* described her clear, earnest style and her "awful statistics."[65]

During the next decade Anna Dickinson became the most charismatic and highly paid woman speaker in America. In one speech she charged McClellan with treason for losing a battle. For this she was fired from a job in the U.S. Mint. Garrison arranged for her to speak in the large Music Hall in New York with an admission charge of $20. When after her successes in Providence, Newport, and Boston, Wendell Phillips, pleading exhaustion, asked her to substitute for him, she wrote her mother: "Think of that, Mum—this small snip—acting as Wendell Phillipes substitute and at his own request at that."[66] (She was five feet tall.)

In 1863 she was offered $1000 a day for twelve days to campaign for the reelection of Governor Andrew Curtain of Pennsylvania. Her fee was larger than that of Chauncey Depew, Orestes Brownson, and assorted governors, senators, and generals, because she was willing to go to the coal regions where the Molly Maguires were hostile to the draft. She was shot at but held her ground. A man more tolerant of unpopular speakers than are some modern college students said, "Ah, but she's a brave girl, boys; let's hear what she has to say."[67] In Wilkes Barre she remarked that only two animals hissed—geese and snakes. Governor Curtain was reelected but Anna was never paid.

In Chicago she was paid $300 each for two addresses at a time when Beecher got $100 a night. Despite Copperhead opposition the House of Representatives invited her to address that body. The proceeds were turned over to the National Freedman's Relief Bureau.[68] In her speech she criticized Lincoln—who came in while she was talking—but called for his reelection. The legislatures of Ohio, Pennsylvania, and New York asked her to speak. In an interview with Lincoln she disagreed with his policy of reconstruction, but supported him against McClellan. On the platform she said she agreed with the dear old lady who asked: "Why will they keep attacking poor, dear, little George McClellan? I'm sure he never attacked anybody."[69]

Like Susan Anthony and Lucy Stone, she was ferocious when aroused. One reporter wrote that "She showered grape and canister on the heads of inefficient and tenderfooted military leaders." She criticized Lincoln for offering amnesty to Confederate soldiers who would swear allegiance to the Union; she argued that the property of slaveholders should be confiscated and distributed to Negroes; she opposed amnesty for Jefferson Davis and other Confederate leaders. Later she decided that vindictive reconstruction was a failure and should be abandoned.[70]

When the transcontinental railroad was opened in 1869 she traveled to California, sometimes riding in the caboose with the men, and at other times in the locomotive. Of the experience she wrote, "What a ride. If Marmee could have taken it, 'twould have made her young again." She was the first woman to climb Mt. Elbert. In Boston she rode horseback astride. Of her travels on the Lyceum circuit she wrote that, "I have crawled off the cars after a twenty hours ride, shaken to a jelly, banged black and blue, asphyxiated with coal gas and the perfumes of burnt iron and dirty humanity, and been spirited to the hall without rest, food, or a clean face. . . ."[71]

It was the kind of experience endured by other crusaders. In 1869 when Elizabeth Stanton joined the Lyceum circuit, she traveled from Maine to Texas. During the year 1871 Susan Anthony delivered 171 lectures from the East to California.[72] It was not only their convictions which kept them going: there was considerable money involved. By 1872 Anna Dickinson, by far the most highly paid of the women, was earning $23,000 a year.

She was also the most richly dressed of the Lyceum ladies. She wore diamond rings and fine silks; she eschewed crinolines, trailing skirts, and multitudinous beads and geegaws. There was also another motivation hinted at by Anna Dickinson, one that after her loss of popularity as a lecturer caused her to become an actress. In her account of the hardships of the lecture tours, she remarked that she began a talk "so tired that I wanted to prop against some convenient table or wall, and have felt, long before I finished, as though I could never be sick or weary, or disgusted. . . ."[73] It is this sense of power, of self-realization of being fully alive, that makes speakers, actors, and college professors loath to retire from the stage.

The estrangement between Anna Dickinson and Susan Anthony came to a head during the campaign for the reelection of President Grant. Both Susan and Mrs. Stanton were repelled by the corruption during Grant's first term in office, but because the Republican platform had a plank cautiously endorsing the demands of women for equal rights, they took the stump for Grant. Anna Dickinson turned down an offer of $20,000 to speak for Grant, and instead accepted $10,000 to do so for Greeley.[74] In this decision she may have been influenced by Whitelaw Reid, editor of the *Tribune*, who supported Greeley.

At one time she was rumored to be engaged to Reid. However she had turned down various offers of marriage and had been courted by General Ben Butler, a friend of woman's rights. Reid was a wary bachelor and opposed to woman's suffrage. Possibly neither she nor Reid contemplated marriage, but they carried on an affectionate correspondence.

A partly illegible entry in Susan B. Anthony's diary suggests that she was accused of making charges to Anna Dickinson against Reid. In any case she recorded, "It is a plot of Whitelaw Reid's to break her off from me."[75] The personal pronoun is significant.

A contributing factor in the split of the woman's movement was Mrs. Stanton's championship of Victoria Woodhull. The Claflin sisters, Victoria (1838–1927) and Tennessee* (1846–1923), definitely came from the wrong side of the tracks. When as a child Tennessee gave evidence of extrasensory powers, the father, Rubin, set up an infirmary exploiting Tennessee's gift. When he was run out of town, the sisters set up as clairvoyants. Charges were lodged against them for allegedly running a house of assignation. In Cincinnati, Tennessee figured in a suit for adultery and one for blackmail.[76]

At the age of sixteen Victoria ran away with Dr. Canning Woodhull, an educated man but a lush. She went to San Francisco where she was a cigar girl in a saloon. Then she met Colonel James H. Blood, a real colonel wounded five times in the Civil War. Although he was an advocate of free love, he married Victoria after their respective divorces. People were scandalized that she permitted Woodhull to live in the same house. Another intimate was Stephen Pearl Andrews. Andrews, a radical nearing sixty, was a learned man: he knew thirty languages, had written a textbook on Chinese and another on a system of shorthand. He knew history, government, politics and science.[77] He also was active in the free love movement and an advocate of a kind of state socialism.[78]

In the meantime the sisters, with the help of Commodore Vanderbilt, had set up as stock brokers in New York. Tennessee is reported to have been the Commodore's mistress, but in view of the fact that he was seventy-six and ailing, it seems more likely that she performed the function of the young woman who warmed the aged King

* She sometimes wrote it "Tennie C."

David. In 1870, possibly with financial help from Vanderbilt, the sisters launched *Woodhill & Claflin's Weekly*.[79] Fifty thousand of the first issue were distributed.

For two months the *Weekly* was a restrained woman's paper, then it became flamboyant. It published serially George Sand's *In Spite of All* and carried a bold editorial on prostitution, deploring midnight raids and the ecclesiastical ownership of whore houses. It advocated police licenses and vigorous inspection.[80] In 1871, speaking in Steinway Hall, Victoria declared, "Yes! I am a free lover! I have an inalienable, constitutional, and natural right to love whom I may, to love as long or as short a period as I can, to change that love every day if I please!"[81]

That same year she appeared before the Judiciary Committee of the House to present a memorial asking Congress to pass laws giving women the right to vote, a right she claimed was authorized by the Fourteenth Amendment. The New York *Herald* reported that other speeches were made but that Mrs. Woodhull had captured the committee. Not quite—the majority report held that Congress had not the power to clarify the Fourteenth and Fifteenth Amendments; the minority, consisting of General Ben Butler and William Loughridge, argued that Victoria had presented the strongest official statement to date in favor of women's rights under the Constitution. In fact it is possible that Butler wrote Victoria's petition; Johanna Johnston says he "almost certainly" did.[82]

Susan Anthony's paper, *Revolution*, endorsed Mrs. Woodhull's position, but Lucy Stone's *Woman's Journal* decried the menace of Victoria's type. Elizabeth Stanton came to the defense: "We have crucified the Mary Wollstonecrafts, the Fanny Wrights, the George Sands, the Fanny Kembles of all ages. . . . Let us end this ignoble record."[83]

With the help of Andrews and Blood, Victoria announced her candidacy in 1879 for president of the United States. The proposal for a People's party was signed by Mrs. Stanton, Mrs. Hooker, Mrs. Gage, and Miss Anthony. As Susan Anthony had not actually signed it, she was enraged—apparently Mrs. Hooker (she was a Beecher) and Mrs. Stanton had simply used her name. The meeting of the People's party convention in 1872 drew delegates away from the

National Woman Suffrage Association meeting at the same time. The new party nominated Victoria Woodhull for president and Frederick Douglass for vice-president—without his consent. As with so many of Victoria's actions, there is always a suspicion that publicity outweighed principle.

On November 1 of that same year Susan B. Anthony and fifteen other women registered to vote in Rochester, New York, arguing their right to do so under the Fourteenth Amendment. Four days later they voted. The women were duly arrested and tried. The judge directed a verdict of guilty and fined them a hundred dollars each. However, no effort was made to collect the fines. When the election board was convicted and fined, Susan appealed to Senator Aaron Augustus Sargent and Congressman Benjamin Butler for help. President Grant ordered the release of the men and the remission of their fines. After all, the election officials were Republicans, and Susan had campaigned for Grant.[84]

Susan Anthony and Elizabeth Stanton unwittingly got involved in an even more sensational affair—the Beecher-Tilton case. Just who told the story to whom is not clear. Susan's biographer says that Elizabeth Tilton told Susan of her involvement with Henry Ward Beecher, perhaps the most prominent clergyman of the time. According to this version Susan told Elizabeth Stanton who in turn told Victoria Woodhull.[85] Mrs. Stanton's biographer says that Theodore Tilton, who was infatuated with Victoria, told it to her directly.[86] In fact both Theodore and Elizabeth Tilton seem to have confided in several people.

Victoria had no reason to like the Beechers: both Catharine Beecher and Harriet Beecher Stowe had attacked her in the press, and Mrs. Stowe had caricatured her in a novel (see below p. 144). Furthermore, Henry Ward Beecher seemed to be practicing what Victoria preached. She first broke the story in a speech, then when the newspapers kept silent she published it in *Woodhull & Claflin's Weekly*, November 2, 1872. Beecher retaliated by defaming the Tiltons and the suffragists as "human hyenas" and "free lovers." When his sister, Isabella Hooker, advised him to confess, his henchmen branded her as "deluded, weak minded, and insane."

In the summer of 1874 Beecher appointed a committee of six

members of his church to investigate the charges against him. They exonerated him; possibly he had selected them carefully for that purpose. Mrs. Tilton was expelled from the church. This was too much for Mrs. Stanton, whose views were published in the *Transcript* of Earlville, Illinois, and in the Chicago *Tribune*. She defended Mrs. Tilton; she quoted Beecher's epithets against the National Woman Suffrage Association; and she used the case as an argument for divorce when couples were incompatible.[87] This was a view rejected by the more conservative American Association.

Theodore Tilton sued his wife for divorce on the grounds of adultery. Tilton asked Mrs. Stanton to appear as a witness, but she declined. Under the law at that time Elizabeth Tilton was not permitted to testify. In her lectures Mrs. Stanton used this as an example of the helplessness of women under existing statutes.

The jury disagreed, and Tilton could not afford to carry the case further. He spent the rest of his life in Paris, and his wife lived out hers in obscurity.[88]

The whole brouhaha did the suffrage movement no good. The Tiltons, Victoria Woodhull, Elizabeth Stanton, and Susan B. Anthony, all active in the movement, came out of the scandal with diminished stature. It widened the gulf between the American Association, whose *Woman's Journal* was favorable to Beecher, and the National Association, represented by Mrs. Stanton and Miss Anthony.

Woodhull & Claflin's Weekly ceased publication in 1876. By that time Victoria was preaching the sanctity of marriage. In 1883 she married a wealthy Englishman, became a lady of the manor, manufactured a bogus genealogy for herself, and instituted law suits against those who published statements about her earlier advocacy of free love.

For the Centennial in Philadelphia the National Association prepared a declaration of women's rights which they handed to the vice-president immediately after the reading of the Declaration of Independence. The women also maintained a suffrage headquarters at the Centennial with eighty-three-year-old Lucretia Mott acting as hostess during a broiling Philadelphia summer.

Probably the most important activity of Mrs. Stanton and Miss

Anthony in the 1880s was the writing of the three-volume *History of Woman Suffrage* which appeared between 1881 and 1886. In Volume II they included a history of the American Association written by Mrs. Stanton's daughter Harriot. Lucy Stone had refused to submit material and years later her daughter Alice charged that the *History* was one sided. In any case the work was praised on both sides of the Atlantic.[89] Both Elizabeth Stanton and Susan Anthony were well known in England. In 1882 both were featured speakers at a meeting in Princess's Hall at which John Bright presided.

Whereas Susan Anthony seems to have mellowed in her later years, Lucy Stone became if anything increasingly harsh. During the railroad strike of 1877 she wrote "This insurrection must be suppressed, if it costs a hundred thousand lives and the destruction of every railroad in the country." The *Woman's Journal*, edited by Lucy and her husband, carried articles praising Anthony Comstock and protesting the appearance of Sarah Bernhardt, who, as the unmarried mother of four children, besmirched the sanctity of marriage. Lucy argued that Oberlin's use of expurgated texts was "as much in the interests of the boys as of the girls." She suggested that Boston University do the same. When Henry took their daughter Alice to England in 1899, Alice wrote that the ballet in *Lucia di Lammermoor* was "utterly uncalled for" and "The first time Mother saw it, she says she put her head down on the seat and wouldn't look." To Frances Willard, head of the WCTU, Lucy deplored a request by women to see President Cleveland—"a male prostitute."[90]

Shortly before her death she wrote Henry mentioning that it was their thirty-eighth anniversary, but went on to say that she wanted all her rents, etc. put in her bank. "I never liked having it put in your bank, but as I have said, you did so much for women that I had allowed it."[91]

The politicking which led to the reunion of the two suffrage organizations in 1890 is outside the scope of this study. Suffice it to say that Mrs. Stanton was elected as the first president of the new National American Association. On her resignation two years later, Susan B. Anthony was elected in her place. Miss Anthony continued to travel and speak for some years but the reins were passing to a new generation with new rivalries—the struggle for leadership between Anna Shaw and Carrie Chapman Catt.

It is not strange that in the 1890s the women tended to move into the Populist camp. Long before that the farmer's Grange had given voting and speaking rights to women, and the Grange was a pillar of the Populist party, a party which attacked some of the same evils the women deplored.

It would be a mistake to overemphasize the controversies within the woman's rights and suffrage movements; they were certainly no greater than those in any important social or political movement. And it would be misleading to suggest that the women's movements were the sole creation of a few major figures like Lucretia Mott, Elizabeth Cady Stanton, Susan B. Anthony, and Lucy Stone. Others like Antoinette Brown and Anna Dickinson were also important, but so too were a host of lesser people: the women who helped to organize the first Seneca Falls Conference and scores of later meetings, women in obscure communities who made the arrangements for Lyceum lectures and turned out to hear the speakers.

All the evidence suggests that the great majority of women were indifferent to woman's rights and suffrage just as a majority of both sexes were indifferent to abolition or more recently to the war in Vietnam. As always the conservatives were actively hostile to the advocates of change. Also in the nineteenth century, men had almost unchallenged control of the press, medicine, law, and the pulpit.

Therefore the achievement of the crusaders is all the more remarkable. They did not get national woman suffrage until 1920 but they gained it in a few western states and almost everywhere north of the Mason-Dixon line they gained various property rights. Equally important, the women demonstrated that they could organize effectively, could be successful and even sensationally successful public speakers. Quite a number of them disproved the theory that political activity unsexed women. Among the women discussed in the present chapter only Susan B. Anthony and Anna Dickinson remained unmarried. The suffrage leaders of the middle decades of the nineteenth century bore a considerable number of children.

Like Abigail Adams, several of the women, notably Lucretia Mott and Elizabeth Stanton, were superior homemakers.

After the failure of prohibition it is easy to be scornful of the tendency of the woman's rights pioneers to have been involved in the temperance movement and the WCTU. But in an era of cheap whiskey, heavy drinking was common—and it was a masculine prerogative. As late as 1935 Faulkner could write in *The Bear*: "There was always a bottle present, so that it would seem to him that those fine fierce instincts of heart and brain and courage and wiliness and speed were concentrated and distilled into that brown liquor which *not women, not boys and children, but only hunters drank*" (italics mine). Faulkner's anachronistic sensibility caught the nineteenth-century ethos: drinking was a part of male chauvinism. It was the women who had to deal with drunken husbands and scrimp on groceries and children's clothes.

The women also faced other social problems: slavery; outrageously unequal pay, especially for teachers; sweated labor; and prostitution, which both Anna Dickinson and Victoria Woodhull recognized as an economic rather than as a moral problem. Anna even visited a brothel to gather statistics on the number of clients a woman served, a number exceeding what she might do for pleasure. With considerable justice at the time Anna Dickinson argued that the Pennsylvania Railroad, not the people, governed Pennsylvania. But she also attacked trade unions for restrictive membership: the struggle was not labor against capital but skilled labor against the unskilled.[92] Similarly Elizabeth Stanton's views on divorce were relatively modern. In an era of moralistic judgments on sex and Horatio Alger views of economic problems, the crusading women were far ahead of their time. They were laying the foundation for the social reformers of the next generation—women like Jane Addams and Margaret Sanger.

The pioneers did not have the vote but they were listened to in Congress and the White House. When in 1872 some Indian leaders were sentenced to be hanged, seventy-nine-year-old Lucretia Mott went to Jay Cook's mansion to call uninvited on President Grant. He explained the pressures he was under to hang them but leaned down to say, "Madam, they shall not all be executed."[93]

Considering the restrictions on women of the Victorian era, the independence of mind and initiative of the nineteenth-century crusaders and the Civil War organizers of the Sanitary Commission and the hospital nurses, one has a feeling of awe.

NOTES

1. Otelia Cromwell, *Lucretia Mott*, Cambridge, 1957, pp. 56, 96–97.
2. Ibid., pp. 30–31, 32–49.
3. Ibid., p. 53.
4. Ibid., pp. 56–57, and Gerda Lerner, *The Grimké Sisters from South Carolina, Rebels against Slavery*, Boston, 1967, pp. 246–47.
5. Cromwell, p. 92.
6. Ibid., pp. 42–46.
7. Ibid., pp. 130–31, 125, 29.
8. Alsop, *History of the Women's Medical College*, p. 40.
9. *History of Woman Suffrage*, ed. by Elizabeth Cady Stanton, Susan B. Anthony, and Matilda Joslyn Gage, New York, 1881, I, 419, 423.
10. Elizabeth Cady Stanton, *Eighty Years and More (1815–1897)*, London, 1898, pp. 24, 17.
11. Ibid., pp. 20–22.
12. Ibid., p. 33.
13. Ibid., pp. 36–37.
14. Ibid., pp. 31–34.
15. Ibid., pp. 45–46.
16. Alma Lutz, *Created Equal: A Biography of Elizabeth Cady Stanton*, New York, 1940, pp. 16–17.
17. Ibid., pp. 20–23, and Stanton, *Eighty Years*, pp. 59–60.
18. Stanton, *Eighty Years*, pp. 72–74, 80.
19. Ibid., pp. 98, 93.
20. Ibid., pp. 111–22.
21. Ibid., p. 138.
22. Ibid., p. 147
23. Margaret Fuller, *Woman in the Nineteenth Century*, Boston, 1855, p. 176.
24. Earnest, *Expatriates*, pp. 128–29.
25. Fuller, pp. 41–42.
26. Cromwell, p. 133.
27. *Elizabeth Cady Stanton*, p. 148.
28. *History of Woman Suffrage*, I, 79.
29. Katherine Anthony, *Susan B. Anthony: Her Personal History and Her Era*, Garden City, N.Y., 1954, pp. 38, 69–70.
30. Stanton, *Eighty Years*, p. 156.
31. Anthony, *Susan B. Anthony*, p. 102.
32. *Elizabeth Cady Stanton*, p. 174.
33. *Dictionary of American Biography*, I, 320.
34. Lerner, p. 19.
35. Ibid., pp. 18–32.
36. Ibid., pp. 37–38, 77–78.
37. Ibid., pp. 47–64.
38. Ibid., p. 112.

39. Ibid., pp. 161, 162.
40. Ibid., p. 142.
41. Ibid., pp. 173, 184.
42. Ibid., pp. 157, 195, 227.
43. Ibid., p. 218.
44. Ibid., pp. 242–45.
45. Ibid., p. 255.
46. Ibid., p. 229.
47. Ibid., pp. 357–58.
48. Ibid., pp. 363–65.
49. Anthony, *Susan B. Anthony*, p. 147.
50. *Elizabeth Cady Stanton*, pp. 196–99.
51. Anthony, *Susan B. Anthony*, pp. 151–52.
52. *History of Woman Suffrage*, II, 265–70.
53. Anthony, *Susan B. Anthony*, pp. 186–88.
54. Lutz, *Created Equal*, pp. 186–88.
55. Elinor Rice Hays, *Morning Star: A Biography of Lucy Stone*, New York, 1961, p. 92.
56. Ibid., p. 14.
57. Ibid., p. 28.
58. Ibid., p. 70.
59. Ibid., p. 98.
60. Ibid., p. 107.
61. Ibid., pp. 106–13.
62. Ibid., p. 150.
63. Anthony, *Susan B. Anthony*, pp. 177–78, 197–200.
64. Giraud Chester, *Embattled Maiden: The Life of Anna Dickinson*, New York, 1951, pp. 13–15.
65. *History of Woman Suffrage*, II, 42.
66. Chester, pp. 29, 36.
67. Ibid., p. 72.
68. *History of Woman Suffrage*, II, 47, 48n.
69. Chester, p. 82.
70. Ibid., pp. 48, 77–83.
71. Ibid., pp. 151, 90.
72. Anthony, *Susan B. Anthony*, p. 268.
73. Chester, pp. 89–90.
74. Ibid., p. 130ff., and Anthony, *Susan B. Anthony*, p. 275.
75. Anthony, *Susan B. Anthony*, pp. 276–77.
76. Johanna Johnston, *Mrs. Satan: The Incredible Saga of Victoria C. Woodhull*, New York, 1967, p. 33.
77. Ibid., p. 63.
78. Emanie Sachs, *The Terrible Siren: Victoria Woodhull*, New York, 1928, p. 65.
79. Johnston, *Mrs. Satan*, p. 69.
80. Sachs, p. 69.
81. Johnston, *Mrs. Satan*, p. 133.
82. Ibid., p. 84, and Sachs, pp. 90–92.
83. Johnston, *Mrs. Satan*, p. 92.
84. Anthony, *Susan B. Anthony*, pp. 292–302.
85. Ibid., pp. 312–14.
86. Lutz, *Created Equal*, pp. 312–14.
87. Ibid., pp. 223–26.

88. Ibid., pp. 229–30.
89. Anthony, *Susan B. Anthony*, pp. 341–48.
90. Hays, pp. 253, 261, 272, 294–95.
91. Ibid., pp. 301–2.
92. Chester, pp. 155, 146.
93. Cromwell, pp. 202–3.

Seven

Through a Glass Eye Darkly

> Novelists are great in proportion to the accuracy and full-
> ness with which they portray women.
>
> William Dean Howells

During the era when American women as educators and
reformers were turning the world upside down, the novelists stuck
to the tired formulas of the past. As Mark Twain said of James
Fenimore Cooper, they "saw through a glass eye darkly." In his
study of the popular book, James D. Hart estimates that between
1840 and 1850 there were almost a thousand novels and tales. Hawthorne complained of "a d----d mob of scribbling women." In the
tradition stemming from Richardson and Jane Austen, the novel
became feminized. As Hart says, "It excluded business . . . it
neglected politics, it was ignorant of social movements . . . ethical
and theological problems were viewed only in the simplest Sunday
School terms." Only in their minor details were novels realistic. As
Mrs. Gaskell observed, "These American novels unconsciously reveal all the little household secrets; we see the meals as they are put
on the table, we learn the dresses which those who sit down to them
wear . . . we hear their family discourses, we enter into their home
struggles. . . ."[1]

The vast popularity of this kind of novel suggests that perhaps
a majority of American women were only lightly touched by the
intellectual, political, and social ferment of their times. This is of
course true of the lumpen populace, male and female, of any era. But
a national literature is evaluated chiefly by the quality of its best
works. The early 1850s are not remembered for two of the most
popular novels, *Tempest and Sunshine* by Mary Jane Holmes and
The Lamplighter by Maria Susanna Cummings, but for *The Scarlet*

Letter, *The House of Seven Gables, Uncle Tom's Cabin, Walden, Moby Dick,* and *Leaves of Grass.* The Holmes and Cummings novels far outsold all of these except *Uncle Tom's Cabin.* The poetry of the 1920s is not judged by the vastly popular Eddie Guest but by the work of such poets as Pound, Frost, Eliot, Moore, Cummings, and Stevens; the novel not by Zane Grey, whose books sold by the millions, but by Dreiser, Lewis, Glasgow, Hemingway, and Fitzgerald.

It is also easy to overlook the fact that many intelligent people read light fiction along with more solid stuff. As has been mentioned, many diaries of nineteenth-century girls and women record a larger proportion of good reading than of trash. Judging by the record, Scott and Dickens were the outstanding favorites. Histories and biographies are constantly mentioned.

Even light fiction can be subversive of the established order. In his introduction to *Tempest and Sunshine* and *The Lamplighter,* Donald A. Koch argues that sentimental fiction gave a thrust to the feminist movement. Despite the fact that the heroines were home-makers rather than crusaders, they tend to dominate the men in the story. As Koch says, "In each case, the heroine emerges as a strong character and the hero a moulded figure whose design is nearly always determined by the female."[2] Howells used this formula as late as 1885 when he pictured Mrs. Lapham acting as her husband's conscience and compelling him to make restitution for forcing the treacherous and incompetent Rogers out of the partnership. The chief difference between Howells and the feminine writers is that he makes Mrs. Lapham abysmally stupid.

Despite the absence of open propaganda for such causes as temperance, abolition, and woman's rights, these topics were mentioned. As Koch says, these "warmly sentimental stories leavened the popular mind to constructive action against a variety of social injustices."[3] The outstanding example is of course *Uncle Tom's Cabin.* Unlike most of the contemporary novelists, Mrs. Stowe introduced obvious propaganda. The novel has elements of the sentimental tradition, but no one except a dedicated punster could call it escape literature. Its huge circulation is a refutation of the notion that the reading public wanted only fictional fluff.

It took male novelists a long time to discover the kind of women who had pioneered in education, opened the professions, organized for woman's rights, worked for the Sanitary Commission, spoken on the political stump. Hawthorne, whose two sisters-in-law, Elizabeth Peabody and Mary Mann, were pioneers in education and were active in various causes, was unsympathetic to women reformers. In *The Blithedale Romance*, based on his Brook Farm experience, he makes his alter ego Coverdale speak bitterly against philanthropy and utopian schemes. Margaret Fuller, whom he once called a great humbug, was possibly the painter's model for Zenobia in the story. Like Margaret, Zenobia writes for magazines and speaks out for woman's rights, but in the novel all this is subordinated to Zenobia's sex appeal, her hopeless love for Hollingsworth, and her suicide.

In *The Scarlet Letter* Hawthorne dipped a timid toe in the water by having Hester speak "of her firm belief, that, at some brighter period, when the world should have grown ripe for it, in Heaven's own time, a new truth would be revealed, in order to establish the whole relation between man and woman on a surer ground of mutual happiness." It is the perennial argument of the stand-patter: the time is not ripe for a change. Certainly Hawthorne disapproved of the Fourieristic idea of "a truth" preached by the Blithedale Society (Brook Farm): "While inclining us to the soft affections of the golden age, it seemed to authorize any individual of either sex, to fall in love with any other, regardless of what would otherwise be judged suitable or prudent."[4]

In the 1860s, '70s, and '80s novelists were usually hostile to woman's rights. With some justice Bayard Taylor in *Hannah Thurston* (1864) linked the movement to spiritualism and the Graham diet fad.* Hannah is a Quaker girl whose mother used to preach in meeting. Hannah speaks on woman's rights; she argues in favor of women physicians, for women's education, and for equal pay for equal work. She cites the example of Maria Mitchell, who after her discovery of a new comet in 1847 had gained an international

* For instance, Victoria Woodhull spoke at several spiritualist conventions, and at Oberlin, crusaders went in for the diet of Sylvester Graham, who advocated a vegetable diet as a cure for intemperance, and the use of coarsely ground whole-wheat flour.

reputation as an astronomer. However Taylor gives a burlesque picture of a woman's rights meeting. Of Mr. Bemis, who quoted the Declaration of Independence and attacked laws which kept women from representation and the control of their property or earnings, Taylor's comment was that the talk had "a certain specious display of logic." He makes Hannah appear as something of a prig, far different from a real-life Quaker reformer like Lucretia Mott.

Harriet Beecher Stowe presented a more balanced view in *My Wife and I* (1871). Although she was a conservative on the subject of woman's rights, she seems to have been less rabid in her opposition than was her sister Catharine. In the novel Caroline is probably abler than her cousin Harry Henderson; at school she helps him with his algebra. When he is about to leave for Europe, she wishes she were a young fellow free to make her way in the great world. He replies with the traditional masculine argument that with her beauty and talents she should be satisfied with a woman's lot. "A woman's lot! and what is that, pray? to sit with folded hands and see life drifting by—to be a mere nullity...."[5]

She asks her Uncle Jacob to take her through a course of medical study, but he refuses to take her seriously. With justice she complains that there are richly endowed colleges for men but only poor schools for women.* What she would like would be to attend a western coeducational college and then study medicine. She does finally get to Paris for medical study.

The rich Van Arsdel girls, Eva and Ida, who had had a European education, are both bored with the social whirl at home. Ida complains that fashionable young women never read a serious book through, and that they never read or write the French or German they have been taught. When Ida's father gives her a job managing the foreign correspondence for his business, she saves her money for a medical education. When Eva speaks of the unhappiness of women "buried under eternal commonplaces and trifles," Harry answers that "The life of the great body of men is a succession of ignoble drudgeries." Mrs. Stowe was trying to hold the scales even. It is

* Wellesley, Smith, and Bryn Mawr were not yet in existence; Vassar was only six years old.

the social butterfly Alice who deplores women speaking in public and says, "For my part, I have all the rights I want."

Mrs. Stowe covers a wide spectrum of the feminine scene. The rich Mr. Van Arsdel allows his womenfolk to surround him with luxuries and works of art about which he is indifferent. A simple, quiet man, he is secretly proud of the superior culture of his wife and daughters. "The Van Arsdel household, like most American families, was under feminine rule."

Two kinds of women are amusingly satirized: the phony publicity-seeking Dacia Dangyereyes—obviously Victoria Woodhull—and the society woman Mrs. Cerulean who takes up causes as a fad: "Problems which old statesmen contemplated with perplexity, which had been the despair of ages, she took up with a cheerful alacrity."

Everything would be solved "by giving the affairs of the world into the hands of women, forthwith. . . . Women were the superior sex. Had not every gentleman of her acquaintance, since she could remember, told her this with regard to herself?"[6]

It was characteristic of Henry James to deal with Victoria Woodhull's siege of London society after she wrapped around herself the cloak of responsibility. His Mrs. Headway is far less vivid than Mrs. Stowe's Dacia Dangyereyes, who drops in at Harry's room, strokes his shoulder caressingly and remarks, "You ain't really hatched yet." She says she *takes* her rights and does what a man would do: smoke, drink, "have a good time with you, if I please. . . . Now I'm a woman that not only dares say but I dare *do*. Why hasn't a woman as much a right to go around and make herself agreeable to men as to sit still at home and wait for men to come and make themselves agreeable to her?"[7]

Granted that this is caricature, it is difficult to paint Victoria Woodhull in bolder colors than she wore in the flesh. As a friend told Harry, "be comforted; you're not the first reformer that has to cry out, 'Deliver me from my friends.' " It was a sentiment Susan B. Anthony and Elizabeth Stanton could have echoed in regard to Victoria. Mrs. Stowe's satire and an attack by Catharine Beecher were contributing causes of Mrs. Woodhull's exposure of Henry Ward Beecher's alleged sexual shenanigans.

My Wife and I is not a very good novel: it is didactic on a variety of topics, like drinking and mildly erotic English poetry; the love story is rather conventional; the whole thing lacks focus. But it is one of the few of its era to take the woman's rights doctrines seriously. Despite her conservatism, Mrs. Stowe presented them more justly than did James fifteen years later in *The Bostonians*. The two girls who want to study medicine are not ridiculed: in fact the expectation is that Caroline will finish her course and that Ida will use her savings to begin the study.

In the nineteenth century much of the debate about women as physicians centered on the question of marriage versus a profession. Almost no one thought the two could be combined. In *The Gilded Age* (1873) by Mark Twain and Charles Dudley Warner, the Quaker girl, Ruth Bolton, studies at the Women's Medical College of Philadelphia. Ruth's suitor, Philip Sterling, asks her if she would not do more good as a homemaker. She answers, "What is to hinder having a home of my own?" He points out that as a doctor she would be out on calls night and day. In an era when physicians actually visited their patients, this was not an academic question for women who wanted to practice medicine. Ruth counters by saying, "What sort of home is it for the wife whose husband is always away riding about in his doctor's gig?" Philip replies, "The woman makes the home."

Novelists usually took the either/or choice—possibly the most realistic solution in the nineteenth century. Ruth nearly dies from an infection picked up in the hospital, and after a slow recovery, marries Philip. It is suggested that a contributing cause of her illness was that the work had been too much for a woman's physical stamina. This was of course part of the mythology of the age. Even late in the century prominent physicians preached that even a college education was dangerous to the physical and mental health of women. Everyone seemed to forget that during the Civil War women had survived the drudgery and horror of working in military hospitals even during battle.

Howells, with his usual insistence on women's incompetence, makes his Dr. Breen in *Dr. Breen's Practice* (1881) little better than a quack. She had no genuine medical education, only some training under a homeopath. Like many of Howells's women she is also stupid and pigheaded. She admits that her only reason for studying medicine was a broken love affair. Thinking that Mr. Libby had lied about an approaching storm, she urges Mrs. Maynard to go sailing. After nearly being drowned, Mrs. Maynard comes down with what Dr. Breen diagnoses as a cold. Dr. Mulbridge recognizes the illness as pneumonia and demotes Dr. Breen to a role as nurse.

It was to be her only case. She tells her mother, "I lament the years I spent in working myself up to an undertaking that I was never fit for. . . . I like pleasure and I like dress; I like pretty things."[8] For some incomprehensible reason Mr. Libby persuades her to marry him. After all sorts of Victorian hesitations she accepts, gives up medicine, and goes on a honeymoon to Europe.

Howells does show the prejudice of other women against a physician of their own sex—something Elizabeth Blackwell and other pioneers had to contend with. Of course in his Dr. Breen's case, their suspicions of incompetence were only too well founded.

Oddly enough it was Henry James who depicted a competent woman physician, Dr. Helen Prance in *The Bostonians*. She is of course unmarried. So too was the heroine of Sarah Orne Jewett's *The Country Doctor* (1884). But as Edward Wagenknecht points out, Miss Jewett makes no attempt to trace the heroine's intellectual or professional growth.[9]

Neither Howells nor James was much interested in women's intellectual growth. Although both men wrote their major novels between the 1870s and early 1900s neither one depicted a woman who had been to college, even though by the 1880s there were half as many women as men in institutions of higher learning. The first novel to deal with a woman's collegiate experience was Hamlin Garland's *Rose of Dutcher's Cooley* (1895).

Howells sprinkled his novels with comments and examples showing women's ignorance, irrationality and incompetence.[10] He never shrank from a generalization. Of Isabel March:

> Like all daughters of a free country, Isabel knew nothing about politics. [*Their Wedding Journey* (1871), p. 19.]

Isabel treats Basil's consent to travel by sleeper

> as a matter of course, not because she did not regard him, but

because as a woman she could not conceive of the steps to her conclusion as unknown to him. [Ibid., p. 5.]

They did not stop to ponder . . . but with the heedlessness of their sex, pushed the door wide open. [Ibid.]

The first quarrel of the newly married pair grows out of Isabel's insistence on hiring two horses for an excursion despite the driver's advice that one was enough. When Basil finally gives in, Isabel says:

I don't care particularly for the two horses, Basil . . . it was your refusing that hurt me. [Ibid., p. 130.]

They overhear a woman scolding her husband:

If you'd let me have my own way without opposition about coming here, I dare say I should have gone to the other place. [Ibid., p. 82.]

Of a woman who tries to be a physician Dr. Mulbridge says:

You would not fail individually, you would fail because you are a woman. [*Dr. Breen's Practice* (1881), p. 222.]

Cornelia Root sums up the case against professional and working women:

I don't know whether I want to join in any cry that'll take women's minds off gettin' married. It's the best thing for 'em, and about all they're fit for, most of 'em. [*A Woman's Reason* (1883), p. 316.]

Silas Lapham would have agreed. About girls who work for a living he remarked:

Don't any of 'em like to do't. . . . They think it's a hardship, and I don't blame 'em. They have got a right to get married and they ought to have the chance. [*The Rise of Silas Lapham* (1885), p. 105.]

The evidence of the novels, particularly Howells's interpolated comments, suggests that these characters were speaking his own views. For instance:

Mrs. Lapham had a woman's passion for fixing responsibility. [Ibid., p. 279.]

When Marcia Gaylord married Bartley Hubbard:

> Marcia entered into his affairs with the keen half-intelligence which characterizes a woman's participation in business. [*A Modern Instance* (1882), p. 141.]

> Women like to be understood even when they try not to be understood. [Ibid., p. 184.]

In the nineteen years between *Their Wedding Journey* and *A Hazard of New Fortunes*, Isabel March does not become less illogical. She tells Basil:

> "I was always willing to live more simply than you. You know I was."

Basil answers,

> "I know you always said so, my dear. . . . I remember that when we were looking for a flat you rejected every building that had a bell-ratchet or a speaking tube, and would have nothing to do with any that had more than an electric button; you wanted a hall-boy with electric buttons all over him." [*A Hazard of New Fortunes* (1890), p. 487.]

Here as elsewhere she

> was one of those wives who expect a more rigid adherence to their ideals from their husbands than from themselves. [Ibid., p. 81.]

Margaret Wyman, who made an exhaustive and exhausting study of thirty-four Howells novels, wrote that "they abound in women as exasperatingly, if not always so delightfully, illogical as Isabel March. Most of these well-meaning, scatterbrained ladies are middle-aged matrons—often mothers, guardians, or cousins of young girl heroines."[11] She suggests that the heroines are often more sensible than the older women. As will appear, this is not true of *Indian Summer*, in which neither Mrs. Bowen or Imogene Graham has much judgment. Forty-one-year-old Colville musing on a conversation with twenty-year-old Imogene

> remembered how the minds of girls of twenty had once dazzled him. And yes, he mused, "she must have believed we were talking

literature. . . . Certainly I should have thought it an intellectual time when I was that age." [*Indian Summer* (1886), p. 86.]

Thirty-six years after Howells had commented on the political ignorance of Isabel March, he described Mrs. Markley:

> . . . as a cultured American woman, she was necessarily quite ignorant of her own country, geographically, politically, and historically. [*Through the Eye of the Needle* (1907).] [12]

Not only did Howells fail to put even one college-trained woman in his novels, it would almost seem that he had never met one.

Similarly, except for a couple of essays written late in life, he was oblivious of the whole woman's rights movement. The nearest he came to representing women's concern with humanitarian causes was in *Anne Kilburn*. However, Anne Kilburn is a fearful bumbler who almost causes the death of a child sent to the shore against a doctor's advice. Her idea of social reform never gets beyond the lady bountiful concept.

As with Mrs. Root, quoted above, Howells seemed to think women were fit only to be wives and mothers, and not very fit at that. Against all common sense Mrs. Lapham conceives the idea that young Tom Corey is in love with the pretty but moronic Irene, who never cracks a book. It is obvious to anyone but a Howells woman that Corey visits the Laphams to see the intelligent daughter Penelope. And although Mrs. Lapham has been a schoolteacher, she delivers herself of such remarks as "I don't know as it's good for a girl to read so much, especially novels. I don't want she should get notions." [13]

Yet apparently Howells approved Bartley Hubbard's description of Mrs. Lapham "as one of those women who, in whatever walk of life, seem born to honor the name of American Woman, and to redeem it from the national reproach of Daisy Millerism." [14] Howells did not expect a woman to have brains but he did honor integrity and the household virtues.

He took a dim view of the study of art for girls. Margaret Wyman notes, "Responsible characters in two Howells novels remarked that someone should marry the girl and put her out of her misery." [15] Yet in the five years he was in Italy he must certainly have known of

Harriet Hosmer, the most famous woman sculptor of the day. As the account of her (pp. 63–64) shows, she was far different from the pitiful artists portrayed by Howells.

His notion of the ideal young girl is probably best represented by Lydia Blood in *The Lady of the Aroostook* (1879). Possibly she is the most charming heroine Howells ever created. An orphan, she has been brought up in South Bradfield by an aunt and her grandfather. After Lydia teaches school for two years, another aunt living in Venice invites her to come for a visit. Lydia, with instinctive good taste, has made herself some stylish clothes copied from *Harper's Bazaar* and the costumes of summer boarders. Brought up in a small town and accustomed to going about unchaperoned, nineteen-year-old Lydia is not much disturbed to find herself the only woman on board the *Aroostook*, a sailing vessel.

She plays shuffleboard and ringtoss with two young men, Dunham and Staniford. Dunham is on his way to Dresden to marry a girl who will, according to Staniford, sacrifice him to her ailments. Staniford himself never expects to marry. He has been a dabbler in the arts and literature, but having lost his money, now plans to try to make enough to take care of his sister's boy. As has been mentioned, he upsets Lydia by kissing her hand.

In Venice she accepts her aunt's advice on the proper behavior of a young girl in Europe, but she is shocked when her aunt and uncle go to an opera on Sunday. Lydia herself will not even read a novel on Sunday—no great hardship because she admits that she doesn't read much anyway. She is so appalled on learning of married women who go out with other men or separate from decent husbands, and on hearing a woman swear, that she decides to go back home.

Of course Staniford comes to Venice as promised. Not knowing that he had been nursing the ill Dunham, Lydia is piqued by his delay in getting there, as her contemporary Daisy Miller is piqued by Winterbourne's delay in getting to Rome. Both Howells and James thought of the American woman as rather demanding. When Staniford proposes, Lydia has qualms about accepting him because she thinks he will be shamed by the unconventional way in which they had met. A maidenly shilly shallying was *de rigueur* at the time.

On the whole, Lydia Blood is a believable character despite her Howellsian squeamishness about a kiss on the hand. Her revulsion against European morals is thoroughly in character for a girl from a remote American village. Her beauty, style, and self-reliance, and innocence are in accord with the description of American girls by a variety of European travelers.

If Lydia Blood is the most attractive of Howells's heroines, Marcia Gaylord of *A Modern Instance* (1882) is perhaps the most repulsive. It is as if Howells wanted to point up the dangers in the freedom given to American girls. In the opening scene, Bartley Hubbard escorts Marcia home at midnight, and she asks him in. "The situation, scarcely conceivable in another civilization, is so common in ours, where youth commands its fate and trusts solely to itself that it may be characteristic of New England civilization wherever it keeps its simplicity." The village would not have been censorious of the unchaperoned visit, but when Bartley kisses Marcia good night, any reader of Howells would realize that they were headed for disaster.

Marcia has been indulged by a mother who "spoke with that awe of her daughter and her judgments which is one of the pathetic idiosyncrasies of a certain class of American mothers." Her father, although disapproving of boarding schools, let her attend one for two years. "What resulted was a great proficiency in the things that pleased her, and ignorance of other things." She had come in contact with people who, according to Howells, "had begun to make such fools of themselves about Darwinism and the brotherhood of all men in the monkey." As might be expected, Maria seldom played on the piano father had bought her.[16]

The squire warns Marcia that Bartley is a scamp but she accepts him anyway; then asks, "Did you despise me for letting you kiss me before we were engaged?" They marry on the spur of the moment, and Marcia proves to be an extravagant housewife. Bartley, a newspaper man, takes her to lectures, concerts, and plays, all of which soon bore her. But she is a fiercely possessive wife who makes a scene whenever Bartley looks at another woman.

Bartley lives up to Squire Gaylord's prediction; he drinks beer, and eventually steals money and absconds. Although Marcia has no money, she rejects the lawyer's advice to sell the house: she must keep it for Bartley's return. When her father tries to take her home, she refuses. "I will stay in Bartley's house till he comes back to me. If he is dead, I will die here."[17]

The novel has been described as Howells's attempt to deal with the question of divorce. For years some of the advocates of woman's rights had demanded more liberal divorce laws. Howells clearly sides with the puritanical lawyer Atherton. Thus when her admirer, Ben Halleck, tells Marcia that Bartley, absent for two years, must be dead, but if not, she should get a divorce, Atherton says, "has that poison got into you Halleck? You might ask her if she were a widow, to marry you, but how will you ask her, if she is still a wife to get a divorce and then marry you? . . . You would have to corrupt her soul first." Even when Ben learns that Bartley had applied for a divorce in Indiana, Marcia at first refuses to believe it; then goes out to contest it. After Bartley's death Ben asks Atherton if he now has the right to ask her to marry him. Atherton, who once told his wife that "as compared with the highest love her husband ever felt for her, Ben's passion was as light to darkness," now says, "Don't you think his being in love with her when she was another man's wife is what he feels it to be—an indelible *stain*?"[18]

Howells said that the marriage of Bartley and Marcia had been "based in the first place on the unreasoning passion of the woman." So too was the engagement of Colville and Imogene Graham in *Indian Summer*. As has been noted, Imogene was the temporary ward of Mrs. Bowen, a supposedly sophisticated expatriate. As William M. Gibson remarks in his introduction to the Everyman edition of the novel, "Colville is fallible enough . . . but he is a paragon of sense compared to Miss Graham and Mrs. Bowen."[19] This is somewhat too kind to Colville, but it well describes the ladies. Twenty-year old Imogene, denied normal youthful contacts, fancies herself in love with Colville, twice her age. It is she who more or less proposes. Partly because of her beauty, partly out of chivalry he drifts into a tacit engagement.

Imogene writes to her mother saying she does not know if she is engaged or not, but she tells her "Dear Diary" she is. "O dear Di! I cannot write his name yet, and you must not ask me till I can. . . ." (Not a single diary in the many examined for this book has anything resembling this.) Possibly out of jealousy Mrs. Bowen refuses to give Colville any advice. "There is no way to please me—as you call it—except to keep her from regretting what she has done." Nor will she help Imogene. Colville, half realizing his mistake, nevertheless feels duty bound to honor the engagement.

On one occasion Imogene pulls him to the sofa and puts his arm about her "with a simple fearlessness, and matter-of-fact promptness that made him shudder." Then she does something that damns any Howells heroine: in the dim corridor

> She put her arms about his neck and sweetly kissed him.
> Colville went out into the sunlight feeling like some strange, newly invented kind of scoundrel. . . . He was the betrothed lover of this poor child, whose affection he could not check without a degree of brutality for which only a better man would have the courage.[20]

Eventually Imogene's mother demands that Colville release Imogene from "a fate that would be worse than death for such a girl." While he is laid up after rescuing Mrs. Bowen and Effie from a carriage accident, Imogene breaks the engagement. In the sick room, " 'I will pray for you,' she said, her face . . . intense with the passions working in her soul! . . . she crushed his hand against her lips and ran from the room. He sank into a deathly torpor. . . ."[21]

After a talk with Lina Bowen in which she admits that she did not interfere because her reasons would have been selfish, Colville tells her he loves her and says farewell. " 'Oh, you must stay!' said Lina, in the self-contemptuous voice of a woman who falls below her own ideal of herself."

She could well be self-contemptuous, for with Howells, marriage was not a happy ending but a comedown. In the autobiographical *Their Wedding Journey* he wrote, "Marriage was not the poetic dream of perfect union that girl imagines. It was a state of trial, of probation; it was an ordeal, not an ectasy. If she and Basil had broken each other's hearts and parted, would not the fragments have been on a much finer, much higher plane? Had not the commonplace, every-day experiences of marriage vulgarized them both?"[22]

Some modern critics defend Howells by arguing that he was

shackled by the mores of his time. But even by Victorian standards he was excessively puritanical—witness his comments on the kiss which Imogene Graham gave Colville. As far back as 1886 a writer in *Lippincott's Monthly Magazine* complained of the vacuity of Howells's women:

> All his heroines are beautiful, affectionate, and almost morbidly conscientious, but they are idle, inconsequent, and more or less jealous, incapable of earning a living, incapable of philanthropy, incapable of hard thinking, or decided action. . . .
> The wives sketched in "Private Theatricals" and "Dr. Breen's Practice" are, indeed, rich chiefly in headaches and nervous troubles, and their world does not seem much wider than that of an Oriental.[23]

About 1862 Emily Dickinson satirized the kind of women Howells later portrayed:

> What soft, cherubic creatures
>   These gentlewomen are!
> One would as soon assault a plush
>   Or violate a star.
> Such dimity convictions,
>   A horror so refined
> of freckled human nature
>   of Deity ashamed,—[Published 1896.]

He would have been horrified by her poem "Wild nights," suggesting sexual ectasy.

Certainly no other novelist between 1870 and 1900 except Henry James made such a thoroughgoing attempt to delineate the American woman. The limitation of Howells can be summed up in the aphorism, "You can take the boy out of the country, but you can't take the country out of the boy." Howells's concept of the American woman was essentially that of rural Ohio before the Civil War. His ideal woman is typified by Lydia Blood, beautiful, charming, self-reliant within prescribed limits, thoroughly good, but puritanical and completely without intellectual interests. Thus his women are almost untouched by the great social changes of the later nineteenth century.

NOTES

1. James D. Hart, *The Popular Book: A History of America's Literary Taste*, New York, 1950, pp. 9–91.
2. Donald A. Koch, Introduction to *"Tempest and Sunshine"* and *"The Lamplighter,"* p. xi.
3. Ibid., p. xii.
4. *Complete Novels . . . of Hawthorne*, p. 481.
5. Harriet Beecher Stowe, *My Wife and I*, Cambridge, Mass., 1871, p. 105.
6. Ibid., pp. 210–11, 226, 245.
7. Ibid., pp. 250–51.
8. William Dean Howells, *Dr. Breen's Practice*, Boston and New York, 1881, p. 234.
9. Wagenknecht, *Cavalcade of the American Novel*, p. 172.
10. William Dean Howells, *Their Wedding Journey; Dr. Breen's Practice; A Woman's Reason*, Boston, 1883; *The Rise of Silas Lapham; A Modern Instance*, ed. by William M. Gibson, Cambridge, Mass., 1957; *A Hazard of New Fortunes*, Everyman edition, New York, 1952; *Indian Summer; Through the Eye of the Needle*.
11. Margaret Wyman, "Women in the American Realistic Novel, 1860–1893; Literary Reflection of Social Life," Ph.D. dissertation, Radcliffe College, 1950, p. 487.
12. Quoted in Wyman, p. 779.
13. Howells, *The Rise of Silas Lapham*, p. 135.
14. Ibid., p. 19.
15. Wyman, p. 765.
16. Howells, *A Modern Instance*, pp. 4, 29, 25.
17. Ibid., p. 313.
18. Ibid., pp. 317, 332.
19. Howells, *Indian Summer*, p. xvii.
20. Ibid., p. 229.
21. Ibid., p. 292.
22. Howells, *Their Wedding Journey*, p. 199.
23. "Our Monthly Gossip," *Lippincott's Monthly Magazine*, 36 (January–June, 1886), 107, 109.

Eight

The Two Nations

Our hearts were touched with fire.
Oliver Wendell Holmes, Jr.

Even before the first shot was fired at Ford Sumter on April 12, 1861, the United States was in reality two nations with two completely different social systems. This situation particularly affected the lives of women. It is no accident that the woman's rights and suffrage movements were confined to the North and West until well after the Civil War. One reason for this was the close links between the abolition and woman's rights movements. Another was the patriarchal tradition described by Ann Firor Scott (see p. 58). In any case the experience of northern women in creating and running organizations enabled them to develop a more organized response to the war than that of their southern sisters.

This is not to belittle the efforts and sacrifices of the women of the South. They endured greater hardships and were called upon for greater individual enterprise than most northern women. But their war effort was fragmented by the regionalism which helped to defeat the Confederacy, and by the hedonistic tradition of the South. Their diaries record both the making of uniforms and ball dresses; hospital work alternated with dances and flirtations.

It is this kind of picture one gets from the reminiscences of Mrs. Burton Harrison (1843–1920) who wrote novels under her maiden name, Constance Cary. On the death of her father the family moved in with her grandmother. It was a not untypical southern household: two widowed daughters, six children, and an endless procession of aunts and cousins who stayed as long as they wished. At boarding school she found that many of the girls from the deep South were pretty, languid creatures who had never put on a shoe or stocking for themselves, and whose views on owning and chastising offending servants were abhorent to her.[1]

With the coming of the war her fifteen-year-old brother rushed off to join the Confederate army. She says that her mother nursed from dawn to dusk in a hospital and slept on an army bunk; yet found time to make for Constance a costume of a lady of the court of Louis XV; she found spangles for the shoes and fan, and a pearl necklace. During that gay winter of 1862 in Richmond, Constance met Burton Norwell Harrison, the man she was to marry after the war. He was about to enlist but was made secretary to Jefferson Davis. Together Burton and Constance rode seventy miles to and from the Natural Bridge. At other times, "We rode races, jumped hurdles, improvised tourneys, spearing a ring of plaited willow hung upon a bow."[2]

In the winter of 1863 she stayed in a pleasant country house near the headquarters of a crack cavalry division, "with a dozen gallant knights ready to do one's slightest bidding." The girls were bitterly disappointed when the general called off a tournament "in which the prowess of Ivanhoe and Brian de Bois Guilbert were to be emulated."[3] (As late as 1864 Mary Chesnut noted that her son "rode in a tournament in Columbia and crowned Natalia Howard queen of love and beauty." She said that she herself "went in for the war-like Scott's *Marmion* and Campbell's stirring odes. I forget to weep my dead." Mark Twain had a point when he said that Scott was responsible for the Civil War.)

In her *Recollections* Mrs. Harrison remarked, "Even now writing it after so many years, I seem to feel again the pulse of that stirring time." There was the occasion when she rode twelve miles through rain and snow to meet a woman who wanted to penetrate the Union lines. Her companion, a hardened cavalryman, told her that he kept wondering "if girls were not of tougher build than men."[4] She remembered General Lee calling upon her mother and herself and kissing them both on leaving.

The Carys often went to receptions given by Mrs. Jefferson Davis. Even President Davis took part in the festivities. At a costume party he cut off his mustache and dressed as an Arab sheik. The evening ended with a supper prepared by a chef.[5] That same year her new evening dress was ruined at the "smartest party of the season" when a man spilled oysters and chicken salad on it. Rumor had it that the champagne cost $10,000.* This was the winter after the Battle of Gettysburg and the fall of Vicksburg.

With Lee's permission the girls arranged dances for the officers. One of them who had galloped to town night after night to get back to camp at two in the morning wrote her a reminiscent letter about what she called that "brilliant winter."

> To you and to me, looking back, it was such a blending of a real "Heroic Age" and a real "Golden Age" as could come but once in a million years . . . there was youth, and beauty, and devotion, and splendid daring, a jealous honor and an antique patriotism, an utter self-abregation and utter defiance of fate, a knightly chastity and beautiful surrender of the coyest maid when her love was going to certain death.[6]

He had an uneasy remembrance of having been engaged to all of the girls.

The southern girl's habit of multiple "engagements" has baffled outsiders until at least as late as the Scott Fitzgerald era. (Zelda was "pinned" to four others besides Scott.) As Mary Chesnut remarked in her diary, "An engagement in Richmond means so little." In a journal kept during the Civil War, Kate Stone (1841–1907) makes constant references to wartime engagements. Her friend Mollie "would not tell me the names of any of her lovers.† She must have had scores. She says she has four on hand now, all waiting in trembling apprehension of yes or no."[7]

Unlike Constance Cary's nostalgically gilded reminiscenses, Kate's journal is a record of immediate experience. Her beautiful mother, widowed at thirty-seven, managed a plantation in Louisiana which comprised 1,260 acres and 150 slaves. There were eight living children. Had it not been for the war the crops of 1861 would have paid off all the debts on the estate.[8] Mrs. Stone had planned a northern tour that winter and one in Europe the following year. Eventually,

---

* It is not always clear in southern memoirs whether or not dollars represent Confederate money but, in view of the amounts, this is probably the case in most instances, e.g. $20 for a turkey in 1863.

† In nineteenth-century novels and diaries *lover* meant *suitor* or even a frequent caller.

as the Union armies approached, General Beauregard ordered the plantation owners to burn their cotton. Mrs. Stone burned $20,000 worth.

Although Kate finished school at fifteen, she, like many of her northern sisters, did a substantial amount of good reading. The editor of her journal counted thirty authors, among them Scott, of course, but also Shakespeare, Jeremy Taylor, Lamb, Victor Hugo (in French), Bulwer-Lytton, Thackeray, Tennyson, Poe, Hawthorne, Irving's *Mohamet and His Successors*, and Motley's *Dutch Republic*, a book she found well written and interesting. From time to time she mentioned such magazines as *Leslie's*, *Harper's*, *The Living Age*, and *Blackwood's*. On reading a book on King Arthur she commented that he gave the impression of "a henpecked Don Quixote."[9]

As with Constance Cary and Mary Chesnut there is the paradox of Kate Stone's hatred of slavery and ardent secessionism. Even under the best owners she thought slaves had a hard life. As she grew older she would wake at night thinking about slavery and "would grow sick with the misery of it all." Tales of cruelties on neighboring plantations were constantly circulated, "tales that would make one's blood run cold. . . . Always I felt the moral guilt of it, felt how impossible it would be for the owner of slaves to win his way into Heaven." Yet when the war began, she described the young men rushing off "Bravely, cheerily, they go, willing to meet death in defense of the South, the land we love so well, the fairest land and the most gallant men the sun shines on. May God prosper us. Never again can we join hands with the North, the people who hate us so."[10]

Suddenly men who could not win their way to Heaven had become "the most gallant men the sun shines on," of a secessionist government which had riveted slavery irrevocably into its constitution, she wrote, "Our Cause is right and God will give us the victory."[11]

At first the war touched the Stones lightly. Kate rode to hounds, ran the sewing machine to make a dress and hem towels, knitted, and read. In January of 1862 the Stones got a new piano. Soon, however, their cotton was burned to prevent it falling into Yankee hands. Kate noted that "it is not such hard living";[12] they had molasses, sugar, varieties of cornbread, fresh vegetables, lots of eggs, chickens, occasional partridges, and often venison. The girls caught messes of fish. But in the distance they could often hear the guns at Vicksburg.

By March of 1863 Kate noted that all the Negroes were running away and her aunt's cook had set a fire. Some of the families lost every Negro on the place. The Stone women learned to make the uppers of shoes out of broadcloth or velvet. Late that month the family evacuated the Brokenburn plantation. After a four weeks stay with friends they embarked in an immense dugout holding Mrs. Stone, Kate and her sister and two young brothers, an aunt, an assorted cargo of corn, bacon, hams plus Negroes and their baggage, dogs, and cats. "It was a dreadful trip."[13]

At Delhi they caught up with their furniture, which had been loaded pell-mell into a wagon. There were soldiers drunk and sober climbing all over it. From there the party started out for a plantation which Mrs. Stone owned in Texas. On the way, when they found a road impassable for a wagon, they loaded their baggage onto horses. At one bayou Kate, carrying her sister Beverly, had to swim her horse. Fastened to her waist she carried a bag with her Aunt Laura's gold. After a three-weeks stopover at Dr. Carson's in Trenton, Alabama, at a home filled with books, music, and pleasant company, Mrs. Stone bought an unsprung Jersey wagon for the rest of the journey. They spent seven weeks with Mrs. Wadley, another friend.

Their hostess arranged a dance for the young people, where some of the girls made such a fuss over the officers that Kate thought another week would have ruined them: "They would have felt superior to their general." For some of the girls it was their first experience with soldiers and they "ran wild."[14]

When the Stones eventually reached Texas, Kate at first hated the place. People wore shoes only for state occasions; there were no bowls, pitchers, or washtubs; the people were ugly and rough; there were ticks, bedbugs, fleas by the millions, and hundreds of snakes. Within a week four or five men were shot nearby. The people "take it as a matter of course that an obnoxious person should be put to death by some offended neighbor."[15]

This pattern of a refugee family kept together despite hardships was often repeated in the South. Those in the path of Sherman's army lost their homes entirely. In a number of ways the Stones were fortunate: they had the Texas plantation to go to, and although the Negroes occupied Brokenburn during the war, it was still there when the family returned. Unlike the women living in or near urban centers the plantation wife could not take part in organized war efforts; she had to survive by means of her own efforts. As a widow Mrs. Stone had more experience as a manager than had most plantation women, but as Anne Scott shows, the wartime South became a matriarchy.

She quotes an old soldier, reminiscing in the eighties, who thought the war had been harder on the women than on the men: a soldier at least knew if he was alive whereas his wife lived in a state of anxiety. One family had twelve sons in the army, nine of whom were killed.[16] A South Carolina woman lost five brothers. Three of the Stone boys died in the Army—one from pneumonia, one from a horse falling on him.

Despite all this, Kate's warlike fever was unabated. "We do not hold nor have we destroyed a single Northern city, as we so much hoped." When a number of Yankees who had commanded Black troops were captured, she wrote, "It does seem like they ought to be hanged." When the news came of the death of her third brother, she paraphrased Tennyson's "Tears, idle tears." On hearing of Lincoln's assassination she wrote, "All honors to J. Wilkes Booth, who has rid the world of a tyrant and made himself famous for generations."[17] (This sentiment was echoed by seventeen-year-old Emma Le Conte who noted in her diary, "Hurrah! Old Abe Lincoln has been assassinated."[18] On the other hand Eliza Frances Andrews of Georgia, aged twenty-four, recorded a different view: "Some fools applauded, but wise people looked grave and held their peace. It is a terrible blow to the South, for it places that vulgar renegade Andy Johnson, in power, and will give the Yankees an excuse for charging us with a crime which was in reality only the deed of an irresponsible madman.")[19]

Meanwhile, for Kate Stone, there were compensations: she mentioned several suitors. Her first Texas beau was "A smooth-faced, rosy-cheeked young dandy, proud of his jet-black imperial." A Captain Empy had "a stock of ready-made compliments that he weighs out ot every young lady as a grocer weighs out sugar." It is obvious that she kept her satiric humor. Before her brother Coley's death she had commented on the loss of his first love: "Like most boys he lost his heart to a girl several years older—fortunately a disease that never kills a boy of that age."[20]

Kate's most serious suitor was Lieutenant Henry Holmes, "such a dissipated man. He is gay and pleasant and a gentleman. Why will he drink?"[21] Her mother wanted Kate to send him off. She and the other girls resolved "to change their war customs, stop flirting, and only engage themselves when they really meant something." Then she embarked on the age-old gambit—she would marry Lieutenant Holmes to reform him. She did marry him in 1868, but did not continue her diary to record the result.

At the war's end the family returned to Brokenburn, where Mrs. Stone set about restoring the plantation. It was easy to get credit to plant cotton, but the worms devastated the crop. Nevertheless, Mrs. Stone kept going. As Anne Scott shows, this was the pattern all over the South. "The war had created a generation of women without men."[22] Many of the men who did return were broken in health and body. Negroes now had to receive wages, and could walk off when they pleased. As might be expected, the war and reconstruction profoundly influenced the position of women in the South.

For instance, there was Eliza Frances Andrews (1840-1931) of Georgia, the daughter of Judge Garrett Andrews, who owned two hundred slaves. As late as 1864 she mentioned dancing at Albany, Georgia, until two in the morning, or going to a friend's house to rehearse for tableaux and theatricals. "I never enjoyed an evening more. We had no end of fun, and a splendid supper, with ice cream and sherbert and cake made of real white sugar." She got home from another party at 4 A.M. In the fall she ruined a riding habit in a fox hunt. On the way home from a declamation contest at a chase through the woods, jumping their horses over every log they came to "just to see what he would do."[23]

By 1865, when their household was reduced from twenty-five servants to five—two of them sick—she got up early to sweep and clean the house. After the war she edited a country newspaper, taught in the public schools of Yazoo, Mississippi, then at the Wesleyan Female College at Macon, Georgia, where she remained on the faculty until 1897. Using the pen name Elzey Hay she published stories, essays, criticism, four novels, and two textbooks on botany. In 1918 she became a Socialist.[24] The pre-war southern belle had traveled a long way.

In her study of the southern lady Anne Scott argues that even before the war "a psychological Geiger counter would have detected a growing discontent with woman's assigned role." However, for a variety of reasons this discontent had not led to organized movements as it did in the North. The connection between abolition and woman's rights is too simple an answer. After all, the temperance organizations had also spilled over into the rights movement. Possibly the more rural nature of southern life had something to do with the absence of women's organizations. When people got together it was a gathering of the clan—cousins, aunts, uncles, married children and their offspring. There is also a real possibility that the southern woman was a victim of the mystique of the belle and the lady.

Many years after the event, Constance Cary Harrison quoted the description of her cousin in the *New Orleans Crescent*:

> Look well at her, for you have never seen, and will probably never see again, so beautiful a woman! Observe her magnificent form, her rounded arms, her neck and shoulders perfect as if from a sculptor's chisel, her auburn hair, the poise of her well-shaped head. Saw you ever such color on a woman's cheek? And she is not less intelligent than beautiful. . . . It is worth a king's ransom, a lifetime of trouble to look at such a woman. No wonder Beauregard pronounced her the most beautiful in that city of lovely women—Baltimore.[25]

Apparently Mrs. Harrison did not throw up at this, for in 1912 she quoted it nostalgically.

As Mrs. Scott's study shows, the newspapers and public speeches were full of this sort of thing. She is probably right in seeing it as a masculine gambit to keep women in their place. This was not part of a conscious male plot: it was part of the mystique fostered by Walter Scott. Thus of Ellen in *The Lady of the Lake*:

And ne'er did Grecian chisel trace
A Nymph, a Naiad or a Grace
Of finer form, or lovlier face! ...
A foot more light, a step more true,
Ne'er from the heath-flower dash'd the dew;
E'en the slight harebell raised its head
Elastic fom her airy tread. ...

Ellen of course has "a breast of snow," which literally and figuratively was supposed to be a mark of the southern lady as well. An often repeated incantation becomes an article of belief.

This magnolia-scented prose infected countless sentimental novels of the period. By contrast there is the excellent and realistic journal kept by Mary Boykin Chesnut during the Civil War. To a considerable degree it supports Anne Scott's hypothesis of the southern woman's dissatisfaction with her role. Mrs. Chesnut's disillusioned view of slavery and slave owners has already been referred to. She described slavery as "a curse in any land"; she was sickened at a slave auction where a handsome mulatto girl was sold. Like Jefferson she thought that "Slavery does not make good masters."[26]

She was also critical of the southern gentleman. "The race have brains enough, but they are not active minded. . . . Our planters are nice fellows, but slow to move, impulsive, but hard to keep moving." She recorded various young men killed in duels. "Dueling has been rife in Camden." And later, "These foolish hair-brained [*sic*] Southern lads have been within an ace of a fight over their camping ground with a Maryland company. That is too Irish, to be so ready to fight anybody, friend or foe."[27] On the same page she mentioned that a Georgian killed a Carolinian on the train because of a quarrel over watermelons.

Mrs. Chesnut was very much a part of the Southern establishment. Her father was a South Carolina nullifier, a United States senator, and a governor of the state. In February 1861, her husband, against her wishes, resigned his seat in the Senate. He helped to draft the Confederate Constitution with its irrevocable article on slavery. Offered a position on the staff of Jefferson Davis he said his duty was in Columbia, South Carolina. She was critical: "I do not like the endless rows of pins stuck into me in this grand court of the Great Buzzfuzz."[28]

She may well have been a more intelligent person than her husband. Certainly her knowledge of literature was impressive; she knew Shakespeare, Jonson, Milton, Sir Thomas Browne, Lady Mary Montagu, Coleridge, Schiller, Goethe, Hume, Creasey, and Oliver Wendell Holmes; she mentioned novels by Thackeray, George Elliott, Kingsley, Meredith, Wilkie Collins, and Disraeli. Before the war she subscribed to *Blackwood's*, *Cornhill*, the *Atlantic*, and *Harper's*. More surprisingly for a Victorian lady, she read Balzac, and *Fanny Hill*. To criticize "Fanny," as she referred to it, "one must be as shameless as the book itself. . . . It is not nastier or coarser than Mrs. Stowe, but then it is not written in the interests of philanthropy." [29]

Her comments on *Uncle Tom's Cabin*, which she read twice, indicate her ambivalence about the South. Earlier, after her bitter description of plantation concubinage, she added, "Mrs. Stowe did not hit the sorest spot. She makes Legree a bachelor." With a mixture of anger and envy she wrote:

On one side Mrs. Stowe, Greeley, Thoreau, Emerson, Sumner. They live in nice New England homes, clean, sweet-smelling, shut up in libraries, writing books which ease their hearts of their bitterness against us. . . . Think of these holy New Englanders forced to have a Negro village to walk through their houses whenever they see fit, dirty, slatternly, idle ill-smelling by nature. [30]

Her bitterness against the North is scarcely less than against the patriarchal male. On rereading Milton she said she saw the speech of Adam to Eve in a new light. "Women will not stay at home, will go out to see and be seen, even if it be by the Devil himself." In one entry she wrote, "James Chesnut has been so nice this winter, so reasonable and considerate—that is for a man." She told Mrs. Jefferson Davis that her husband had ordered her to give no more parties "and he is decidedly master in his own house. . . ." And in her diary, "To hear is to obey." Later on she wrote "All married women, all children and girls who live in their father's houses are slaves. . . . Does a man ever speak to his wife and children except to find fault? Does a woman ever address any remark to her husband that does not begin with an excuse?" [31]

In all societies there is a gap between the ideal and the realities.

However it is hard to escape the conclusion that the southern lady was faced with a peculiarly schizophrenic society. As a girl she was assured that she was a belle, and was courted with romantic gallantry. As a wife she had to close her eyes to a husband's philandering with slaves on his own plantation. As a wife and mother she had to accept the possibility that her husband, brothers, or sons would be killed in duels. Yet she was trained to praise the ideals of honor and bravery. It may be that this need to accept the gulf between the ideal and the real in southern society caused women like Constance Cary, Kate Stone, and Mary Chesnut—all of whom hated slavery—to become ardent secessionists.

Many years later Ellen Glasgow, a Virginian, wrote, "I hated—I had always hated—the inherent falseness in much of the Southern tradition. . . ."[32] But it was not until the 1920s that she could satirize it in such novels as *The Romantic Comedians* and *They Stooped to Folly.* For the southern women of the mid-nineteenth century there was no escape hatch from the social system. It was not the first time that the prisoners of a system have become its most ardent defenders—nor will it be the last.

Furthermore, as wars do, this one shook people out of a routine which, without realizing it, they had found dull. A month after Fort Sumter, Kate Stone mentioned that her brother was wild to go to Virginia; he was afraid that the fighting would be over before he got there. The Confederate veterans who reminisced to Mrs. Harrison about the winter of 1863 in Richmond felt that for both of them it had been a blend of a Heroic Age and a Golden Age. After all the hardships of her stay in Texas, Kate Stone feared she would look back upon her last year there with regret: "The happiest year of my life."[33]

As Anne Scott says, "The challenge of war called women almost at once into new kinds of activity."[34] They had to take over plantations, mills, businesses. "Soldiers' aid societies sprang into being as if southern women had all their lives been used to community organizations." Nearly a thousand societies sprang up. Mrs. Scott cites examples of women who set up and managed hospitals. Phoebe Yates Pember, who became a matron of one in Richmond, ran into the usual masculine opposition from the chief surgeon, who feared "petticoat government." In her four years of service she gradually won him over. She performed every kind of service from administration to taking charge of the whiskey barrel—a source of trouble. When some drunken soldiers came in search of it, she held them off with a pistol. But even as late as her reminiscences in 1879 she felt it necessary to defend women against the charge that hospital work coarsened them.[35]

In the North, women who wanted to organize and participate in hospital work faced the same kind of opposition from physicians and military brass. There was some justification for this. William Quentin Maxwell says in his history of the United States Sanitary Commission, "Prima donnas of self-righteousness came to nursing with little or no training; they took matters into their own hands and disregarded orders."[36] Some women distributed delicacies to enhance their own prestige.

However, at the beginning of the war there was one woman, Dorothea Dix (1802-87), who probably knew more about hospitals than anyone else in the United States. She was so prominent that on April 23, 1861, Secretary of War Simon Cameron accepted her offer to select nurses for the army. In June of that year she was commissioned as superintendent of United States Army Nurses—the first such commission ever issued.[37]

Dorothea Dix was one of those persons whose neurotic compulsions lead them to channel their energies into various causes. This is not to imply that all crusaders are neurotic, but Miss Dix certainly was. At about the age of twelve she left an unhappy farm home in Maine where her father drank to excess and her mother was a semi-invalid. Dorothea had felt unloved at home, and she believed that her Boston grandmother disliked her. While going to school in Boston she had no intimate friends or playmates. After two years her grandmother sent her to an aunt's where she found tact and sympathy. But throughout her life she felt unloved.[38]

When she began teaching school at sixteen, she used the whip freely. Like many able women she had a lust for knowledge: she read extensively, in her grandfather's library, the Boston library, and various circulating libraries; she attended public lectures by Harvard professors. To her friend, Ann Heath, she wrote that she had little time for amusements: her days were taken up with business, teaching, learning, reading, and writing. This last included a book on education which went through sixty editions, a volume of hymns for children, and a series of moral tales. In the school she ran in her grandmother's mansion she maintained rigid discipline: pupils never ran in the streets or laughed boisterously. Some of them later said they were spiritually revolutionized; others remembered exhaustion and sleeplessness.[39]

In a letter to Ann Heath she referred to her grandmother as "Medusa." The fifty-year long correspondence between Dorothea and Ann has obvious lesbian overtones. Dorothea's contained effusive declarations of affection, and sometimes ended, "Do not show or read anyone this note." She enclosed locks of her own hair.[40]

In 1836 she suffered a complete nervous and physical collapse. Using a small annuity and some savings she sailed for Europe. With a letter from William Henry Channing she visited the home of William Rathbone, a well-to-do humanitarian. Dorothea had a habit of making self-invited protracted visits—in this case eighteen months. Despite the fact that she was her grandmother's heir, she did not return to look after the old lady in her last days.

It was not until 1841 that she began the work which was to make her famous. Teaching a Sunday School class for women in the East Cambridge jail, she discovered that the insane were kept in unheated cells: the jailer said the lunatics did not feel the cold like other people. At that time there were only fourteen mental hospitals in the United States and the insane were usually handled like animals.

With the encouragement of Samuel Gridley Howe and Charles Sumner she began a tour of Massachusetts jails. Within eighteen months she had visited every almshouse, workhouse, and prison in the state—some of them many times. In her inspections from cellar to attic she discovered horrible conditions were the rule. In 1843 Howe presented her report to the legislature. A committee called for immediate action, and a relief bill passed by a good margin.[41]

During the next two years she traveled over ten thousand miles to visit eighteen state penitentiaries, three hundred jails and houses of correction, and over five hundred almshouses. By 1847 she had covered thirty thousand miles from Canada to the Gulf and from the

Atlantic to the Mississippi. Within a surprisingly short time her efforts began to pay off. In 1845 the New Jersey legislature passed a bill to establish an asylum in Trenton—her first-born child as she called it. That same year the legislature of Pennsylvania voted to establish the Pennsylvania Lunatic Hospital in Harrisburg.[42]

So it went in state after state after she presented her petitions: Illinois, Tennessee, North Carolina, Mississippi. The hospital in North Carolina was named Dix Hall. Presidents of railroads and steamboat lines gave her annual passes; express companies transported supplies free; she became a friend of presidents Polk, Fillmore, and Lincoln.[43] The Swedish novelist Fredrika Bremer visited her in 1851 and traveled with her. When during a visit she learned of the many wrecks on Sable Island, Newfoundland, she collected money in Boston, New York, and Philadelphia to buy and outfit four lifeboats, plus a mortar and harness.

In 1854 when she went to Europe, the president of the steamship line gave her free passage and came to see her off. As usual her activity was incredible: she visited hospitals for the insane in Scotland, Paris, Rome, Florence, Naples, Genoa, Milan, and Constantinople, covering fourteen countries and hundreds of institutions. The Pope granted her an audience and at her request restored a Dr. Gulini to a hospital post.

Back in the States, the proprietor of a small hotel in Texas refused to take money: "Make sure now there's a home for you in every house in Texas."[44] In Columbia, South Carolina, she was given a public ovation. For one thing, Miss Dix had taken no interest in abolition or woman's rights. Even as late as 1863 when the Confederates stopped a train in Pennsylvania, an officer, recognizing her, released the train.

Thus when in 1861 she was appointed superintendent of United States Army Nurses she already had national and international fame as an expert on hospitals. As superintendent she introduced the same moralistic discipline that she had used as a teacher. In her famous call for nurses she said, "No woman under thirty need apply. . . . All nurses are required to be plain looking women. The dresses must be brown or black, with no bows, no curls, no jewelry, and no hoop-skirts." There was some common sense in this: some women tried to become nurses to follow their own men or to find husbands; there was as yet no established nurse's uniform. Miss Dix applied her strictness to the men as well: she got a dishonorable discharge for any surgeon found drunk.[45]

When Louisa May Alcott came down with pneumonia while nursing, Dorothea brought her wine, tea, medicines, and cologne. In her journal Miss Alcott wrote, "She is a kind old soul, but very queer and arbitrary." Among other things Miss Dix discriminated against Catholic nurses, despite the fact that surgeons often preferred the nuns. The Sanitary Commission, a well-financed volunteer organization, tended to stay out of Miss Dix's realm: she was essentially a loner; she lacked tact, and did not work well in a team.

The idea of an organization similar to the British Sanitary Commission was conceived by the Rev. Dr. Henry Bellows (1814-82). With Dr. Elisha Harris he went to Elizabeth Blackwell's New York Infirmary for Women, where some fifty or sixty women were meeting to discuss ways of helping the soldiers. Bellows was elected chairman and at once called a meeting of women at Cooper Union. Out of this grew the Woman's Central Association of Relief. A committee headed by Bellows went to Washington to visit Miss Dix, who had already been appointed superintendent of nurses. With her backing the committee persuaded the acting surgeon general, Colonel Robert Wood, to support the plan for a Sanitary Commission. Secretary of War Simon Cameron signed an order after considerable hesitation and sent it to Lincoln, who feared the organization might become "a fifth wheel to the coach." Eventually he approved the order.[46]

The long history of the commission's struggles with the hidebound Medical Department of the army is outside the province of this study. Basically it was an organization run by men and concerned with obtaining ambulances and supplies, and especially with sanitary provisions for camps and hospitals. Bellows's colleague Frederick Law Olmsted (1822-1903) was its administrative genius. The role of women throughout the country was in organizing the great Sanitary Fairs which raised millions of dollars and provided mountains of supplies. The commission, and not the over-publicized Clara Barton, was the ancestor of the American Red Cross.[47]

The war effort of Clara Barton (1821-1912) was considerable and important, but she lacked the training and organizing genius of Dorothea Dix. As a child in North Oxford, Massachusetts, she was close to her father: he told her stories of his service as an Indian fighter under General Wayne; he talked Jacksonian politics, and taught her to name the men in public office. She did math problems with her brother Stephen and rode bareback with her brother David. Many years later Civil War officers found it a challenge to ride with her.

Hers was the characteristically American pattern of so many outstanding women: close association with the men in the family, a striving for knowledge, and the participation in household tasks. She learned to paint and varnish furniture, to hang wallpaper, to milk, to use a hammer and saw, and to throw a ball like a boy. At eighteen she began teaching school. But as she said, she "had the habit of study ... with a burning anxiety to make the most of lost time." Thus after ten years she entered the Liberal Institute of Clinton where junior professors from Hamilton College tutored the girls.[48]

She seems never to have thought of marriage, although a suitor gave her $10,000 from the gold rush. Like Dorothea Dix she thought of herself as friendless. Throughout her life she had several nervous breakdowns, one of them lasting ten years.

As has been suggested, the coming of the Civil War gave a release from drab routine. When it began, Clara Barton had a job in the Patent Office; almost at once she rented a warehouse and began collecting and distributing supplies to soldiers. After the battle of Fredricksburg she dressed wounds in military hospitals.

As her fame spread, soldiers greeted her with cheers and waving caps. However she was not amenable to hospital routine and Miss Dix's nurses were critical of her. Finding herself a supernumerary in the area controlled by Miss Dix and the Sanitary Commission, she appealed to Senator Henry Wilson, an opponent of the Commission. With his help she got into the Wilderness campaign, and General Butler appointed her as superintendent of nurses for the Army of the James. "Honor any request that Miss Barton makes without question," Butler ordered, "she out-ranks me." Clara described Butler as "dignified, wise, and princely, and still, perhaps, the most kindly and approachable personage on the grounds." She had to supervise the preparation of huge quantities of food; however, Ishbel Ross contrasts Clara Barton's solitary operations with Dorothea Dix's much greater organization.[49]

Despite the partisanship of their biographers, it would be a mistake to represent the remarkable achievements of women like Dorothea Dix and Clara Barton as the only enlightened medical work of the Civil War. The surgeon general, William A. Hammond, was a man of vision who worked out a design for military hospitals—long white pavilions with many windows. Before the war he had done research with Dr. S. Weir Mitchell. In Philadelphia Hammond set up the Turners Lane Hospital with four hundred beds for the treatment of nervous diseases and injuries to the nerves. Here the team of doctors Weir Mitchell, George R. Morehouse, and W. W. Keen developed methods of treatment recorded in *Gunshot Wounds and Other Injuries to the Nerves* (1864), a book which in a later amplified edition was still in use by the French in World War I.

In this hospital and probably in others under Hammond's jurisdiction each bed had a card identifying the patient and carrying information about the ailment and treatment. Walls were whitewashed and floors kept scrupulously clean. As the wounded were brought in, each one was questioned by a surgeon, given iced lemonade, and assigned to a bed. The Sanitary Commission insisted on rigid inspections, and Mitchell was occasionally employed as an inspector of other hospitals.[50]

Conditions in improvised field hospitals could be terrible—witness Whitman's *Drum Taps*—but nowhere in the world up to that time had there been such enlightened care of the wounded as that organized by Dorothea Dix, Clara Barton, and William A. Hammond.

After Appomattox Clara Barton, through Senator Wilson's efforts, got a letter from Lincoln authorizing her to search for missing prisoners of war. Then she went on the Lyceum circuit. Susan B. Anthony enlisted her in the suffrage movement, but, as Ishbel Ross points out, Clara had worked too long with men to feel that they were natural enemies. But by 1869 she had a breakdown and sailed for Europe.

With the start of the Franco-Prussian war she had a new spurt of energy. In a revealing statement she wrote:

The bugle-call to arms again sounded in my war-trained ear, the bayonets gleamed, the sabres clashed. . . . I remembered our own armies, my own war-stricken country, and its dead, its widows, and its orphans, and it nerved me to action for which the physical strength had long ceased to exist, and on the borrowed force of love and memory, I strove with might and main.[51]

It was not with the widows and orphans she was concerned: she tried unsuccessfully to get to the French front.

Then the Grand Duchess Louise of Baden, daughter of Emperor William I, summoned her to Carlsruhe, to get her to work with the Prussians. Clara found that she liked the Germans better than the French. When Strassburg surrendered, Clara worked there for forty days with the wounded and the starving refugees. In the workrooms she organized the women who turned out fifteen hundred garments a week. Then she went on to shattered Paris. But at the peak of her service she fell victim to a nervous prostration which left her nearly blind during 1872. In 1875 she went to a sanitarium, and again in 1879 and most of 1880.[52]

It was during her European service that she became acquainted with the Red Cross, an organization conceived in 1862 by Jean Henri Dunant, and established by the Treaty of Geneva in 1864. It became prominent during the Franco-Prussion War and was already spreading across Europe when Clara took up the cause in America. The opposition to signing the Geneva Convention was based on the argument which later defeated participation in the League of Nations— no entangling alliances. However, presidents Hayes and Garfield were receptive to Clara Barton's lobbying, and under President Arthur the American Red Cross was chartered. In 1882 the United States ratified the Geneva Convention.

Miss Barton had skillfully emphasized the role of the Red Cross in national disasters, where it performed great services. However until the end of the century the organization suffered from being too greatly identified with a single person—Clara Barton.[53]

The immense role of women in the Civil War was almost completely neglected by the novelists. By contrast, Lincoln in 1864, addressing a Sanitary Fair held in Washington, after saying somewhat inaccurately that he was not accustomed to the language of eulogy, went on, "I must say that if all that has been said by orators and poets since the creation of the world in praise of women were applied to the women of America it would not do them justice for their conduct during this war."[54] Even allowing for the oratorical hyperbole there is a basis of fact for the statement. There were of course plenty of fictional heroines in novels of the war, but the usual type was a girl separated from a soldier sweetheart—often across sectional lines. The southern belle finally surrendering to a Union officer was a stock character: the will-she-won't-she? made for delicious suspense.

The two best nineteenth-century Civil War novels, William De Forest's *Miss Ravenel's Conversion* (1869) and Stephen Crane's *The Red Badge of Courage* (1895), are thoroughly realistic in their treatment of war, but do little or nothing with women's role in it. In Crane's novel this omission is justified by his donnée: the events of a single battle. De Forest painted a much larger canvas: along with scenes of courage and horror on the battlefield and in military hospitals, he dealt with the Union occupation of New Orleans, the drinking and wenching of the officers, the political and military corruption in speculative ventures. The book lacks the concentrated unity of Crane's much shorter novel, but its characters are more complex; it deals with issues as well as events, and its scope is immense.

Furthermore, his title suggests that a woman is central to the story. In presenting Miss Lillie Ravenel, De Forest starts out on a realistic level. Her father, a Connecticut-born physician, has been practicing in New Orleans until the outbreak of the war. Despite his Union loyalty, Lillie has absorbed the seccessionist sentiments of that city. Early in the story the Ravenels attend a dinner party in New Boston given by the mother of Professor Whitewood, described as "that pale bit of human celery." At the party, "Miss Ravenel, accustomed to far more masculine men, felt a contempt for him at the first glance, saying to herself, How dreadfully ladylike! She was far better satisfied with the appearance of the stranger Lieutenant-Colonel Carter . . . with a full chest, broad shoulders and muscular arms, brown curling hair, and a monstrous mustache . . . brown eyes at once audacious and mirthful. . . ."[55]

As the description suggests, Colonel Carter is not a model of propriety. Before his wife's death he had been an affectionate but neglectful husband. In preparation for the stuffy dinner at the Whitewoods he had fortified himself with a number of drinks which were then supplemented by the professor's sherry. The puritanical hero of the novel, Edward Colburne, rather hoped that Miss Ravenel would be shocked by the Colonel's boisterous behavior, but she "had been too much accustomed to just such gentlemen in New Orleans society to see anything disgusting or even surprising in the manner of the Colonel."[56]

Obviously Lillie Ravenel seems rather unlike the usual Victorian heroine. Her attitude was more like that of the Georgia girl Eliza Andrews, who recorded in her diary that as men were likely to do when there were no ladies present to keep them straight, a party came back from a barbecue "with more liquor aboard than they could hold. . . . Our Beau Brummel [apparently her brother] protested that he was not drunk but only a little tight. It was all so absurd that I fairly roared in spite of myself."[57]

However, Lillie was less clear sighted than Eliza Andrews: she married the bibulous colonel despite her father's warnings. From that point on she becomes the typical sentimental heroine, mooning over her husband's letters and failing to discover that he is a roué. For a brief period she teaches reading to the Negroes on a plantation operated by her father as a kind of experiment with free labor. But she is very much the fluttery female: she can't or won't learn the rules at cards: exposes her hands, trumps her partners' aces.

When she becomes pregnant, she hesitates for a long time before blushingly telling her secret to her husband. When the baby is born, she asks the doctor how long before it will talk; it seems strange to her that it cannot do so almost at once. She is so happy with the baby that she finds she does not greatly miss her husband. "Like most women she was born for maternity more distinctively and positively even than for love."[58]

Understandably, Colonel Carter has become involved in an affair with the fascinating widow, Mrs. Larue, who thinks that Don Juan was an ideal man. In many ways she is a far more interesting character than Miss Ravenel, her cousin by marriage. She is amoral:

in seccessionist circles she is a rebel; in the North on a visit she is a displaced loyalist. When Lillie finds out about the affair, Mrs. Larue thinks that a wife should forgive her husband's peccadillos. Easy going and kind hearted, she pulls wires to have Dr. Ravenel made head of a hospital.

Granted that Mrs. Larue is a type who has managed to survive and even to flourish in all wars, she is hardly representative of the American women of the Civil War. And Lillie Ravenel's shift of loyalty is not ideological but personal. In New Orleans she had been ostracized; in the North she was well treated. And any reader of nineteenth-century novels could foresee from the start that she would eventually marry the fine, upstanding war hero Colburne.

Even so, De Forest's realism was far less popular than historical romance.* Thus two novelists who had known the war first hand—General Lew Wallace and Dr. S. Weir Mitchell—produced, respectively, the hugely popular *Ben Hur* laid in ancient Rome and the best seller of 1896, *Hugh Wynne*, a story of the American Revolution.

Mitchell, who had served as a contract surgeon at Gettysburg and had helped to run a military hospital in Philadelphia, did write of the Civil War in three novels: *In War Time* (1884); *Roland Blake* (1886); and *Westways* (1913). He pictured war without glamour: the opening scene of *In War Time* is of the wounded from Gettysburg pouring into a Philadelphia hospital. A brave soldier, Colonel Fox, admits that he has been terribly afraid in battle, and the young daredevil Arthur Morton tells his brother, "I never realized until now how dreadful is war . . . Anyone who says that he likes it is stupid or lies." Both *Roland Blake* and *Westways* give vivid pictures of the Wilderness campaign.

However, Mitchell's heroines are very much in the Victorian tradition. The beautiful and witty Alice Westerly of *In War Time* appears in a hospital only as a lady bountiful distributing goodies to

---

* In a letter to Howells in 1879 De Forest blamed his lack of sales "on the theory that our novel-reading public is mainly female or a very juvenile public, and wants something nearer to . . . *Helen's Babies* and *That Husband of Mine*" (quoted by Gordon Haight, introduction to *Miss Ravenel's Conversion*, Rinehart edition, N. Y., 1955, p. xviii). However, General Grant sat up half the night to read *Ben Hur*.

soldiers. Mitchell even causes her to speak his own prejudices. When a Miss Clemson says, "Let us educate women as well as men are educated . . ," Alice replies, "I should like to start a rival college with professors in the art of pleasing."[59] Often his minor characters are the more real: the dominating Mrs. Morton, whose husband first found refuge in a mistress, then entered the war with enthusiasm, and Mrs. Grace, a busybody who is a fearful nuisance to the other ladies working for the Sanitary Commission.

Mitchell's failure to represent the kinds of women who were emerging in the last half of the nineteenth century is a particularly significant illustration of the gulf between the fiction and reality of the period, especially in the treatment of women. Probably no man of his time had a greater opportunity to study the feminine psyche. In 1877 he had published *Fat and Blood*, a medical work largely devoted to the problem of the semi-invalid woman suffering from "nervous exhaustion." For over three decades until his death in 1914 he was probably the leading psychiatrist in America. His Rest Cure method of treatment was widely used in England and in the 1890s by Sigmund Freud. In his *Doctor and Patient* (1888), which he described as a series of lay sermons addressed to women, he told of the need for the physician to listen to long confessions in order to learn the lives, habits, and symptoms of the patient. "The doctor who does not know sick women does not know women."[60]

NOTES

1. Mrs. Burton Harrison, *Recollections Grave and Gay*, New York, 1912, pp. 23, 42.
2. Ibid., pp. 69, 88.
3. Ibid., pp. 98, 125.
4. Ibid., pp. 57, 101.
5. Ibid., pp. 129–30.
6. Ibid., p. 151.
7. *Brokenburn*, p. 155.
8. Ibid., p. xi.
9. Ibid., p. 43.
10. Ibid., pp. 8, 14.
11. Ibid., p. 36.
12. Ibid., p. 109.
13. Ibid., p. 191.
14. Ibid., p. 213.
15. Ibid., pp. 223–27.

16. Scott, *The Southern Lady*, p. 86.
17. *Brokenburn*, pp. 233, 245, 262, 333.
18. *When the World Ended: The Diary of Emma Le Conte*, ed. by Earl Shenck Miers, New York, 1957, p. 91.
19. *The War-Time Journal of a Georgia Girl, 1864–1865*, ed. by Spencer Bidewell King, Jr., Macon, 1960, pp. 172–73.
20. Ibid., p. 232.
21. Ibid., p. 336.
22. Scott, p. 106.
23. *The War-Time Journal*, pp. 76, 83, 105.
24. Ibid., pp. 113–14; Scott, p. 119.
25. Harrison, p. 59.
26. Chesnut, *A Diary from Dixie*, pp. 10–11, 21, 169.
27. Ibid., pp. 238, 102.
28. Ibid., p. 213.
29. Ibid., p. 254.
30. Ibid., p. 163.
31. Ibid., pp. 207–8, 489.
32. Ellen Glasgow, *The Woman Within*, New York, 1954, p. 77.
33. *Brokenburn*, p. 358.
34. Scott, p. 81.
35. Ibid., pp. 81–84.
36. William Quentin Maxwell, *Lincoln's Fifth Wheel*, New York, London, Toronto, 1956, p. 66.
37. Helen E. Marshall, *Dorothea Dix, Forgotten Samaritan*, Chapel Hill, 1937, p. 203.
38. Ibid., pp. 7–15.
39. Ibid., pp. 39–44.
40. Ibid., pp. 26–27.
41. Ibid., pp. 62–98.
42. Ibid., pp. 98–107.
43. Ibid., pp. 107–13.
44. Ibid., p. 129.
45. Ibid., pp. 206, 219.
46. Maxwell, pp. 1–8.
47. Ibid., p. 314.
48. Ishbel Ross, *Angel of the Battlefield: The Life of Clara Barton*, New York, 1956, pp. 4–9, 18–19, 103.
49. Ibid., pp. 55, 65–77, 86.
50. Earnest, *S. Weir Mitchell*, p. 53.
51. Ross, p. 110.
52. Ibid., pp. 113–28, 134.
53. Ibid., pp. 130–39.
54. Philip Van Doren Stern, *The Life and Writings of Abraham Lincoln*, New York, 1940, p. 805.
55. John William De Forest, *Miss Ravenel's Conversion from Secession to Loyalty*, ed. by Gordon Haight, New York, 1955, pp. 19–20.
56. Ibid., p. 26.
57. *The War-Time Journal*, pp. 324–25.
58. Ibid., p. 429.
59. S. Weir Mitchell, *In War Time* (originally 1884), New York, 1909, p. 325.
60. S. Weir Mitchell, *Doctor and Patient*, Philadelphia, 1888, pp. 10–11.

Nine

Daisy and Jennie—The American Girl in Europe

"What are your American girls made of?"

An English gentleman to
Elizabeth Cady Stanton

Daisy Miller and Jennie Jerome were about the same age. From the first, Daisy became a symbolic myth figure; more recently Jennie has become so. In many ways they represent the polarities of the American girl's experience in Europe. The one, a brash innocent, was ostracized by fashionable society; the other—definitely not an innocent—married an English lord, lived in an immense palace, and bore the most famous British statesman of the twentieth century. Jennie was born in 1854 and married Randolph Churchill twenty years later; Daisy Miller, presumably in her early twenties, acted out her drama about 1875.* Together the two women symbolize the social history of an era.

It is difficult to think of Daisy Miller as a fictional character. Like Huckleberry Finn and George F. Babbitt, she has been discussed as both a person and a symbol. In 1879, when the story first appeared in America, Howells wrote to James Russell Lowell: "Harry James waked up all the women with his Daisy Miller. . . . The thing went so far that society almost divided itself into Daisy Millerites and anti-Daisy Millerites."[1]

In the late nineteenth-century books on etiquette studied by Arthur M. Schlesinger, she "became a stock example of what American girls should not be and do."[2] A writer for the *North American*

---

* *Daisy Miller* was first published in 1878 but James laid the scene two or three years earlier.

Review stated that James's "witty sketch . . . has helped innumerable other Americans, who learned through this delicate satire more than they would through a volume of well-intentioned maxims." In 1904 Margaret Sanger said that because of the development of chaperonage the Daisy Miller type no longer went to Europe.[3]

James Huneker gave a different picture. In *Painted Veils* (1920) an American man brought up in Paris described Daisy Miller as a "reticent aristocrat" compared to twentieth-century expatriated girls.

From the time of its publication the story embedded the name Daisy Miller in the language almost to the extent that Simon Legree and Babbitt became descriptive words. Howells was probably right in saying that the story was misinterpreted. James had not intended it as a lampoon on the American girl but, as he called it, "a study"—a study of the different mores of European and American society. Two remarks at the end of the story make this clear. Giovanelli, who had taken her on the ill-fated excursion to the Colosseum said, "She was the most beautiful young lady I ever saw, and the most amiable . . . and she was the most innocent." Winterbourne, who had misinterpreted the moonlight excursion, told his aunt, Mrs. Costello, "I was booked to make a mistake. I have lived too long in foreign parts."[4] With all her faults Daisy is treated far more sympathetically than is Mrs. Costello, a snobbish Europeanized American who ostracized Daisy.

Why, then, did the story cause such a commotion? Partly because James had hit a sore spot. There were girls like Daisy Miller, daughters of the uncultivated new rich of the Gilded Age. Even Howells, who often defended American women against the charge of "Daisy Millerism," eventually pictured some of her type. Hjalmar Hjorth Boyesen, a Norwegian novelist who taught at Cornell and Columbia from 1874 to 1895, described a Daisy Miller type he had met: "She had about as much idea of propriety (in the European sense) as a cat has of mathematics." He cited European writers who had caricatured the type in fiction and added, "it is of no use to deny her existence. She is very prevalent in Europe; and though she rarely invades the so-called best society of our seaboard cities, you need only go abroad or sufficiently far west to find her in all her glory."[5]

Granting that girls like Daisy Miller existed, there was neverthe-less validity to the charge that James had pictured her not only as a person or even a type, but as *the* national type. Boyesen did not thus categorize her: beginning with his first experience in America in 1869 he described other kinds of American women, particularly those bent on self-improvement. That James intended to portray Daisy as the typical American girl becomes clear from Winter-bourne's reverie: "Never, indeed, since he had grown old enough to appreciate things, had he encountered *a young American girl of so pronounced a type as this* . . . were they all like that, the pretty girls who had a good deal of gentlemen's society?" (italics mine). Daisy had boasted, "Last winter I had seventeen dinners given me; and three of them were by gentlemen. . . . I have more friends in New York than in Schenectady—more gentlemen friends. . . ." This is caricature despite James's sympathy for Daisy, a sympathy he heightened in his revisions of the story. And James was clearly type-casting her.

Thus Winterbourne "had heard that all his pretty cousins in New York were tremendous flirts." He tells Daisy that her habits are those of a flirt. "Of course they are," she cried. . . . "Did you ever hear of a nice girl that was not?" He replies inaccurately that "Flirting is a purely American custom; it doesn't exist here." Mrs. Costello says of Daisy ". . . she is very common," but "She has that charming look they all have. . . . I can't think where they pick it up; and she dresses to perfection . . . I can't think where they get their taste."[6] Not *she* but *they*, meaning American girls.

A year later, in "A Bundle of Letters," James pictured Miranda Hope of Bangor, Maine, as even more crude than Daisy Miller. In Paris she meets Violet Ray of New York. A young man from Boston described the girls to a friend: "they're very much alike too. . . . They're both specimens of the practical positive passionless young thing we let loose on the world—and yet with a certain fineness of knowing, as you please, either too much or too little . . . no more mystery, either of them, than the printed circular thrust into your hand on the street-corner."[7] It should be noted that both girls are identified as typical Americans.

Violet Ray has a headstrong quality that James seemed to regard as a national trait. She and her mother have refused to return to America with Mr. Ray: "we succeeded in making him understand that we wouldn't budge from Paris and that we'd rather be chopped into small pieces than cross that squalid sea again." In *The Europeans* (1878) Felix described Gertrude Wentworth: "she whirls me along!" Of her temperament: "it pulls—it pulls—like a runaway horse."[8] Daisy behaves very much like a runaway horse. When Winterbourne warns her that she is behaving in a way that offends sophisticated ladies, she says, "I have never allowed a gentleman to dictate to me, or to interfere with anything I do."

With all her charm she is almost unbelievably insensitive to the opinions of other women. She scornfully rejects the advice of the kindly Mrs. Walker. And she is extremely ignorant. Asked if the Millers are going to Italy by way of the Simplon, she says, "I don't know. . . . I suppose it's some mountain." In an era when American girls were avid readers of Byron she had never heard of *The Prisoner of Chillon*. Winterbourne tries to tell her of Bonnivard, but the story goes in one ear and out the other.

James continued to draw the Daisy Miller type for at least a decade. Pandora Day of *Pandora* (1884) is described by a lady as "the new type. It has only come up lately." When Count Otto Vogelstein asks about the new type, the lady's husband explains, "she's the latest freshest fruit of our great American evolution. She's the self-made girl." James says the type is not fast, nor crude, nor loud. The daughter of small burghers, she raised herself by honest exertion and "got into society more or less by reading." In the story Pandora is so much a type as to be scarcely a person.

Francie Dosson of *The Reverberator* (1888) is perhaps James's most repulsive version of Daisy Miller. Francie, befriended by the Proberts, an aristocratic French family of American descent, tells the yellow journalist, Flack, about them—family skeletons included. To the consternation of the Proberts he publishes all this in *The Reverberator*. James said that the story was based on a real incident. Francie is described as extraordinarily pretty with a typical American grace. The portrait painter tells Gaston Probert to go ahead and marry her: she is of the finest material and only needs someone to mold her into a perfect thing. Gaston acts on this highly dubious theory.

James was less interested in developing the character of Francie than, as the title suggests, writing a diatribe against American newspapers. The importance of Francie is that James regarded her as a typical specimen. In 1908 he wrote, "In the heavy light of Europe thirty or forty years ago there were more of the Francie Dossons and the Daisy Millers . . . and the Pandora Days than all of the other attested American objects put together. . . ." Americans overreacted to *Daisy Miller*, but they were not wrong in seeing it as James's picture of a typical American girl.

Whatever he may have intended in *Daisy Miller*, James portrayed Isabel Archer in *The Portrait of a Lady* (1881) as a representative national type. In describing Isabel her aunt, Mrs. Touchett, says, "She thinks she knows a great deal of [the world]—like most American girls; but like most American girls she's ridiculously mistaken." And James says of her: "Like the mass of American girls Isabel had been encouraged to express herself; her remarks had been attended to; she had been expected to have emotions and opinions. Many of her opinions had doubtless but a slender value, many of her emotions passed away in the utterance. . . ."

James's description of Isabel Archer could apply almost equally well to Daisy Miller. There is some justice in Margaret Wyman's statement, "The pictures of the American girl which James presented in thirteen novels and novelettes between 1871 and 1904 show variety of detail and coloring, but the essential features did not change."[9] Thus of Isabel:

Altogether, with her meagre knowledge, her inflated ideals, her confidence, at once innocent and dogmatic, her temper at once exacting and indulgent, her mixture of curiosity and fastidiousness, of vivacity and indifference, her desire to look very well and to be if possible even better, her determination to see, to try, to know, her combination of the delicate, desultory, flamelike spirit, and the eager and personal creature of conditions: she would be an easy victim of scientific criticism if she were not intended to awaken on the reader's part an impulse more tender and more purely expectant.

Much of this could apply to Madame de Mauves, Christina Light (who became the Princess Casamassima without developing any common sense) and Maggie Verver. Isabel's gentler qualities appear in Milly Teale. It is significant that both Isabel and Milly were partially drawn from Minnie Temple, for whom James as a young man had a platonic affection. Very possibly novelists tend to pattern their heroines after the girls of their youth.

There are two crucial questions about James's representation of the American girl, one raised in his own time, the other more recent. Were American girls as ignorant, brash, and "common" as Daisy, Miranda Hope, Francie Dosson, and the much later Sarah Pocock of *The Ambassadors*? Isabel Archer is not "common" but she is certainly ignorant, headstrong, and full of inflated notions. James may not have been aware of the aptness of his remark about Isabel "affronting her destiny." Very likely he was using what Twain called the "second cousin" of the right word. James had little of Twain's sensitivity to humorous linguistic nuances. But both Daisy and Isabel did "affront" their destinies, largely because of their lack of sophistication.

In another story, Euphemia, who became Madame de Mauves,

> dreamed of marrying a man of hierarchical "rank" . . . because she had a romantic belief that the enjoyment of inherited and trans-mitted consideration, consideration attached to the fact of birth, would be the direct guarantee of an ideal delicacy of feeling. . . . She was essentially incorruptible and she took this pernicious conceit to her bosom very much as if it had been a dogma revealed by a white-winged angel. Even after experience had given her a hundred rude hints she found it easier to believe in fables.

The other question is: were American girls as sexually naive and puritanical as James represented them?

In order to evaluate the accuracy of James's portrayal of the American young woman of the 1870s and 1880s it is useful to look at some of the records of the period. For instance, Julia Newberry, born in 1853, was almost exactly contemporary with Daisy Miller. Like Daisy she had a very rich father and was taken to Europe as a young girl.

Julia's diary began when she was sixteen. She was born in Chicago, a city she liked "much better than any other place."[10] In describing her home she mentioned that her father had rebuilt it at a cost of $60,000. (Isabel Archer told her aunt that she had no idea of the value of the house she had inherited. "I don't know anything about money.") Julia had a private staircase from her dressing room to a studio with a beautiful view of the lake. When her mother took her to Europe for the third time, Julia said she hated to leave her home. (By contrast, Isabel Archer, who had been abroad three times before she was fourteen, told Mrs. Touchett that she would promise almost anything to go to Florence.)

Julia's athletic activities have been recorded (p. 64 above). Not given to self-pity, she joked about her serious illness. Trying on a dress at Stewart's in New York, she fainted. "I always wanted to faint once, just to know how it felt; and it's very nasty; however heroines always faint, but authors never say it is because they are bilious." At a party: "Being excited I had a bright color, and no one . . . would believe that I was sick and going to Florida for my health. Everyone was so kind and I enjoyed myself immensely. . . ."[11]

The Florida trip did not effect an improvement. Thus at a later party:

> Everyone I met has a different cure, that effected marvels with one's cousin, or that one's grandmother. And then the sighs and groans "and oh how strong and well you used to be." And "oh how pale you are! and how big your eyes are! and do you take port wine, brandy, iron, salt baths, bordeaux, San Moritz, cod-liver oil, raw meat, beef-tea, sea-bathing, horse-back, donkey-back, brandy cock-tail, beer, ale, quinine, Nib, pyramids, and egyptians."[12]

Unlike Madame de Mauves with her romantic view of titles, Julia wrote that she found Disraeli's *Lothaire* horrid: "His plebeian adoration of the English aristocracy is disgusting."[13] Isabel Archer was not repelled by Gilbert Osmond's statement that he had never earned a penny or by Madame Merle's remark that "he's very in-dolent, so indolent that it amounts to a sort of position."[14]

Julia Newberry's reaction in Nice was more typically American: "The lazy lives these foreigners lead, enough to disgust one." She would not have been attracted as Isabel was to a Gilbert Osmond. Describing a similar character, she wrote that he was "superlatively clean . . . clean. Oh so clean, so clean . . . A selfish, pleasure-seeking over-refined, blasé man of thirty-nine, whose life had narrowed down to eating, drinking, washing, fishing, shooting, and sleeping; a very highly pampered human animal. . . ." She quoted him as saying, "I think one always feels so cross and nasty if one gets up before noon, and then besides the world is not well aired before that time."[15]

There is no evidence that Daisy Miller ever cracked a book. Mrs. Touchett found Isabel "reading a heavy book and boring herself to death." As James said, "She had a great desire for knowledge, but she really preferred almost any source of information to the printed page. . . ." Julia Newberry bemoaned the fact that her illness had kept her from reading "anything deep," but her list of favorite books included *Jane Eyre*, *Vanity Fair*, all of Byron's poems, *The Ancient Mariner*, Longfellow's *Hyperion*, *Henry IV* and *V*, *Romeo and Juliet*, *The Mill on the Floss*, *She Stoops to Conquer*, Cooper's *The Spy*, "Ruskin's book of beauties," *Pickwick Papers*, Bacon's *Essays*, Irving's *Sketch Book*. She disliked Disraeli, Shelley, Bulwer, Victor Hugo, and Mrs. Browning. Her taste was not undiscriminating.

Isabel Archer and her sisters had been sent to "superficial schools, kept by the French, from which, at the end of a month, they had been removed in tears." Obviously Isabel could not have got into nearby Vassar even if she had ever heard of it. There is no evidence that any Jamesian heroine had ever heard of it. By contrast Julia Newberry complained that being abroad so much had prevented her from studying chemistry, astronomy, botany, and natural philosophy.[16]

Unlike Daisy, Julia refused to go driving with a young man because she did not think it proper. "And yet all most all girls here and elsewhere do it!" As the *here* refers to Nice, one wonders if James did not exaggerate the scandal of Daisy's drive with Winterbourne. Julia had a realistic view of men: they would amuse themselves by making a giddy girl do and say foolish things, and pretend to approve what they secretly despised. She did not blame them, for if she were a man she would do the same. Daisy had boasted about being a flirt; Julia wrote, "I hope I am not a flirt and yet sometimes I believe I am."[17]

Julia's visit to the Colosseum was less tragic than Daisy's: "We visited the Coliseum and dug up a live ruin in the shape of Mr. G. W. Wurtz."[18]

The women in the novels of James and Howells are completely oblivious of world affairs; in fact Howells emphasized the political ignorance of American women. The diaries tell a different story. On December 31, 1870, three days after her seventeenth birthday, Julia listed the dynastic changes in Europe during the year, and mourned over the suffering caused by the seige of Paris, and the 350,000 French prisoners of war in Germany. Then came the news of the Chicago fire of 1871, a more personal disaster, for her beloved home was destroyed. "But oh the misery of the people, and the destitution of the poor, the sick people, and the little babies. And all the people who are just comfortably off, and now have lost their all."[19]

Julia listed the Newberry losses: her father's favorite books and his letters to her, her mother's jewels, and letters from Cooper, Van Buren, Irving, and Burr. The seventeen-year-old girl knew what had been in that library. For years she had looked forward to going back, but now she had nothing to look forward to. "Papa bought the land; Papa built the house, Papa planted the trees, Papa lived there, and now what is left in the wide world of association with him?"[20]

Before her father's death on his way to Paris in 1868, the father-daughter relationship had evidently followed the American pattern of a close association which so often developed able women.

By contrast, James in the two novels which explore a father-daughter relationship represents it as destructive. In *Washington Square* Dr. Sloper refuses to allow his plain daughter to marry the only man who offers. The man is a fortune hunter, but Catherine loves him. Even when she is middle-aged, her father, still angry about her refusal to promise not to see the man again, reduces her inheritance by four-fifths. After Dr. Sloper's death, Townsend returns but Catherine has become disillusioned with him.

In *The Golden Bowl*, the bond between Adam Verver and his

daughter Maggie is almost incestuous—so much so that Maggie's husband resumes an earlier love affair.

In the whole body of James's work it is difficult to find a nourishing family relationship. A number of his heroines are either orphaned or have the most tenuous relationships with parents. It sometimes seems as if the typical Jamesian heroine had been born by parthenogenesis.

As the foregoing chapters show, this was far different from the characteristic American pattern. The reasons for this discrepancy are to be sought not in the American scene but in the psyche of Henry James. One of his first acts on the death of his father was to ask his publisher to remove "Jr." after his name. Late in life he wrote to his brother's widow, saying how little Cambridge and Boston had ever been his affair, "but an accident for me, of the parental life there to which I occasionally and painfully and losingly sacrificed. . . ."[21]

Julia Newberry resembled a Jamesian heroine to the extent that she rarely mentioned her mother. Julia's resentment about being dragged around Europe must have produced some hostility to her frequently expatriated mother; the references to her sister are affectionate.

Unfortunately Julia Newberry did not live to fulfill her early promise: she died in Rome before she was twenty-three. Her sister had died two years before. Julia had known numerous prominent people at home and abroad. General Philip Sheridan had often danced with her (she said he was homely but a fine dancer.) On her seventeenth birthday she summed up her life to date: "I have been twice in Florida, and three times to Europe. I have been to two boarding schools. . . . Have been run-away with twice, and had my portrait painted. I have learned to paint and have inherited a fortune.* Have been through a long illness and had a terrible sorrow. And I might have been married if I had chosen."[22]

With her wealth, sorrow, and illness she resembled the later Milly Theal, but she had none of the dovelike character of James's heroine. She was less naïve than Milly, far more sensible than Daisy Miller or Isabel Archer, wittier and better informed than any girl

---

* Walter L. Newberry left about $4,000,000, half of it to found the Newberry Library in Chicago.

portrayed by either Howells or James—perhaps more typically American.

The same American qualities appear in the brief diary of Fanny Knight, another rich girl who was taken abroad—in her case at sixteen. The time is fifteen years earlier, but the social milieu is the same: a world of wealthy American expatriates. The two girls had a similar gift for amusing comment and both were interested in the political situation.

In Paris in 1854 Fanny noted that hoops were still in fashion. In carriages "the poor gentlemen's heads . . . are peeping out from the flounces which envelop them. The men always remind me of so many modest little daisies afraid to show their heads."[23] On seeing Jerome Bonaparte she commented: "It is hard to believe that this old man was once the dashing lover of Mistress Betsy Patterson in Baltimore."

Not only was she aware of a bit of American history, she looked with disillusioned eyes at Louis Napoleon: "The Emperor has a twofold design in view, the embellishing of the city and keeping the people out of mischief, for he well knows that his security lies in keeping the working class employed so that it will not meditate revolution."[24]

In Rome she attended a reception for former President Fillmore. At a Swiss hotel a fellow guest was Charles Sumner. She did not think him "a flattering specimen of an American senator." In her view Congressman Brooks had acted in a most ungentlemanly fashion, but "Mr. Sumner deserved what he got." She thought it in very bad taste for him to sign the register "The Hon. Charles Sumner, Senator of the United States"[25]—as of course it was.

In Russia she saw political prisoners leaving for Siberia. "The prisoners shed not a tear; they seemed to have lost all emotions of any kind, just a numbness remained. Thank God, I was born neither a serf nor a prince in this land."[26]

Evidently Fanny Knight was an attractive girl. In Rome her instructor in Italian wrote her a sonnet on a card embellished with a pink Venus surrounded by cupids. In Alexandria she went to an apothecary shop for hand lotion. The apothecary's assistant, a young

Egyptian, was so smitten that he called that evening with a love letter proposing mariage. She did not reply.

After five years abroad she expressed her feelings on reaching America: "New York looks very lively and bustling and somewhat shabby, but how glad I am to be at home again. . . . I tell Pa that after being so long in Europe, I will be entirely forgotten by all my friends, and in my old age will feel myself a stranger in my own land. . . . I am still proud of being the daughter of America, and will ever prefer my mother country to any other. . . ."[27]

The brief diary gives a picture of an attractive, sensible girl who took her studies seriously and who was knowledgeable about political matters. If she had any of Daisy's crudity, it does not appear in the diary.

The same qualities are revealed in the journal of Louise Stoughton,[28] a contemporary of Julia Newberry and Daisy Miller. She was born in 1851 in Bellows Falls, Vermont, and was educated in a New York finishing school. While there she lived in the home of her uncle, Edwin Wallace Stoughton, whose wife was the mother of the historian John Fiske by an earlier marriage.

When Edwin Stoughton was named minister to Russia in 1877, he and his wife took Louise along, apparently as a kind of secretary. Her journal, begun on the steamship, in the form of letters to her married sister, was designed for circulation among members of the family.

As she was the only young woman aboard, the captain became her "most devoted attendant." He showed her over the ship, let her steer, and while watching the moon and Venus set quoted Byron to her. She found him by far the greatest fun of anyone on the ship. But in London she cried from homesickness.

Her comments are those of a tourist with a knowledge of English history. Thus she complained of the lack of furnaces and gas lights but also noted that at Temple church the organ had been selected by "the bloody Judge Jeffries, who must have had a taste for music in his young and innocent days, if he ever had any, which from Macaulay's account of him, one might be inclined to doubt" (December 16, 1877). At the Inner Temple a Mr. Rose pointed out a spot where a barrister had been murdered by his laundress for unknown reasons. She suggested that perhaps he had not paid his bill. A Mr. Dawson called and sat on the edge of his chair nervously twirling his hat. He had two horned toads that he planned to show in England. "While he was calling, there came one of those terrible pauses, which neither Aunt Mary nor I filled up. After a few seconds, he gave a nervous little laugh & remarked in quite a loud voice and impressive voice 'The toads are very well' " (December 16, 1877). Her uncle engaged a six-foot-tall courier with an immense black beard. "He calls Uncle 'Excellency.' His bows of respect are something quite awful to behold; I feel quite overpowered. . . ." With her aunt she went to Albert Hall to hear the *Messiah*. "Mr. Foulkes took us there, but he had promised to go to a party (I daresay to meet some girl) & could not stay. He bade us goodbye, but refrained from tears. The Oratorio was magnificent" (December 20, 1877). None of this is very profound but neither does it suggest the unsophisticated Jamesian heroine.

In Paris, Louise, like Fanny Knight and Julia Newberry, was fitted for a dress at Worth's. Louise described Worth as "a disgusting man with big fat hands & quantities of enormous rings." Young Frank Hooper of Boston escorted her around Paris, gave her books, took her to the opera and to the circus. He told her that he was thankful to meet a woman who liked to walk. (She later married his brother William.)

The Stoughtons stopped off in Germany, which Louise hated, but she found St. Petersburg beautiful. She and her aunt bundled up and took a droshky ride in January. They were there not as tourists but as members of the diplomatic corps. Louise recognized that "the American Minister is rather small potatoes compared with the Ambassadors," but she managed diplomacy very well. When the Italian ambassador called while her aunt was dressing, Louise acted as interpreter. She was presented to Princess Orbelinsky and Countess Gale, both "quite nice. . . . They were a good deal like Western girls." However, "Titles are as common as dirt here, you know." Five weeks after Louise had arrived, the Grand Duchess came up to shake hands and, in English, ask if she had made any acquaintances. Louise said that she had. The duchess asked her to thank her uncle for money from American women to the Red Cross. In March she was presented to the empress, who during a ten-minute interview in French also thanked the American ladies for gifts to the Red Cross. They talked of Longfellow and Whittier.

Despite her pleasant association with titled Russian girls Louise remained very much the American. At St. Isaac's church she and her aunt were excluded from two chapels reserved for men. "It made me so angry that I would not look at anything." At a church service two English people sat beside her and talked aloud all through the prayers. "I never saw such a performance in my life. I was in such a state of fury that I could not enter into the service at all" (March 3, 1878). At the place she got into conversation with "such a smart girl. You ought to have seen her open her eyes when I told her we went out walking all alone in America."

Much of her life was routine. She studied Russian, filed papers for her uncle, and worked over visiting lists until one or two in the afternoon. From five until seven o'clock dinner she read and studied. In the evening she played California Jack or watched her uncle and aunt play cribbage with a Colonel (unnamed). "Exciting is it not. I lose my temper at cards almost every night. You ought to see the Colonel's eyes twinkle when he takes a trick away from me. He is simply *lovely* and I am awfully fond of him" (February 1, 1878).

On various other occasions she looked at herself with ironic amusement. On an excursion to Venice she took a gondola ride by moonlight: "If there had only been a young man or two along it would have been quite romantic." At the Bridge of Sighs, "I had the regulation shudder as we passed under it." Her description of a sightseeing party in the Doge's Palace is timeless:

> Each one had a guide book. Many wore spectacles and they all had that anxious grasping expression that a searcher of information invariably has. They scurried across the room pîle, mîle, helter-skelter, chins up, finger in book, ears pricked up to catch the guide's first word, trying at the same time to get a hurried glimpse round the room as they passed through it. There were tall, thin ones, & short, fat ones, & there were old men & young women & the

women all wore veils. It was one of the funniest sights I ever saw. [April 13, 1878]

Back in St. Petersburg she struck a more somber note. A Russian pamphlet mailed to the legation was headed "Death for Death." In it the Socialists claimed credit for the assassination of the chief of the Gendarmes, and threatened further violence unless the government changed. It made her blood run cold. "I would rather be almost any one I know than the Emperor of Russia."

There was a great scare about the Nihilists, and extra police and two mounted Cossacks were stationed at each street. The papers from New York carried frightening stories about the Knights of Labor; from Boston came news of a large turnout in Faneuil Hall to hear the labor leader Denis Kearney, whom she considered a disgusting creature.

Louise Stoughton was not a profound thinker on political and social questions; her remarks tend to reflect the middle-class attitudes of the 1870s. She liked clothes and dancing and the attention of attractive men, but all these occupy a very small portion of her journal-letters. Naturally she was pleased by the friendliness of titled Russian ladies, whose manners as she described them seem to have had a pleasant informality. Although she never boasted about her social skills they must have been considerable, for she became friendly with numerous girls of her own age. She had none of Daisy Miller's contempt for the opinion of other women.

Nowhere in her letters home is there anything remotely like those of James's character Miranda Hope, who wrote her mother

There's one thing I hope—that you don't show my letters to William Platt. If he wants to see my letters he knows the right way to go to work. I wouldn't let him see one of these letters, written for circulation in the family for anything in the world. If he wants one for himself he has got to write me first. . . . You can show him this if you like: but if you show him anything more I'll never write you again.[29]

In contrast to James's view that in the 1860s and 1870s the Francie Dossons, Daisy Millers, and Pandora Days outnumbered all other American types put together, Anthony Trollope drew a more sympathetic picture. In several respects his American heroines in two novels resemble Louise Stoughton more than they do Daisy Miller. In *He Knew He Was Right* (1869) Caroline Spaulding accompanies her uncle, who is American minister to Florence. He is a crude, demagogic politician from Nubby Creek, Illinois. At a dinner party Caroline meets the Honorable Mr. Glascock, who is due to inherit an English peerage. She tells him that he would not like it in America because as an aristocrat, half the people would run after him and half away from him. She then gives him an ironic account of American customs. After dinner while the gentlemen sit over their wine Spaulding sounds off in a boasting fashion. When Glascock joins the ladies, Caroline remarks dryly: "My uncle has been saying a few words to you perhaps."

"Yes he has," said Mr. Glascock.

"He usually does," said Cary Spaulding.

With the Spauldings is a Miss Petrie, "the Republican Browning," who argues that aristocrats "are dishonest and rotten to the core"; no free American should trust one. Many of her speeches could be transferred without change to Henrietta Stackpole of *The Portrait of a Lady* nine years later. It is difficult to escape the suspicion that James's caricature of Henrietta was based on Trollope's of Miss Petrie.

With mock seriousness Cary asks Glascock, "Do you mean to look me in the face and tell me that you are not acquainted with Miss Petrie's works,—that you don't know pages of them by heart, that you don't sleep with them under your pillow . . . ?" She then admits that she had never read a word of them herself.[30] Trollope caught the jocular tone which appears in the diaries of American girls but rarely in James.

Caroline's feelings about Glascock are more believable than those of Isabel Archer about Lord Warburton. Cary falls in love with Glascock, but hesitates to accept him for fear his aristocratic family will cold-shoulder her. In the end, of course, she marries him. Isabel rejects Warburton largely because she would have to surrender her self-image as an independent being. Isabel's only real love affair in the story is with herself.

Trollope, in *The Duke's Children* (1880), had an English lady say of the American Isabel Boncassen, "I think she is the loveliest person to look at and the nicest person to listen to that I ever came across." Isabel is the daughter of a shy father who spends all his time in the British Museum gathering material for a book.

Isabel says frankly that her grandfather had been a day laborer, but unlike Daisy Miller, she is aware of social usages. At a garden party she tells Silverbridge, the eldest son of a lord, that in America a girl might walk about with a young man but that judging the English customs she has already walked with him too long. Trollope says of her "there was no doubt as to the charm of her wit and manner. And she had no touch of that blasé used-up way of life of which Lady Mabel was conscious herself." Indeed she is vital enough to beat Silverbridge at tennis.

With the British love of a lord, Trollope described Silverbridge through Isabel's eyes: "She had never seen anything like him before —so glorious in his beauty, so gentle in his manhood, so powerful, and yet so little imperious, so great in condition, and yet so little confident in his own greatness. . . ."[31] So far in the story his greatness had been chiefly demonstrated by getting kicked out of Oxford for an outrageous prank, and later by losing 70,000 pre-war pounds in idiotic bets on a horse.

He does have the good judgment to see Isabel's good qualities. In his mind he compares her with the English girl he might have married. "Lady Mabel with all her grace, with all her beauty, with all her talent, was a creature of efforts . . . a manufactured article. She strove to be agreeable and clever. Isabel was all this and infinitely more without struggle."[32]

Long before, this ease of manner had impressed the English. In 1840 when Mr. Stanton was in London for an anti-slavery convention, the Duchess of Sutherland and her brother Lord Morpath wanted to meet the American abolitionists. Their wealthy English host was nervous about having these titled visitors. When the Reverend Mr. Green's daughter discovered that her father had not been presented, she quietly brought him forward and introduced him. A gentleman standing next to Mrs. Stanton said, "What are your American girls made of? Not a girl in England could have gone through that ceremony with such coolness and dignity."[33]

Even Henry James gave Daisy Miller "a natural talent for making introductions."

One reason for this ease in adult company was that American girls were not banished to the nursery and later sent for years to some St. Trinian's school. By contrast Trollope wrote of the Duke of Omnium: "he had no knowledge of his daughter's character. She had been properly educated—at least he hoped so. . . . She had been left to her mother—as other girls are left. And his sons had been left to their tutors."

Trollope's contrasting pictures of American and English girls help to explain why so many titled Europeans married American girls. In many cases money was a consideration, as when Mrs. Vanderbilt practically bought the Duke of Marlborough for Consuelo,[34] but the beauty and spontaneity of American girls was a factor. The duke's cousin, Lord Randolph Churchill, met Clara and Jennie Jerome at a ball. As Jennie's biographer, Anita Leslie,* says, "Those girls were quite different from anything that ever came out of a schoolroom of a British country house." After the ball, Randolph told a friend that if possible he meant to make "the dark one" his wife. Two nights later he proposed and was accepted.[35]

When Prince Cantacuzene of Russia met Julia Grant, granddaughter of General Grant, he was a little more dilatory than Churchill had been: it was two weeks before he proposed. Certainly in this case money was not the object: Julia's father Robert Dent Grant had a diplomatic post in Vienna but not much money.[36]

In 1850 the Honorable Edward Twisleton, younger brother of Lord Saye and Sele, arrived in Washington with a letter of introduction from the historian, George Ticknor. In answer to his knock, the door was opened by a lovely girl in a dressing gown. She was Ellen Dwight, a Ticknor relative. Six weeks later Twisleton proposed. At first she refused, but when in the following spring she gave him some encouragement, he dashed back from England and married her—certainly not for her money. Two years after their marriage they spent the winter in Paris studying chemistry in a laboratory three hours a day. On a visit to the States she told a friend that the main consolation for leaving home was to have "captured a

* Anita Leslie's grandmother was Jennie's younger sister Leonie.

husband to whom you can give your whole heart and soul forever."[37]

Even the notorious Claflin sisters, Victoria and Tennessee, married into the British gentry—Tennie's husband was a baronet. By that time the sisters were in their forties and certainly without money, but both of these beautiful and uninhibited women had always fascinated men.

Another prominent American woman, Annie Oakley,[38] who made her living for seventeen years in Buffalo Bill's Wild West Show, could have taken her pick of European suitors had she not been already married. Only five feet tall and weighing ninety-eight pounds, she could outshoot any man on either side of the Atlantic. When at twenty-seven she went abroad with the show in 1887, she still looked like a teenager. Twelve years before, as little Annie Mozee, she had defeated Frank Butler, a vaudeville performer whose specialty was shooting. He fell in love with her and took her as a partner, then married her. When she outshone him, he became her manager. Raised in poverty in Ohio, Annie, who adopted the name Oakley, was then almost illiterate, but Frank, who loved poetry, tutored her in literature, geography, and history. Together they joined the Sells Brothers Circus, then Buffalo Bill's Wild West Show. During the winters Annie studied books and practiced shooting.

After several successful seasons in America Bill Cody took his show abroad. When it opened in London, the Prince of Wales prevailed upon Queen Victoria to see it. She was so delighted that she asked to have Cody and Annie presented to her. "You are a very, very clever little girl," she remarked.

In England and on the Continent Annie Oakley became a heroine. A French count proposed marriage, an English sportsman wanted her to become the mistress of his estate, a Welshman sent her a proposal by mail. (She set up his photograph and at thirty paces put six bullets between the eyes, then mailed it back to him.) A twenty-one-year-old English gentleman wrote saying that it was "your gentle bearing, and sweet face" that led him to adore her. When he learned that she was married, he said he could not trust himself to keep entirely away from her and so left for South Africa. Twenty-five years later he called on the Butlers in their Chesapeake Bay home, bringing along a collection of horns from Kenya.

Neither her skill nor her charm was an illusion. Using a knife blade as a mirror, she could hit the center of a five of spades held up by Butler behind her back; she could reach down from a galloping pony, pick up a revolver and shoot targets swung by a cowboy. At thirty-three while standing on the back of a galloping horse she could break glass balls with a rifle. In one nine-hour period, using a sixteen gauge shotgun, she broke 4,772 out of 5,000 balls tossed into the air. In Germany at the demand of the crown prince, later Wilhelm II, she shot off the end of a cigarette held in his mouth. During World War I she is reported to have written asking for a second chance.

In America, Sitting Bull had so much admired her that in a special ceremony he adopted her as his daughter. To her he deplored the poverty he saw in the cities: the white man did not know how to distribute his great wealth. In London, admirers sent letters of praise, filled her tent with flowers, clamored for her autograph, and went away impressed with her gentle charm. When not in her buckskin costume, she dressed tastefully and was graceful in serving tea and wine to visitors. On her table were signed photographs of the Prince of Wales, the Emperor of Austria, and the Duke of Monaco. In Munich she and Frank were the Duke's guests in his box at the opera.

On leaving for a visit to the States, Buffalo Bill wrote in her autograph book, "To the lovliest and truest little woman, both in heart and aim in all the world." In her autobiography she wrote that a crowned queen was never treated with more reverence than she was by the cowboys in the show. For seventeen years she was their little sister, sharing their good and bad news from home.

After a train wreck in 1901, which left her temporarily paralyzed, she and Frank gave exhibitions and ran a gun club—part of the money going for the support of numerous orphans. At sixty-two she could still break 100 clay pigeons for a perfect score.

Unlike some of the European husbands of American women, Frank Butler was a devoted husband, having sacrificed his career to hers. Although he was ten years her senior, Frank was still writing love verses to her when she was in her fifties: "her presence would remind you/Of an angel in the skies."

Annie Oakley was more uniquely American than any heroine

drawn by Howells or James, and by all accounts a more charming one.

It is difficult to determine the extent to which money or charm, or both, led to European marriages. Randolph Churchill's family at first vigorously opposed his love match with Jennie Jerome, then turned around and demanded a large marriage settlement. Dixon Wecter cites a computation of 1909 showing that more than fifty American women had married titled foreigners and had brought to Europe about $220,000,000. A professor of history who had made a canvass of England county by county told Wecter that in almost every small community, the vicar or innkeeper remarked, "There's a countrywoman of yours living hereabouts, the American wife of Sir ———, who years ago brought him the money to mend his house." An innkeeper might add, "And they do say, sir, that she's had a bit of a hard life of it, too."[39]

It was inevitable that a social phenomenon of such dimensions should become a topic of discussion in the press and should engage the attention of Howells and especially of James, whose staple was the international scene. As Margaret Wyman shows, Howells represented marriages across social boundaries as likely to be unhappy, but the worst were international unions, which he envisioned as between relatively innocent American girls and mercenary European bounders. . . . To Howells, the international marriage was always a profanation, and against it his stand was uncompromising."[40]

Henry James, despite his preoccupation with the international theme, gave few instances of international marriage. In several of his stories such marriages fail to come off, for instance in *An International Episode*, *The Portrait of a Lady*, *The American*, *The Wings of the Dove*. Isabel Archer's marriage to Gilbert Osmond is not really international: he is an expatriated American. James is hardly less puritanical than Howells in his picture of European husbands, whether married to their countrywomen or to Americans.

In *Madame de Mauves*, Mrs. Draper tells Longmore that Richard de Mauves is "a shining sinful Frenchman" who married Euphemia for her money and is spending it on his own pleasures. He is consistently unfaithful. M. de Vionnet in *The Ambassadors* is described as a brute; he and his charming French wife live apart. In *The Golden Bowl* Prince Amerigo is unfaithful to Maggie Verver.

There is no reason to doubt the accuracy of James's picture of upper-class European marriage and morals, but there are grounds for questioning the responses of his heroines. Thrown into a hedonistic society they adhered to the Puritan code of middle-class America. The mother of Count de Mauves tells Euphemia, "If you wish to live at ease in the *doux pays de France*, don't trouble too much about the key of your conscience or even about your conscience itself. . . ." Later on the Count himself says, "I'm faithless, I'm heartless, I'm brutal, I'm everything horrible. . . . Take your revenge, console yourself; you're too charming a young woman to have anything to complain of. Here's a handsome young man sighing himself into consumption for you. Listen to your poor compatriot and you'll find that virtue's none the less becoming for being good natured."[41]

Nevertheless she does not console herself with her compatriot, Longmore. Two years later he learns that the count had repented his follies and on his knees begged forgiveness. "All in vain! She was stone, she was ice, she was outraged virtue." De Mauves blew out his brains.

When Isabel Archer realizes that her husband Gilbert Osmond hates her, James describes her state of mind:

> But there were certain things she could never take in. To begin with they were hideously unclean. She was not a daughter of the Puritans, but for all that she believed in such a thing as chastity and even as decency. It would appear that Osmond was far from doing anything of the sort: some of his traditions made her push back her skirts. Did all women have lovers? Did they all lie and even the best have their price? Were there only three or four that didn't deceive their husbands?[42]

Even her knowledge about Osmond's cynical views on morals had not prepared her for the revelation that his daughter Pansy was the illegitimate child of Madame Merle. When Isabel says she had never guessed, the Countess Gemini, Osmond's sister, says, "That's because you've such a beastly pure mind. I never saw a woman with such a pure mind!"[43]

Isabel has at least the gumption to disobey Osmond and go to the bedside of the dying Ralph Touchett, who had sacrificed a fortune for her. While she is in England, her former suitor, Caspar Goodwood, tries to prevent her from going back to a despicable husband who hates her. She tells Goodwood to leave, but he takes her in his arms. "His kiss was like white lightning, a flash that spread, and spread again, and stayed, and it was extraordinarily as if, while she took it, she felt each thing in his hard manhood that had least pleased her. . . ." She goes back to Osmond.

Throughout the novel Isabel's behavior can only be explained as a rejection of sex. She turned down two fine young men—a British lord and an American manufacturer—to marry a middle-aged dilettante, who, as his sister says, is incapable of loving anyone. Her revulsion against Goodwood's kiss is told on the last page of the novel.

In *The Princess Casamassima* (1888) the lady has not seen her husband for three years. She considered "that in the darkest hour of her life she sold herself for a title and a fortune." According to her, the Prince is the greatest bore in Europe. "You know people oughn't to be corrupt and dreary." To alleviate her boredom she takes up revolution. As one character says, "she must try everything; at present she's trying democracy, she's going all lengths in radicalism." Thus she takes the well-named Hyacinth Robinson for long rides in her barouche. He is supposed to be an anarchist, socialist, or nihilist—James was apparently not clear in his own mind about the difference. That practiced revolutionaries would have entrusted an assassination to such a delicate flower is incredible. But so is the whole novel. The point of discussing it here is to bring out the sexlessness of the relation between the Princess and Hyacinth, who may not be really interested in women. Alone in Paris or Venice he just watches them go by.

This sexlessness was not solely due to nineteenth-century prudishness: as the foregoing account shows, James dealt with adultery. In *The Ambassadors* (1903) his heroine, Mme. de Vionnet, is involved in an adulterous affair with Chad Newsome, who under her tutelage has became a much finer man. James's alter ego Strether tells Chad that he would be a "brute" to abandon her. As early as *Madame de Mauves* James took an enigmatic position about Euphemia's puritanical rejection of her repentant husband. On hearing that she was a widow, Longmore had an impulse to return to Europe. But after he delayed for several years, "the truth is that in the midst of all the ardent tenderness of his memory of Madame de Mauves, he has became conscious of a singular feeling—a feeling of wonder, of uncertainty, of awe."

There is no denying the vividness of the portraits of Daisy Miller, Madame de Mauves, Isabel Archer, Milly Teale, Maggie Verver, and even some of the lesser women characters whose innocence contrasted with European sophistication. The question is: were American girls abroad so innocent and so puritanical?

Much of the evidence suggests that girls who married abroad adopted the mores of the social groups in which they found themselves. Elizabeth Vassall, whose father built the Craige-Longfellow house in Cambridge, was taken to England as a child when her loyalist father fled the country. At fifteen she married Sir Godfrey Webster. To break off her love affair with Lord Pelham, her husband took her to Italy, where Lord Pelham followed. Then she fell in love with the third Lord Holland by whom in 1796 she had an illegitimate child—at which point her husband divorced her.[44] Married to Lord Holland she bore four more children and became a famous hostess to literary celebrities, including Irving and Cooper.

In 1803 eighteen-year-old Elizabeth Patterson of Baltimore married Jerome Bonaparte, brother of Napoleon. After living for a time in England she went home to astonish the natives with the daring style of dress described by Margaret Bayard Smith (p. 50).

In the era of Henry James the most notorious social set in England was that of the Prince of Wales, later Edward VII. It was what today would be called a jet set, constantly moving about from place to place and from bed to bed. When Edward and his friends descended on a country house, the hostess tactfully assigned adjoining rooms to lovers. Because of the rapid changeovers, this necessitated a knowledge of current gossip. The lavish expenditures for entertainment, gambling, clothes, and jewels rivaled that of American multimillionaires.

Some of the money came from those multimillionaires. Consuelo Vanderbilt, married to the Duke of Marlborough, listed at least four American ladies in the prince's circle. The most glamorous of these was Lady Randolph Churchill, the former Jennie Jerome. The Vanderbilt and Jerome fortunes had helped to bail out the Churchill family. Randolph Churchill and the Duke of Marlborough were first cousins.

The story of Jennie's marriage has already been told. One of the most beautiful women of her time, she became a great favorite of the Prince of Wales, who often called on her of an afternoon. Jennie's biographer, Anita Leslie, could not find in Edward's many letters to her any evidence that they became lovers, but does not reject the possibility. Certainly Jennie was very much a part of a set where "it was the smart thing to go to bed with the Prince of Wales, and boast about it afterwards." After Lord Randolph Churchill became incapacitated with syphilis, she had at least two extended extramarital affairs.* Her sister Clara, married to Morton Frewen, had a long affair with King Milan of Servia. Jennie and Clara wrote to each other and their younger sister Leonie about their love affairs.[45]

The Jerome girls had been brought up in a home where their mother apparently took a tolerant view of her husband's philandering. By contrast, Consuelo Vanderbilt's divorced mother acted as a kind of jailor, seizing her daughter's letters from the man she loved and not permitting her to get outside the gate until Consuelo consented to marry the Duke of Marlborough.[46] In Consuelo's memoirs the duke appears as a stuffy, arrogant aristocrat, interested in his wife only for her money and as brood mare for a male heir. In many ways he resembles Gilbert Osmond of *The Portrait of a Lady*. But unlike Isabel Archer, who returned to a husband who hated her, Consuelo, after eleven years of marriage, obtained a legal separation from the duke and devoted herself to philanthropic and political work. As she says, "in Edwardian social circles divorce or separation were not recognized as a solution for marital discord." Although she does not say so, divorce was regarded as a characteristically

* George Moore credited her with 200 lovers (Ralph G. Martin, *Jennie*, Englewood Cliffs, N.J., 1971, II, 389).

American institution. In the more tolerant 1920s she did get a divorce and found happiness in a second marriage.[47]

A puritanical upbringing, like a convent education, did not insure conventional behavior. Mary Smith, born in 1864 in Philadelphia, was the daughter of Hannah Whitall Smith, a Quaker evangelist. Mary married an Oxford don who had visited the Smith home. After eleven years of marriage she abandoned her two children to run off with Bernard Berenson.[48] Her sister Alys became the first wife of Bertrand Russell. Alys, who in theory believed in free love, was ashamed of her sister's action. Later, Russell tired of her, and against her will, banished her from his bed. Nevertheless, when he told of his affair with Lady Ottoline Morrell and asked for a divorce, Alys made a scene.[49]

It is unsafe to generalize on the basis of a half-dozen examples, but there is reason to believe that they are to some extent typical. Logan Pearsall Smith, the brother of Mary and Alys, wrote

> And the American women! In what capital of Europe are they not to be found reigning, if not as queens, at least as princesses? They wear ducal coronets in England, they preside at English and other embassies abroad, they are hostesses in many Italian palaces. Seeing thus some American girl, some local Mamie or Maud or Mildred, upon her social throne in Europe, and picturing to oneself her original starting place, some main-street house perhaps where she used to sit with her beaux upon the wooden piazza or pay visits with them to the ice-cream-soda fountain round the corner, one cannot but wonder at the journey she has traveled, the transformation she has undergone, and the marvelous tact she has displayed in adjusting herself to the circumstances, the ways and manners, of that once far-away kingdom of romance which her girlish intelligence has enabled her to conquer.[50]

Smith is wrong in adding that this is all written in the book of Henry James. Daisy Miller, Euphemia de Mauves, Isabel Archer, Henrietta Stackpole, Mamie Pocock, and Maggie Verver did not undergo a transformation and adjust themselves to the ways and manners of Europe. They retained their American values and prejudices, especially a puritanical attitude toward sex. It is an attitude

James seemed to share. Women like Osmond's sister, the Countess Gemini; Mme. Merle; and Kate Croy, who have extramarital affairs are usually represented as evil. Only Mme. de Vionnet escapes his censure, though even she is tinged with dishonesty.

It is even possible that James projected his own sexual inhibitions onto his women characters. In Paris he regarded the Variétés as merely a pretext for bad jokes and undressed *figurantes*. At a watering place he was amazed at the skill with which French women swam, but he felt that Mlle. X's somersault from a diving board was "an impropriety." He was puzzled by the logic of this; white and black were divided by a hair, but "virtue is on one side, and vice on the other."[51] After seeing Daudet, Goncourt, and Zola, he commented on their "handling of unclean things." Isabel Archer muses, "To break with Osmond once would be to break forever; any open acknowledgement of irreconcilable needs would be an admission that their attempt had proved a failure. . . . They had attempted only one thing, but that one thing was to have been exquisite. Once they missed it nothing else would do; there was no conceivable substitute for that success." That is possibly the most unlikely reason for a marriage ever given. Isabel's thoughts are those of an effeminate artist rather than those of a healthy young American girl.

James was a major novelist who within the narrow limits of his social vision created a believable world, but perhaps as idiosyncratic a world as that of a Hemingway or a Faulkner. So convincing are James's portraits of nineteenth-century women that they have often been taken for reality. The evidence presented in the foregoing discussion indicates that the actual women were more sophisticated and full blooded. Few if any of James's American women could have achieved the positions in European society described by Logan Pearsall Smith. *Current Literature* described Lady Randolph Churchill as "the only hostess of genius in the United Kingdom," and the *Daily Mail* remarked in 1911 that "When she first came to England, as Lady Randolph Churchill, she gave London society a fillip."[52] Jennie Jerome was a more fascinating character than either Daisy Miller or Isabel Archer.

NOTES

1. Quoted in Wyman, "Women in the American Realistic Novel," p. 678.
2. Arthur M. Schlesinger, *Learning How to Behave*, New York, 1946, p. 45.
3. Hoxie, "Mrs. Grundy Adopts Daisy Miller," pp. 483–84.
4. Henry James, *Daisy Miller, Pandora, The Patagonia and Other Tales* (New York Edition), New York, 1909, p. 93.
5. Hjalmar Hjorth Boyesen, "Types of American Women," *Forum* VIII (1889–90), 340–41.
6. Ibid., pp. 23–24.
7. Henry James, "A Bundle of Letters," in *The Seige of London, An International Episode, and Other Tales* (New York Edition), New York, 1908, p. 501.
8. *The American Novels of Henry James*, ed. by F. O. Matthiessen, New York, 1947, p. 137.
9. Wyman, p. 650.
10. *Julia Newberry's Diary*, ed. Margaret Ayer Barnes and Janet Ayer Fairbank, Richfield Springs, N.Y., 1933, p. 60.
11. Ibid., pp. 30, 42.
12. Ibid., p. 72.
13. Ibid., p. 73.
14. Henry James, *The Portrait of a Lady*, I, 281.
15. Ibid., pp. 102, 151–52.
16. Ibid., p. 32.
17. Ibid., pp. 78, 133.
18. Ibid., p. 116.
19. Ibid., p. 163.
20. Ibid., p. 170.
21. Van Wyck Brooks, *The Pilgrimage of Henry James*, New York, 1925, p. 28.
22. *Julia Newberry's Diary*, p. 103.
23. Alexandra Lee Levin, "Miss Knight Abroad," *American Heritage* XI, No. 3 (April 1960), 16.
24. Ibid., p. 18.
25. Ibid., p. 24.
26. Ibid.
27. Ibid., p. 28.
28. Louise Stoughton Papers, 1877–79, MS in Arthur and Elizabeth Schlesinger Library, Radcliffe College.
29. James, "A Bundle of Letters," pp. 479–80.
30. Anthony Trollope, *He Knew He Was Right*, London, 1951, p. 527.
31. Anthony Trollope, *The Duke's Children* (originally 1879–80), New York, 1954, p. 379.
32. Ibid., p. 544.
33. *Elizabeth Cady Stanton*, p. 84.
34. Anita Leslie, *Lady Randolph Churchill*, New York, 1969, p. 204.
35. Ibid., pp. 32–33.
36. Princess Cantacuzene, Countess Speransky, "My Marriage," *Saturday Evening Post*, Dec. 4, 1920.
37. Hasketh Pearson, *The Marrying Americans*, New York, 1961, pp. 30–31, 47, 49.
38. Walter Havighurst, *Annie Oakley of the Wild West*, New York, 1954, pp. 117, 128, 143, 146, *et passim*; John Burke, *Buffalo Bill, the Noblest Whiteskin*, New York, 1973, pp. 155–59; *DAB*, VII, 603.
39. Wecter, *The Saga of American Society*, p. 405.

40. Wyman, p. 491.
41. Henry James, *The Reverberator, Madame de Mauves, A Passionate Pilgrim and Other Tales* (New York Edition), New York, 1908, pp. 292–93.
42. James, *Portrait of a Lady*, II, 200–201.
43. Ibid., II, 362.
44. Pearson, p. 9.
45. Leslie, pp. 222, 170, 213–14.
46. Consuelo Vanderbilt Balsan, *The Glitter and The Gold*, New York, 1952, p. 47.
47. Ibid., p. 239.
48. Sylvia Sprigge, *Berenson*, Cambridge, 1960, p. 104ff.
49. *The Autobiography of Bertrand Russell, 1872–1914*, Boston and Toronto, 1967, pp. 112, 315.
50. Logan Pearsall Smith, *Unforgotten Years*, Boston, 1939, p. 289.
51. Henry James, *Parisian Sketches*, ed. by Leon Edel and Elsie Dusoir, New York, 1957, p. 52.
52. Ralph G. Martin, *Jennie*, Englewood Cliffs, N.J., 1971, II, 294, 389.

Ten

The College Girl, the Gibson Girl, and the Titaness

> No country seems to owe more to its women than America does, nor to owe them so much of what is best in social institutions and in the beliefs which govern conduct.
>
> James Bryce

After the Civil War at least four relatively new types of women emerged in American society: the college girl, the titaness,* the office girl and, late in the century, the Gibson girl. To some degree the categories overlapped but the college girl and the Gibson girl represent the polarities. The early college girl was an inheritor of the woman's rights movement; the Gibson girl was a product of an increasingly urban, wealthy, and hedonistic social class.

Of the four types the office girl is the most difficult to describe: as a class she seems to have left few records in diaries and memoirs; novelists before World War I almost totally neglected her. For one thing her occupation was not usually a career, but an interval between school and marriage. She was a product of the invention of the typewriter and the increasing complexity of the business office. In social status she probably ranked with the school teacher who had a normal-school education. Women had begun to enter government agencies during the Civil War. A law in 1864 provided that they receive one-third of what a man was paid. In 1868 a woman stenographer entered the State Department. By 1888 there were sixty thousand stenographers in American offices.[1]

Important as the office girl was as a forerunner of the career

* The term *titaness* comes from Thomas Beer's *The Mauve Decade*, an account of the 1890s.

woman in business and industry who emerged after World War I, she was certainly not among the movers and shakers of her time. However, she was characteristically American to the extent that, unlike working girls in Europe, she was not considered to be a servant like a shop girl or an English governess. She might even marry her employer's son or some rising young executive.

To an even greater extent the college girl was an American invention. She was the logical result of a historical process that began with the Declaration of Independence and was fostered by the unique features of American life which have been discussed in earlier chapters. A society in which many women shared the studies of their fathers, brothers, and husbands would inevitably institutionalize such instruction.

Some of the pioneering work by such people as Emma Willard, Mary Lyon, and Catharine Beecher has been recorded in Chapter 5. As has been suggested, the better seminaries offered a combination of secondary and junior college or normal-school training.

The seminaries were largely the creation of women; the women's colleges and coeducational institutions were usually started by men. Oberlin, the first college to offer women the same course of study followed by men, was founded in 1833 by John Jay Shipherd, with Asa Mahan as its first president. At first women, because of poor preparation, were enrolled in the Female Department, a non-collegiate division. However in 1837 four women were admitted to the Collegiate Course, and four years later three of them became the first women in the world to receive bona fide A.B. degrees.

Oberlin must not be thought of as a tiny, local institution. In the early years a majority of students came from New York and New England. They came by way of the Erie Canal, crossed Lake Erie on small steamboats, then took coaches over terrible roads from Cleveland to Oberlin. In 1852 the railroad reached the town. By 1841 the institution had over 500 students as compared with a few over 200 at Harvard and 400 at Yale. Eleven years later the enrollment exceeded 1,000, making Oberlin at that time probably the largest educational institution in the nation. Many of the students were, of course, in the Preparatory Department.[2]

Oberlin became the model for coeducational institutions throughout the country. Antioch College, which opened in 1853 with Horace Mann as president, followed the Oberlin pattern. When Andrew White was appointed as first president of Cornell in 1865 he visited Oberlin and Michigan to see how coeducation worked. Because of a shortage of men during the Civil War, both Michigan and Wisconsin had admitted women. In that day college women were a civilizing influence. White, who had graduated from Michigan before coeducation, noted that the men were no longer slouchy and unkempt in class. Comparing the periods before and after coeducation, "It was the difference between the smoking car and the car behind it."

The critics were of course manifold. President Fairchild of Oberlin answered those who argued that women would handicap the progress of men: they had not in his experience as a teacher of Latin, Greek, Hebrew, mathematics, and philosophy. Nor did women's health break down more often than men's. Women were neither coarsened nor caused to disdain the usual lot of women. Most of them married. He argued that monastic institutions were more likely to fill the minds of youths with fanciful creations which were unlike actual men and women. Did not the acquaintances formed at school lead to matrimony? "Undoubtedly," answered Fairchild, "and if this is a fatal objection, the system must be pronounced a failure."[3]

In the 1850s the appropriately named Professor Silliman of Yale— a very prominent man in his day—made women's education the subject of a Phi Beta Kappa address. He stated that the best diploma for a woman was a large family and a happy husband. She should place "He" before the "Arts" to obtain the degree of "Mistress of Hearts."[4]

A former Harvard professor of medicine, Dr. Edward H. Clarke, charged in 1873 that "identical education of the two sexes is a crime before God and humanity that physiology protests against, and that experience weeps over." He quoted Dr. S. Weir Mitchell's statement in *Wear and Tear* that female education had made the American woman unfit for her duties as a woman. The next year in a second book, *Building a Brain*, Clarke cited horrendous reports of girls' physical and mental breakdowns from overstudy. Thomas Woody quotes him as saying that if present trends continue, "the mothers of our republic must be drawn from transatlantic homes. The sons of the New World will react on a magnificent scale to the old story of unwived Rome and the Sabines."[5]

As late as 1904 the eminent psychologist G. Stanley Hall, president of Clark University, after praising Clarke, wrote: "It is utterly impossible without injury to hold girls to the same standards of conduct, regularity, severe moral accountability, and strenuous mental work that boys need."[6]

Like the Wife of Bath, Elizabeth Cady Stanton regarded experience as a better guide than the theorizing of the learned: she told of the superheated atmosphere of Miss Willard's seminary after her earlier experience in a coeducational academy. "The healthful restraint always existing between boys and girls in conversation is apt to be relaxed with either sex alone. In all my intimate association with boys up to that period, I cannot recall one word or act for criticism, but I cannot say the same of the girls during the three years I passed at Troy."[7] Throughout her life she preached the value of coeducation.

The two early colleges for both men and women, Oberlin and Antioch, were relatively poverty-stricken institutions where revivalistic religion competed with genuine education. At the former, where Charles Grandison Finney was brought in as professor of theology, he and the new faculty were inauguarated in a huge tent holding three thousand people, over which flew a banner proclaiming "Holiness to the Lord." Finney was an evangelist of hypnotic power. For the next fifteen years there were constant revivals at the college, some lasting several weeks, and one, celebrating Finney's return from England in 1860, going on for months. At Antioch when President Mann refused to permit a revival there was a tremendous uproar led by the Reverend Ira W. Allen and joined by the sectarian press. Insisting that he always maintained a Christian spirit, Allen used such phrases as "dark plot," "despicable injustice" and "Mrs. Mann's sullen and overbearing manner." The *Gospel Herald* in an editorial entitled "Antioch College—A Warning" said that some powerful influence had prevented all religious power from operating: "no revival season has been enjoyed in this College—no conversions made during the whole period of its existence."[8]

As might be expected, this Calvinistic bigotry had an influence on the students. They, and especially the girls, were indoctrinated with the belief that novels were evil. Put down that novel, repeated five times, appeared in the *Advocate of Moral Reform* and again in *The Oberlin Evangelist*. The warning ended, "It will ruin your soul." A male student took a more utilitarian point of view in a satiric poem about a girl who read novels: "the beef is burnt, and the veal is raw,/And all from novel reading." Thus when an Oberlin student gave his fiancee Bulwer-Lytton's *Eugene Aram* she laid it aside, telling herself, "It cannot be wrong not to read it—and I like to be on the safe side."[9] In a period when college literary societies everywhere were the chief sources of student reading matter, the men at Oberlin hotly debated the propriety of the Ladies Literary Society Library Association's ownership of a copy of Byron.

Despite all this religious and masculine nonsense a woman could probably get a better education at Oberlin or Antioch than elsewhere before the Civil War. When in 1857 the Hawthornes left England for a tour of the continent, they engaged Miss Ada Shepard, a graduate of "Mr. Mann's College at Antioch," as a governess for their children. (No doubt Sophia Hawthorne's sister, Mary Mann, had recommended her.) Hawthorne had tried English governesses and found them ignorant and inefficient. Miss Shepard, a girl of twenty-one, gave instruction in reading, spelling, composition, Latin, Greek, German, French, Italian, arithmetic, algebra, geometry, and chronology to the Hawthorne childen and to other expatriate youngsters.[10]

So proficient was she in French that when Hawthorne could not understand the rapid speech of customs officials, Miss Shepard acted as interpreter. To her fiancee, Clay Badger, she wrote, "As they cannot afford a courier, I do not know what would become of them and their baggage if they were left to themselves."[11] Hawthorne was a graduate of Bowdoin in an era when men's colleges did not teach modern languages.

There is considerable evidence that the young women who embarked on a college education during the half century after such a thing became possible tended to be an especially dedicated type. Often they had to overcome parental and even community disapproval. Families were much more inclined to sacrifice to send a son to college. Girls were sometimes expected to help to finance boys' education. Lucy Stone revolted against making shirts for such a project, saying, "let us use our scantier opportunities to educate ourselves."[12] As has been mentioned, her father required her to sign a note to pay for her own schooling—one that took her years to pay off.

A current leftish cliché is that until very recently a college education was available only to the upper classes. Nothing could be further from the truth. From earliest days the student who earned much or all of his own expenses was a ubiquitous American type. At Harvard Emerson and Thoreau largely supported themselves; at the relatively expensive University of Virginia the faculty asserted that in 1844–45, the great majority of students belonged to the middle ranks of society and that a considerable number earned their own money for expenses.[13]

Because of lower wages, girls had a more difficult time than boys. In the 1840s when tuition at Oberlin was $18 a year and total expenses about $100, girls at the college did domestic labor at about three cents an hour and ironed men's shirts at thirty-seven and a half cents a dozen. Thus a girl doing domestic labor would have had to work over 3,300 hours to pay her expenses.[14]

A more practical solution was to teach school for a few years to save money for a college education. This was Lucy Stone's method of paying off the note to her father. Anna Howard Shaw (1847–1919), who became a prominent lecturer and in 1904 took office as president of the National American Woman Suffrage Association, was brought up in a cabin in the wilds of northern Michigan a hundred miles from a railroad. Her father went to Kansas leaving the cabin unfinished, so the young people—three brothers and Anna and her two sisters—installed a floor, windows, and doors, and dug a well. Anna, largely self-educated, began teaching at fifteen, and at seventeen began to preach. Ten years later she entered Albion College for two years, then transferred to the Boston University Theological School.[15]

Lucy Larcom told of the Lowell mill girls saving money to attend Mount Holyoke Seminary before it became a college. Alice Freeman, who later became president of Wellesley, was the daughter of a farmer who said that as he could afford to send one person to college, it should be his son. Alice, who was the eldest, said if he sent her, she would not marry until she could put her brother through college, and give her sisters whatever education they wanted. In her junior year at the University of Michigan she dropped out for a semester to take a job as head of a high school. After getting her A.B. she taught for a time in a high school, then at twenty-four was appointed professor of history at Wellesley. During the summers she studied for her Ph.D.[16]

Undoubtedly the difficulties facing girls who wanted a college education acted as a selective process: only the especially able and highly motivated were likely to try it. Their years in college reinforced the sense of mission of being participants in a crusade. This was especially true at Oberlin, where before the Civil War students and faculty participated in religious activities and abolition. White girls sat in classes with the illegitimate mulatto daughters of Southern planters; students saw fugitive slaves and heard their tales of brutal punishments; Oberlin graduates went to Kansas. Mobs broke up abolitionist meetings, threw rotten eggs, thrashed male students with bullwhips, tarred and feathered them. Because of this sense of participation in crusades, the historian of the college, Robert Fletcher, estimated that 99 out of 100 Oberlinites went out as missionaries for Oberlinism.[17]

Jane Addams (1860–1935), who in 1877 entered Rockford Seminary in Illinois, wrote of the intense enthusiasm of the girls to transform "The Mount Holyoke of the West" into a college. In order that they should be ready for the bachelor's degree when it was offered, they took a course in mathematics, and applied for an opportunity to compete in the intercollegiate oratorical contest of Illinois. When Jane was selected as the orator, she found that she was expected to represent not only her school but college women in general. No personal feeling must be allowed to stand in the way of Woman's Cause.[18]

Miss Addams spoke of the atmosphere of intensity growing out of the "glamour of frontier privations. . . . We worked in those early years as if we really believed in the portentious statement from

Aristotle which we found quoted in Boswell's Johnson. . . . There is the same difference between the learned and the unlearned as there is between the living and the dead."

Something of this same sense of dedicated pioneering inspired both faculty and students in the early years of the great women's colleges. The first one with an endowment comparable to that of institutions for men was founded in 1861 by a sixty-nine-year-old brewer with little formal education, Matthew Vassar. He had been influenced by his niece, Lydia Booth, who ran a female seminary, and he got advice from Professor M. P. Jewett, who had been head of the Judson Female Institute in Alabama. When he decided to go ahead with his scheme, Vassar obtained a charter and appointed a board of trustees. When the act of incorporation became law, he read to the trustees a statement of his views: "It occurred to me, that woman, having received from her creator the same intellectual constitution as man, has the same right as man to intellectual culture and development." He spoke of the need for mothers who would be able to mold the character of citizens and of the importance of training teachers, then added the radical statement: "It also seemed to me that if woman were properly educated, some new avenues of honorable employment . . . might be opened to her."[19]

He went on to outline a curriculum including science ("with full apparatus"), economics, political science, aesthetics, domestic science, hygiene, Moral Science, and the study of the Bible. When he finished reading his statement, he handed over to the trustees a box containing stocks, bonds, mortgages, and a deed for 200 acres of land—a gift totaling over $400,000. Up to that time no woman's college had an endowment of over $100,000.[20]

Most newspapers praised the gift, but expressed the hope that education would not unfit women for their proper duties. The *New York Times* tolerantly said that as long as there were Allopathic, Hydropathic, Homeopathic and patent pill colleges "why not let the girls have one?"[21]

Vassar himself broke ground for the first building, a mammoth affair housing classrooms, laboratories, and dormitory rooms. He soon added an observatory, a gymnasium containing a room for calisthenics, a riding school, and a bowling alley. When the college opened in 1865, there was a faculty of eight men and twenty-two women,* a student body of 353. Under the influence of Sarah Josepha Hale he had adopted the policy of having a preponderance of women on the faculty. One of his appointments was Maria Mitchell, the discoverer of a comet, as professor of astronomy. However, because of the lack of qualified women seven of the nine full professorships were given to men, and Milo Jewett was made president. Vassar's own statement was that he hoped to "inaugurate a new era in the history of the life of women. . . . I wish to give one sex the advantages too long monopolized by the other. Ours is, and is to be, an institution for women—not men."[22]

He was not even daunted when a pious graduate who had gone through college on a scholarship, wrote, "A college foundation which is laid in beer will never prosper." A student who was with him at the time reported that when he read this, he shouted, "Well, it was good beer, wasn't it?" Then he joined the girls in a roar of laughter.

Like Matthew Vassar the students and the faculty had a sense of participating in a revolution. Maria Mitchell judged everything from the standpoint of "How is this going to affect women?" The "Lady Principal," Miss Lyman, impressed on the young women the fact that higher education for women was an experiment, that the world was looking on.

Much the same pattern was repeated at Wellesley. Here too, one wealthy man endowed the college, outlined the course of study, and personally supervised the construction of the original building. However, founder Henry Fowle Durant and his wife, Pauline, put much greater emphasis on piety. The original statute stated that "The College was founded for the glory of God and the service of the Lord Jesus Christ, in and by the education and culture of women." Workmen on the building were forbidden to swear or speak in loud voices. Every trustee and teacher had to be a member of an evangelical church.

Although Durant provided that the president and all the faculty should be women, the student president of the first class wrote to

* The Vassar catalog for 1971–72 showed that 61 percent of the faculty was male.

her parents, "Dr. Durant rules the college, from the amount of Latin we shall read to the kind of meat we shall have at dinner." One of his strictures was against eating between meals. As supper was limited to bread, butter, cookies, molasses and milk, students often complained of hunger. One of his dictums was that "pies, lies, and doughnuts" should never have a place at Wellesley. Even at Thanksgiving girls were forbidden to receive food from home.[23]

Such rules were symptomatic of the traditional view that women needed to be hedged in with more rigid restrictions than applied to men—a view which colleges are only now reluctantly abandoning. At Vassar and Wellesley the student's day was programmed from rising at 6 to retiring at 9:40 or 10. Miss Lyman, principal at Vassar, required that every woman change for dinner and that women should wear gloves for any college function, even for the reading of an essay or poem in chapel. Because many women began their work in the preparatory department at Vassar or Wellesley, they remained in a highly regimented environment for more than four years. Because of cost and distance, many of the students could not get away for holidays, and when they did, they carried with them the marks of their training. A Wellesley girl going home by train at Christmas happened to look at her watch. "It's silent time at Wellesley now," she said to her companions. At once a hush fell over the group.[24]

In addition to a conventlike regimen which tended to produce a somewhat inhibited type of woman, there was the influence of the classical curriculum with its emphasis on Latin and Greek. In the years following the Civil War the creation of technical and agricultural schools gave men an increasing freedom of choice. Vassar did offer a scientific course leading to an A.B., but the tendency of the eastern women's colleges was to follow closely the traditional curriculum in order to give an education like a man's. The all-male board of trustees which established Smith College in 1871 with a bequest from Sophia Smith decreed that "the requirements for admission will be substantially the same as at Harvard, Yale, Brown, Amherst, and other New England Colleges."[25] Smith College tended to put more emphasis on the classics than did Vassar and Wellesley.

At men's colleges the unworldliness of the classical curriculum was somewhat tempered by the fact that it bore some relationship to the law and the ministry—professions largely closed to women. Left for women was chiefly teaching. By 1892, 540 of the 734 graduates of Wellesley were teachers; 12 were practicing physicians; 15, librarians; and 20, missionaries.[26] A study in 1895 by Margaret Shinn showed that of 1,805 college women only 28.2 percent were married as compared to 80 percent for women over twenty in the population as a whole. The figures for college women went up in later age groups: 32.7 percent of women over twenty-five, and 54.5 percent of women over forty. As a considerably higher proportion of graduates from coeducational institutions married than did those from women's colleges, it is evident that the eastern women's colleges tended to produce spinster school teachers.[27]

In fact, a number of women presidents and faculty members had a considerable hostility to men. This was not true of Alice Freeman, the second president of Wellesley, who regarded it as fortunate that she had attended the coeducational University of Michigan. Her subsequent marriage to George Herbert Palmer seems to have been a very happy one. President William Rainey Harper of the University of Chicago made the Palmers the unusual offer of joint appointments to the faculty—he as professor of philosophy, she as dean of women.

By contrast M. Carey Thomas, president of Bryn Mawr from 1894 to 1935, was the kind of female dragon who confirmed masculine prejudices against college women.

As a girl at Cornell she threw over forever a college friend who announced her engagement.[28] Her Quaker mother wrote, "Thee ought to extend to others the same liberty on the subject thee claims for thyself." Miss Thomas was never one to extend liberties to others. She broke off a friendship with another good Quaker when he announced his engagement.

Martha Carey Thomas (1857–1935) was representative of one type of the early generation of college women—a dedicated person with a sense of mission. At fourteen she wrote in her diary. "If I ever live to grow up my aim and concentrated purpose shall *be* and *is* to show that women *can learn, can reason, can compete* with men in the grand fields of literature and science, that a woman can be a woman and a *true* one without all her time engrossed by dress and society."[29]

Born of well-to-do Quaker parents in Baltimore, a city more noted for beautiful than for intellectual women, she was sent to fashionable schools and spent summers at Atlantic City. Outside of school she and her friend Bessie King started the study of Greek. When they wanted to build a telegraph as a college boy had done, her mother said, "Oh you can't, you're only girls." It made Carey grind her teeth and swear (affirm) "that no one should say that of us—as if we hadn't as much sense and perserverance as boys." She read incessantly—sixty-five books in 1871.

Like so many vigorous girls of the supposed era of fainting females, she was something of a tomboy. Because of her Unionist sentiments she got into fist fights with other girls. At recess the boys and girls had a battle with water pistols, spit blowers, and buckets of water: "It was the jolliest fun I've had for ages." She drove the Thomas carriage so fast that Bessie King was forbidden to ride with her; she played baseball with her cousins; she learned to skate so well that she could do figure eights backwards; she said that all the skating roughs in the city knew her on sight.[30]

With encouragement from her aunt, Hannah Smith, a woman's rights advocate, she went to Howland Institute on Lake Cayuga, which had an excellent classical course. It was probably her experience there that caused her to change her objective from Vassar to Cornell, which had recently become coeducational. After some objections, Dr. Thomas gave his consent. Apparently with his support she was later allowed to work for an M.A. at Johns Hopkins, where he was a trustee.

However, she was consistently hostile to her father: she thought he was responsible for begetting too big a family; she even blamed him for her mother's refusal to consult a doctor about a fatal cancer. Mrs. Thomas, apparently very happy in her marriage, accused Carey of being a fault finder and hardly tolerating her father.[31]

In 1879 Carey and her possibly lesbian friend Mamie Gwinn went to Zurich to study for a Ph.D. There they took pains to ignore the men students. Carey got her doctorate *summa cum laude*, the first American woman to get a Ph.D.

Back in the States she was given the deanship at Bryn Mawr, newly founded under a bequest defining it as a college for "young women of the upper classes." Miss Thomas fell into the spirit of this by opposing the appointment of Jews to the faculty. She and Mamie Gwinn lived together in the deanery, and traveled together in the summer. A strange woman, Mamie refused to talk at dinner, even to a visiting Frenchman, although she could speak excellent French. She just sat and gobbled.[32] When Mamie, after a secret engagement, resigned to be married, Carey Thomas turned to Mary Garrett, an old friend from Baltimore.

Miss Thomas was very much the titaness. As dean she was barely civil to the rest of the faculty; she feuded with Professor Woodrow Wilson—not a difficult feat—until he broke his contract a year early. Despite all this she was made president in 1894, possibly because Mary Garrett offered $10,000 a year to the English Department if and while Carey was president.

As president, Miss Thomas tyrannized the faculty and disregarded the expressed wishes of the trustees. One reason she got away with it was the support of Mary Garrett, who on one occasion she made up a deficit of $30,000. Mary brought with her to the deanery silver, linen, and works of art. However, Bertrand Russell said that Miss Thomas ran her dinner parties like a committee meeting.[33]

M. Carey Thomas helped to create the reputation for snobbery that often unjustly came to be attached to the excellent women's colleges in the East. Like her male contemporaries at Princeton and Yale, she favored Collegiate Gothic architecture; she liked May Day celebrations after the English pattern, but of course without the traditional fornication; she distrusted foreigners and found Lothrop Stoddard's racist ideas congenial.

It would be a mistake to leave the impression that the eastern colleges like Vassar, Wellesley, Smith, and Bryn Mawr were representative of women's education throughout the nation. As early as 1870 women had been admitted to 30.7 percent of all colleges other than technical schools and those for women only. Ten years later the proportion of coeducational institutions was 51.3 percent and in 1890 was 65.5 percent. By far the largest number of these were in the West. Between 1875 and 1900 women in coeducational schools increased 600 percent, whereas the number in women's colleges went up 60 percent. By that time there were nearly 20,000 coeds compared to not quite 16,000 in women's colleges.[34] In the 1880s and 90s Harvard, Columbia, Tulane, and Brown set up coordinate colleges for women. At the end of the century one-third of all college students were women.[35]

Hugo Münsterberg, who joined the Harvard faculty in 1892, told of the European attitude toward the American college-trained woman. ". . . next to the twenty-story buildings nothing excites our curiosity more than the women who have the bachelor's degree." As a typical German he stated his belief in the mental inferiority of women, but had to admit that contrary to his expectations the girls at Smith, Wellesley, Bryn Mawr, and Radcliffe were not the repulsive creatures pictured in German comic papers, but were "an enchanting type by Gibson."[36]

Perhaps the chief difference between the Gibson girl and the college girl was that up until the first World War, a high proportion of college-trained women had a sense of mission. In the era when the inequities of an economic system which produced sweated labor and malefactors of great wealth were becoming increasingly evident, many of these women devoted their energies to social amelioration and reform. They became allies of such men as John Peter Altgeld and Theodore Roosevelt. The tendency of American businessmen and politicians to put morality in the wife's name had led many women into the temperance and abolition movements before the Civil War; after it the women addressed themselves to the evils of social injustice. By the turn of the century Mark Twain wrote that he believed the entire population of the United States—*exclusive of the women* [italics mine]—to be rotten as far as the dollar is concerned.[37]

To a considerable degree the college women of the half-century after the Civil War were heirs of the woman's rights movement. As has been mentioned, a number of the early crusaders became concerned with the plight of low-paid women in industry, even with the economic forces that led to prostitution.

Thus in 1889, women from Smith, Vassar, Wellesley, and Bryn Mawr opened a settlement house in New York. Two weeks later, in Chicago, a graduate of Rockford College, Jane Addams, joined Ellen Gates to start the famous Hull House. From time to time other college women were associated with Hull House: Julia Clifford Lathrop (1858–1932), a graduate of Vassar, and Florence Kelley (1859–1932), from Cornell.

Both Julia Lathrop and Florence Kelley had distinguished careers. In 1892 Governor Altgeld appointed Miss Lathrop as the first woman member of the Illinois Board of Public Charities, a post she occupied until 1909. She was active in the mental hygiene movement and worked for laws against child labor. Florence Kelley, one of the few pioneer social workers to marry, in 1884 became the wife of Dr. Lazare Wischnewtzky, a Polish-Russian physician, and bore three children. In 1891 she became a member of the Hull House group, but also found time to earn a law degree at Northwestern University and gain admission to the bar. She moved to New York, where she joined the Henry Street Settlement House. Then Governor Altgeld brought her back to Illinois as the first factory inspector appointed under a new law.[38]

Not all the early social workers were college graduates. Lillian Wald (1867–1940) went to private schools and the New York Training School for Nurses and took courses at the Women's Medical College in New York. She was the developer of two famous institutions: a settlement house and a citywide visiting nurse service, and was the founder of the National Organization for Public Health Nursing.[39] Mary Ellen Richmond (1861–1928) studied stenography at night and attended lectures at Cooper Union. After working for the Charity Organization Society of Baltimore she went to Philadelphia as general secretary of the Society for Organizing Charity. In 1909 she became director of the charity organization of the Russell Sage Foundation.[40]

However, as Jill Conway points out, none of the other pioneer social workers achieved a national reputation comparable to that of

Jane Addams. Miss Conway attributes this to Miss Addams's tremendous drive and charismatic personality.[41] Another reason was that she was a good writer. Such books as *Democracy and Social Ethics* (1902) and especially *Twenty Years at Hull House* (1910) gave an excellent account of her work and ideas. Hull House became an intellectual center: actresses, musicians, authors, royalty, heads of state all came to visit. Despite her charm, Jane Addams seems to have lacked the smallest spark of humor—a limitation shared by most of the early social workers.

However, her record is impressive. She advised Theodore Roosevelt on social problems, and campaigned for him in 1912.[42] During and after World War I she was a pacifist. It is ironic that in 1931 she shared the Nobel Peace Prize with Nicholas Murray Butler, an interventionist who had fired the pacifists on the Columbia faculty. Certainly Jane Addams was a titaness in an era of titanesses.

The activity of so many college women in social work and reform caused some persons to attack the women's colleges. At Wellesley, Vida Scudder brought in a fiery labor leader, Jack O'Sullivan, to speak to the faculty. Even M. Carey Thomas opened a summer school at Bryn Mawr in 1921 for women in industry. That same year Vice-President Coolidge wrote for the *Delineator* a series of articles, "Enemies of the Republic." The first was entitled "Are the Reds Stalking our College Women?" He thought they were. Among other disturbing events at Vassar and Radcliffe he reported that at Wellesley a professor was "said to have voted for Debs."[43] This was no doubt Vida Scudder, who had become a Socialist long before that.

It was not only college women who developed a social conscience. One of the supporters of Hull House was the titaness Mrs. Potter Palmer (1849–1918), whose biography by Ishbel Ross is entitled— and with reason—*Silhouette in Diamonds*.[44] Her wedding gift from her husband was the $3,500,000 Palmer House. It burned the next year in the great Chicago fire, but with her help her husband made another fortune and built a more lavish Palmer House.

Bertha Honoré Palmer seems to have been an unlikely person to develop into an organizer of women's trade unions. Born of a well-to-do Kentucky family which later moved to Chicago, she was sent to a convent school where she took honors in profane history, ancient and modern geography, chemistry, mineralogy, astronomy, botany, logic, philosophy, rhetoric, literature, composition, algebra, geometry, mantua work, and domestic economy. She also took top honors in piano, harp, and vocal music.[45] The variety indicates the wide-ranging superficiality of some of the women's seminaries of the period.

Potter Palmer (1826–1902) attended Bertha Honoré's coming out party. A bachelor of forty-one, he had made $7,000,000 as a merchant, a speculator in cotton, and in real estate deals. After a trip to Europe for his health he had blossomed as a man of the world, making a splash at Saratoga and driving one of the finest turnouts on Broadway. In Chicago he bought a mile of frontage on the lake and planned the wide roadway which eventually materialized. One of his business associates was Henry Honoré, Bertha's father.

Despite his extensive business deals Potter Palmer found time for an extended courtship of Bertha, who was half his age. A portrait by Anders Zorn shows her as extremely beautiful in a kind of Mae West costume, but photographs of her as a girl and mature women suggest that "handsome" would be a better description. Neither John Singer Sargent nor Charles Dana Gibson would have given her such a square jaw. But both would have represented the gowns and the jewels. During her honeymoon in Europe she began her fabulous collections of both. At one of her parties Palmer remarked to Ernest Poole, "There she stands with two hundred thousand dollars worth of jewels on her."[46]

Mrs. Palmer was fond of giving lavish parties and balls, but her husband usually disappeared before the evening was over. At one such occasion Poole, finding him slumped on a sofa, asked if he was tired. "No but my feet hurt." If Mrs. Palmer's feet ever hurt, no one ever heard of it. She bore two sons, Honoré in 1874 and Potter in 1875; she learned about business through discussions with her husband; she became active in the Women's Christian Temperance Union despite the flourishing bar in the Palmer House.[47] And when Mrs. Palmer's sister Ida married Fredrick Dent Grant in 1874, the Palmers arranged a lavish wedding at their home. Potter Palmer showered Ida with diamonds; President and Mrs. Grant came for the occasion; the guests included many Civil War officers, and the plutocracy of Chicago. From this time on Mrs. Palmer was the hostess to the Grants on their visits to the city, and occasionally displayed her gowns and jewels in the receiving line at the White House.[48]

It is understandable that both Palmers should give large sums to charitable causes; her gifts alone were estimated at $25,000 a year. What is remarkable is that Bertha Palmer became active in reform movements. She was one of the leaders in establishing the Chicago Woman's Club in 1876, an organization whose primary purpose was the study of social problems. Working girls as well as social leaders were members. In her own home Mrs. Palmer held meetings for factory girls; she helped to push for protective legislation, and became a patron of the Women's Trade Union League, which helped to organize the millinery workers of Chicago.[49] When Hull House was founded she gave it support.

Meanwhile Potter Palmer was building a half-million dollar castle with a Spanish music room, an English dining room, a Moorish ballroom, and a Louis XVI drawing room ninety feet long and forty feet high. Pictures of the exterior and interior show that it was all in the godawful plutocratic taste of the time and filled with a mishmash of European antiques, Chinese porcelains, and Smyrna rugs. There were Moorish arches, Venetian mosaics, cathedral glass copied from a palace in Cairo, and a bathtub shaped like a swan. In this setting Mrs. Palmer's parties became legendary: they included diplomats, foreign princes, Benjamin Harrison and William McKinley. But she also entertained ward politicians, labor leaders, reformers, shopgirls, and assorted cranks.[50]

Probably Mrs. Potter's most notable achievement was the creation of the Woman's Building at the World's Columbian Exposition in 1893. After the Civil War a generation of men who had made great fortunes were notorious for their absorption in business and politics. As a result their wives and daughters were the true leisure class of America. Many of them devoted their energies to expensive social life and travel, but some, like Mrs. Potter, needed a larger scope. With their money and access to the seats of power they tended to dominate the cultural life of the nation.

Thus, as chairman of the board of lady managers of the Columbian Exposition, Mrs. Palmer set out for Europe to gain the support of women of other nations. In London her old friend Robert Todd Lincoln made appointments for her in court circles. While Potter Palmer went to the races and haunted the clubs, his wife cultivated the titled ladies. The Princess Christian, third daughter of Queen Victoria, was alarmed by Mrs. Palmer's views on women's rights. Echoing her stuffy mother, the princess said that women should be trained only to care for their families, beautify the home, and nurse the sick; she could see no place for women in the learned professions. However, Mrs. Palmer won her over to the extent that she consented to head the women's committee in England under the patronage of the Queen. Mrs. Palmer also managed to get some suffrage leaders into the galaxy of titled ladies.[51]

In France she enlisted the help of the committee of women who had worked for the Paris Exposition, and who "basked in the full sunshine of official power." Beautifully dressed and speaking excellent French, Mrs. Palmer won the support of various statesmen, including the all-important minister of commerce. The resident commissioner in Paris for the Columbian Exposition, Theodore Stanton, son of Elizabeth Cady Stanton, was helpful in opening doors for Mrs. Palmer. Her efforts resulted in the appointment of a women's commission and a government appropriation of 200,000 francs —more than the American women had yet received from Congress.

While his wife was lobbying among influential people, Potter Palmer, somewhat knowledgeable about art, was combing the dealers and studios for paintings for the Woman's Building. Under the influence of Sara T. Hollowell, his wife's Paris representative, he became interested in the Impressionists, whose work the Palmers introduced to Chicago. Bertha commissioned Mary Cassatt, then little known in America, and Mary Fairchild MacMonnies, wife of the sculptor Frederick MacMonnies, to do murals for the Woman's Building.

So it went. In Vienna her brother-in-law, Frederick Grant, was the popular American minister, but Austria had broken off relations with the United States over the McKinley tariff. Even so, Mrs. Palmer managed to form a commission for the fair. In Belgium she was received by Queen Marie Henriette and in Italy by Queen Margherita, both of whom agreed to form committees.

Back in America, Mrs. Palmer conducted a worldwide correspondence which eventually resulted in favorable responses from forty-one countries. In Japan the empress headed a committee; in Russia the empress personally assembled a collection of laces, embroideries, and costumes for the exhibit. As Mrs. Palmer told her board, "We are now possessed of the most powerful organization that ever existed among women."[52]

As might be expected, a dominating woman like Mrs. Palmer ran into opposition from other strong-minded women, and also as might be expected, a Beecher was involved in the controversy. Mrs. Isabella Beecher Hooker wanted Clara Barton as president of the women's committee. Mrs. Palmer fired the corresponding secretary, Miss Phoebe W. Cousins, a lawyer and prominent suffragist, who, supported by Mrs. Hooker, brought suit. Mrs. Palmer won the suit and the presidency. Among her supporters were Julia Ward Howe, Susan B. Anthony, and Anna Howard Shaw.

Probably with justice, Mrs. Palmer's biographer credits her with the creation of the Woman's Building: she insisted on a woman architect for it and filled it with the work of women sculptors and painters; she rejected offerings of local women's arts and crafts groups. The result was a building in the Italian Renaissance style, with balconies, logias, and, at her insistence, a roof garden. It had land and water entrances, and a Hall of Honor seventy feet high inscribed with the names of women important in art, music, science, statecraft, and literature.

The Exposition as a whole was opened on October 20, 1892, with a grand ball and banquet at which Mrs. Palmer presided, wearing a gown of yellow satin and velvet, ropes of pearls, and a diamond tiara. To the strains of the "Coronation March," played by Sousa's band, she led a parade of patronesses. The next day as a chorus of five hundred finished the "Hallelujah Chorus" and the "Columbia March" she was presented by the director general of the Exposition. In her speech she said that the basic intention of the Woman's Building was to create public sentiment for woman's industrial equality with man. "Even more important than the discovery of Columbus, which we are gathered together to celebrate, is the fact that the General Government has just discovered woman."[53]

Her optimism was a little premature. President McKinley appointed only one woman—Mrs. Palmer of course—as a member of the National Commission to represent the United States at the Paris Exposition of 1900. Over the opposition of the French directors she got Jane Addams appointed to an important post. Mrs. Palmer herself was given the Legion of Honor for her part in the exposition, an award heretofore given to only two women, Florence Nightingale and Rosa Bonheur.

Mrs. Palmer also made a splash in England: she played golf with Edward VII; she spent an estimated $200,000 in a single season after she took Hampden House. She brought Chaliapin from Russia to sing for her guests; she had the entire cast of *Salome* give a private performance after it was banned on the English stage. In her Paris home she had Melba to sing and Pavlova to dance.[54]

Whether or not the American government had discovered women, the American public did so. The papers and magazines were full of accounts of titanesses like Mrs. Palmer and Mrs. Jack Gardner—of whom more later—and of American women who married titled Europeans. However the flesh and blood women were overshadowed by the Gibson girl, who on both sides of the Atlantic became the personification of the ideal American girl: tall, slim but well formed, with a chiseled face and an aristocratic bearing. She was usually pictured in a ball room, at a summer resort, aboard an ocean liner, or at a presentation to the Queen.

Gibson's biographer, Fairfax Downey, says she made her debut in 1890.[55] Before that Charles Dana Gibson had been drawing cartoons and satirical sketches for *Tid Bits* and the original *Life*. Then the prestige magazines, *Century*, *Harper's*, and *Scribner's*, began to use his illustrations for stories. A Gibson drawing and a Richard Harding Davis story became as inseparable as a Tenniel illustration for *Alice*.

It was at the Columbian Exposition that Gibson came into his full glory. For the center page of *Life* he drew as a personification of Chicago a beautiful woman accompanied by three ladies in waiting, and being crowned with laurel by an airborne cupid with a strategically placed ribbon across his middle.[56] During the fair he filled double pages of *Life* with faces and figures of celebrities in the lobby of the Palmer House and of performers like Chief Rain-in-the-Face and Buffalo Bill. Writing of the Chicago fair, Mark Sullivan said it developed an appreciation for art that made possible the vogue of Charles Dana Gibson. "Gibson's characters, always clean and fine, composed the models for the manners of a whole generation of Americans, their dress, their pose, their attitude toward life." Robert Bridges, the future poet laureate of England, said that the Gibson girl was the ideal whom many men expected to find some day in flesh and blood.[57]

For one thing, Gibson pictured girls riding bicycles, riding to hounds, playing tennis and golf, and swimming—not merely bathing —in the sea. Before his time it is difficult to find in a magazine or illustrated novel a picture of a girl engaged in any sport more strenuous than croquet. Of course Gibson did not invent athletics for women: the early educational reformers like Catharine Beecher and Mary Lyon had advocated calisthenics; and the more strenuous system of Dio Lewis was in vogue at the women's colleges. But any form of group exercise is likely to be dull and is unsuited to anyone who has left the group. In Gibson's drawings tennis, golf, and bicycling were often linked with romance, like the one showing two infatuated golfers and entitled "Is a caddy always necessary?"

Tennis was from the time of its introduction to America a coeducational sport; in fact it may have been imported by a woman, Mary Outerbridge, who in 1874 brought in rackets and a net from Bermuda for a game she called Shairistiké.[58] A photograph taken in the 1880s by Miss Outerbridge at the Staten Island Cricket Club shows three of the five tennis courts occupied by mixed doubles. The ladies' elaborate hats and voluminous costumes are obviously unsuited to strenuous activity. The Gibson girl's shirtwaist and skirt and small sailor hat were more functional for bicycling, tennis or golf, but clearly not designed for very vigorous sport. But his bathing girls are shown, sometimes blushingly, in costumes that came only to the knee.

Gibson was by no means a pioneer feminist. In two series, *In the Days to Come* and *When Our Betters Rule*, he satirized the woman's rights movements with cartoons such as a women's council of war, with the participants in becoming military tunics; he represented women as ambassadors and cabinet ministers; he pictured a football game between Yale and Vassar with a determined looking amazon about to tackle a frightened looking Yale ball carrier.[59]

The prevailing theme in Gibson's work is elegance: girls beautifully gowned and divinely tall; men wearing evening clothes and top hats. It is essentially the world pictured by Edith Wharton in *The House of Mirth* (1905) and *The Reef* (1912) and in her autobiography, *Looking Backward*. Like Mrs. Wharton, Gibson showed the foibles of fashionable society: the social climbing, the scramble for titled marriages, the gaucheries of the vulgar rich. Among his favorite targets are scheming dowagers and dandified men.

One of his most popular series was the Mr. Pipp sequence of drawings beginning in 1898, a satiric version of the Jamesian theme of Americans abroad. Mr. Pipp is a diminutive, henpecked husband and father who is bulldozed into taking his wife and daughters to Europe. What they describe as "a liberal education" for him proceeds through London, Paris, Rome, Monte Carlo, and rural England. On shipboard a seasick Mr. Pipp is promenaded by his healthy daughters; in Paris he disconsolately watches them being fitted for expensive dresses; at a jewelers the girls cajole him into buying expensive necklaces; at a dinner in the American colony the ladies on both sides of him fawn on handsome gentlemen, leaving him stranded.

Despite Gibson's crusade against marriages of heiresses to noblemen, he allowed one of Mr. Pipp's daughters to marry a titled Englishman, but balanced this by having the other marry the upstanding John Willing, manager of the Pipp Iron Works.[60] A sorrowing Mr. Pipp is practically carried to the wedding by the brides, who tower over him. One of the Gibson's favorite themes was that of a man being bullied by his wife and daughters into attending social events—in one picture being carried in on a stretcher.

The line between the Gibson girl and the titaness was a thin one. In picture after picture she towers over the men; in the satirically titled series *The Weaker Sex* she sits in a theater box like a queen beside a short, fatuous escort, and looks down regally at the handsome man gazing at her from below. It might even be said that the Gibson girl was the young titaness who after marriage would dominate the scene.

Edith Wharton (1862–1937) looked like a Gibson girl and became very much the titaness. Born Edith Newbold Jones, she was brought up in Europe and among the old aristocracy of New York, the latter the milieu of two of her best novels, *The House of Mirth* (1905) and *The Age of Innocence* (1920). After her marriage at twenty-three to Edward Wharton, she adopted a pattern satirized by Gibson, that of a queenly woman dragging a reluctant male to Europe. Until she settled in France in 1907 she made annual four-month visits abroad.

Her English friend Percy Lubbock described the arrival of the titaness. Henry James would be summoned from his house at Rye:

It was magnificent, it was Napoleonic but how little she understood the life of the literary hermit. . . .

Here was America brilliantly flashing upon Europe; here was fine old New York, secure and decent, the right tradition, the real thing, and here upon that well-laid foundation, was her own skill, grace, intelligence, all of the best flashing across to meet this Europe on the highest terms, any terms she pleased—she had only to make her own.[61]

Edith Wharton's world, like that of Gibson, was one of status and privilege. Both of them were contemptuous of the climber and the parvenue. Mrs. Wharton remembered with pleasure the weekday luncheons in New York where the men, having leisure, were as numerous as the women. She boasted that only one of her near relations and not one of her husband's was in business. Similarly Gibson tended to omit the business world. In the early nineties his working girls were the governess, the salesclerk, the seamstress, the artist's model, the chorus girl—always fully clothed—but never the typist or telephone operator. When he began to represent the business and professional woman, he tended to be satiric, as *In the Days to Come*. His college girls in cap and gown shyly and uncertainly confronted a grinning Old Man World. Edith Wharton deplored the tendency of women to get university degrees instead of learning the "more complicated art of civilized living."[62]

For Mrs. Wharton civilized living meant money. The tragedy of Lily Bart in *The House of Mirth* is essentially that of a Gibson girl without money trying to hold her place in New York society. With considerable justice young men suspect her of fortune hunting; she loses much more than she can afford at the almost compulsory bridge games; she is innocently compromised because of gossip about her appeal for help from a wealthy roué; her weak-kneed suitor deserts her. Bereft of money and reputation she kills herself. It never occurred to Mrs. Wharton that Lily chiefly needed an education and a job. Nevertheless *The House of Mirth* is an excellent novel showing the darker aspect of the Gibson-girl era.

Henry James in 1890 had a different name for it: "the age of Mrs. Jack": he saw "the figure of Mrs. Jack, the American, the nightmare . . . the American looming up—dim, vast, portentous—in their millions—the gathering waves—the barbarians of the Roman Empire."[63]

James was, of course, referring to Isabella (Mrs. John) Gardner (1840–1924), who was described in New York's *Town Topics* December 1, 1887: " 'Mrs. Jack' as she is familiarly called, is easily the brightest, breeziest woman in Boston. Though hardly beautiful in the fleshly sense of the word, she is the idol of the men and the envy of the women. She throws out her lariat and drags after her chariot the brightest men in town, young and old, married and single." In a less confused metaphor James compared her to "a locomotive with a pullman car attached."[64]

It was not until she was over fifty that Mrs. Jack began the art collection for which she is now remembered. Before the 1890s she was chiefly noted for her flirtations with men younger than herself, and for her parties, jewels and somewhat daring gowns. Her rumored affair—very possibly a correct rumor—with the novelist F. Marion Crawford, fourteen years her junior, titilated Boston for years. By the time she was in her mid-forties she was very much the titaness. On a tour of the Orient in 1883 with her husband, she managed to get to the nearly inaccessible Angkor Wat; she was entertained by the King of Cambodia and the Nizam of Hyderabad in India. She and her husband took a palace in Venice, to which she returned many times.

It was in answer to her invitation to meet the Gardners in Venice in 1884 that Henry James wrote a revealing letter about his experiences with titanesses:

> You have everything, you do everything, you enjoy everything and if you don't happen to find an extra post-horse at Venice to pull your triumphant car—to tow your gondola—you may be sure that the next patient beast will be waiting at the next stage. In other words, I shall be waiting in London and shall get into harness when you arrive. In the meantime, have pity on the place where the collar rubbed. I wear a collar always: que dis-je? I wear half a dozen.[65]

Although James did visit Mrs. Jack on later occasions, he was not the sort of man to be lassoed behind her chariot or to her gondola. She preferred them young. Throughout her life she acted as a patroness to young musicians and artists. One of them was Bernard Berenson, whose European study she began to support in 1886.

Berenson was a beautiful curly-headed young man and also a very shrewd operator. When in the early nineties he learned that Mrs. Jack wanted to collect paintings of ladies named Isabella, he proceeded to find them. According to Mrs. Jack's biographer, each picture that Berenson recommended was positively the most wonderful that he had ever seen. Unless she bought it quickly, someone else would get it. When he found that she was unwilling to smuggle out a Giorgione for which the Italian government would not grant an export permit, he arranged to have someone else get it to Boston.[66]

Before her husband's death, Mrs. Gardner consulted secretly with a young architect, Willard T. Sears, about building a museum for the Gardner collection. About a year after her husband's death in December 1898 she decided to go ahead with the building of Fenway Court. The architect found her very much the imperious titaness: she made continual changes in plans when she was present and demanded that nothing be done in her absence. Accustomed to firing servants on a whim, she quarreled with the carpenters, who then struck, and she discharged the floor-layers for mimicking her.[67]

When the museum was opened, she hired carefully selected Harvard students as guards; they had to be of good family, interested in art, and on the dean's list. Government officials ruled that a museum open only twelve days a year and charging a $1 admission fee could not be considered a public museum. The Treasury Department assessed her $200,000 in duties and threatened legal proceedings for violations of customs laws. "People seem to hate me! Why?" she asked Berenson. He replied that everyone who went straight for his own goals was hated. "Your enemies are one of the things that attract me to you. They make me think of mine—curse them."[68]

Berenson missed the point: the reason Mrs. Jack made enemies was her arrogance—possibly the one unforgivable sin in America. A case could be made for the theory that the American Revolution was largely due to the arrogance of the British ministry and the colonial governors. The public could envy but admire a Mrs. Palmer or make a heroine of Jane Addams. Women tried to pattern themselves after the Gibson girl and men hoped to marry her. Male chauvinists might laugh at the college girl and at conservative institutions like the University of Pennsylvania might try to ignore her, but she was not often hated except by DAR types. (The Daughters of the American Revolution expelled Jane Addams and joined the Coolidge crusade against the women's colleges.) However, arrogant M. Carey Thomas could raise the hackles of every male she came near. Henry James could like and admire a titaness like Edith Wharton but loathe a Mrs. Jack.

Categories like college girl, Gibson girl, and titaness may be useful for defining certain roles, but in America from the time of Abigail Adams, who could run a farm or the White House, the American woman, like the American male, has often refused to stay in one category or social class. As has been suggested, the types described in this chapter often overlapped. A good example is Alice Duer Miller (1874–1942). She was Gibson girl, college girl, and titaness.

The Duers were an old New York family who moved to an estate at Weehawken after the wreck of the family fortune. Nevertheless she remembered having a dozen servants and fine old furniture and silver. The Duers, like their cousins, the Livingstons, the Van Rensselaers, the Kings, and the Gracies, belonged to a set that held somewhat aloof from the newly rich.

Alice learned to ride a vicious pony, which her grandfather would poke with a stick to teach her "a good seat."[69] However, her two great interests by the time she was fifteen were mathematics and poetry. Math led to the study of astronomy. During a summer holiday she acted as navigator on a friend's yacht.

At the time of her debut in the Gibson-girl era she was considered a beauty. Every evening after dinner she played the piano—Mendelssohn and Tosti. The family had season tickets to the Boston Symphony and later the Philadelphia Orchestra. As a naval officer, her father moved from place to place. When the family fortunes were at a low ebb she decided to work her way through Barnard. This decision shocked her aristocratic friends; Mrs. Astor called to remonstrate with Mrs. Duer.[70]

Alice paid her way by tutoring and writing small pieces for *Harper's*. However, she managed to combine the life of the Gibson girl and the college student. She would cut short her stay at a dinner or a ball to go in her evening gown to the Columbia University observatory, where she would put on a smock and spend long hours.[71] Her prize-winning senior thesis was "Dedekind's Theory of Irrational Numbers."

After her marriage to Henry Wise Miller she shared a life of poverty on a plantation in the West Indies. She taught for a time in a girl's school, but after her husband made money in Wall Street, she devoted her time to writing: short stories, society thrillers under a pseudonym, three novels, editorials, and an occasional poem. Her husband, her biographer, says that she acted as a ghost writer for Woodrow Wilson. An ardent feminist, she was for several years a writer for the *New Republic*, a connection which gained her such friends as Walter Lippmann, Max Eastman, and Dorothy Straight. For three years she wrote a column for the *New York Herald Tribune*. Her story *Manslaughter* was filmed by Cecil B. de Mille.[72]

However, she did not give up her role in high society: the Millers had a box at the opera; they entertained at Newport on gold plate. They spent part of every year abroad, leasing villas in Antibes, Portugal, and Egypt, and houses in London.

Increasingly, however, Alice Duer Miller moved into other circles. One winter she set up housekeeping in Bermuda with Irving and Ellin Berlin. In New York she took up with the Algonquin group: Woollcott, Marx, Benchley, Marc Connelly, Russell Crouse, Frank

Sullivan, Ben Hecht, Harold Ross, Franklin P. Adams, and Dorothy Parker.[73] Her shift of social milieus is symbolic of the differing roles of women before and after World War I. The more decorous world of the Gibson girl gave way to that of the flapper and the type of intellectual who, like Dorothy Parker, thumbed her nose at middle-class mores.

In her role as titaness Alice Duer Miller was a trustee of Barnard for twenty-two years, was made an honorary Phi Beta Kappa in 1926, given the University Medal in 1933, and an LL.D. in 1942.[74]

Her husband's biography of her gives almost nothing of her inner life. It is useful chiefly as a record of the social mobility possible to an American woman—the ability to function in several social classes. This goes as far back as Abigail Adams, who functioned on a farm, at the Court of St. James, in the White House, and again on the farm. A number of the women described in this study rose from very humble beginnings to positions of national and even international prominence.

This suggests that the college girl, the Gibson girl and the titaness were the products of a society which had long given American women a greater freedom than their sisters enjoyed elsewhere. The first college in England to accept women was Griton which in 1869 admitted six; the first German university to accept them was Heidelberg in 1900. As James Bryce said in 1889, "the provision for women's education in the United States is ampler and better than that made in any European countries. . . ."[75] As a result, the American women "feel more independent, they have a fuller consciousness of their place in the world of thought as well as the world of action." He said that women had made their way into most of the professions more largely than in Europe.

Male chauvinism existed in America, of course, but as the lives of the door openers and crusaders demonstrate, many of them had male encouragement and support. As has been pointed out, the development of coeducation and the creation of colleges for women was largely the work of men.

Nevertheless, women in this country still suffered under restrictions on employment, especially in executive positions; their pay scales were unjust and they did not have the vote until 1920. Thus it is understandable that many college women and a number of the titanesses were ardent feminists. But it is significant that the woman's suffrage movement in America did not produce the kind of bitterness which appeared in England in the early twentieth century. American women did not throw themselves in front of police horses, chain themselves to railings, or subject themselves to forced feeding in prisons. It would appear that before World War I, the college girl, the Gibson girl, and the titaness achieved a unique status in America—and realized it. For complex reasons beyond the scope of this study they have not maintained it.*

* The percentage of women on college faculties declined from 38 in 1879 to a little over 20 in 1959; that of women earning professional degrees peaked between 1910 and 1920, and has declined since 1930; as of 1970, 6 percent of American physicians were women as compared to 12 percent in England and 75.5 percent in Russia (Page Smith, *Daughters of the Promised Land*, pp. 295–96).

NOTES

1. Gerald Carson, *The Polite Americans*, New York, 1966, p. 264.
2. Earnest, *Academic Procession*, pp. 60–70.
3. Ibid., pp. 194–95.
4. Ibid., p. 171.
5. Edward H. Clarke, *Sex in Education, a Fair Chance for Girls*, Boston, 1874, pp. 127, 117; Thomas Woody, *A History of Women's Education in the United States*, Lancaster, Pa., 1929, II, 277.
6. G. Stanley Hall, *Adolescence*, New York, 1904, II, 569–70, 623.
7. Stanton, *Eighty Years and More*, pp. 36–37.
8. Earnest, *Academic Procession*, pp. 79–80.
9. Ibid., pp. 94–95.
10. Earnest, *Expatriates*, pp. 168–69.
11. Randall Stewart, *Hawthorne, A Biography*, New Haven, 1948, p. 184.
12. Hays, *Morning Star*, p. 26.
13. Earnest, *Academic Procession*, pp. 127–28.
14. Fletcher, *A History of Oberlin College*, II, 623.
15. Anna Howard Shaw and Elizabeth Jordan, *The Story of a Pioneer*, New York, 1915, pp. 72–83.
16. George Herbert Palmer, *The Life of Alice Freeman Palmer*, Cambridge, 1908, pp. 42, 56–57, 82.
17. Fletcher, I, 431.
18. Jane Addams, *Twenty Years at Hull House*, New York, 1911, pp. 44–55.
19. Lossing, *Vassar College and Its Founder*, pp. 91–93.
20. Ibid., pp. 110–15.
21. Frances A. Wood, *Earliest Years at Vassar*, Poughkeepsie, 1909, pp. 5–6.
22. Wood, pp. 107–8.

23. Alice Payne Hackett, *Wellesley, Part of the American Story*, New York, 1949, pp. 55–64.
24. Ibid., p. 55.
25. Elizabeth Deering Hanscom and Helen French Greene, *Sophia Smith and the Beginnings of Smith College*, Northampton, 1926, p. 115.
26. Hackett, p. 107.
27. Earnest, *Academic Procession*, p. 192.
28. Edith Finch, *Carey Thomas of Bryn Mawr*, New York and London, 1947, pp. 116–17.
29. Ibid., p. 1.
30. Ibid., pp. 20–21, 24.
31. Ibid., pp. 85–86, 203–4.
32. Ibid., pp. 187–89.
33. Ibid., p. 245.
34. Woody, II, 257.
35. Carl N. Degler, "Revolution without Ideology: The Changing Place of Women in America," *Daedalus*, 93, No. 2 (Spring 1964), 662.
36. Hugo Münsterberg, *American Traits*, Cambridge, 1902, pp. 130, 159.
37. Bernard DeVoto, *Mark Twain in Eruption*, New York, 1940, pp. 257–58.
38. *DAB*, XI, 462, 463.
39. *DAB*, XI, 687–88.
40. *DAB*, VIII, 584–85.
41. Jill Conway, "Jane Addams: An American Heroine," *Daedalus*, 23, No. 2 (Spring 1964), 763 (reprinted in *The Women of America*, ed. Robert Jay Lifton, Boston, 1965).
42. Ibid., pp. 763–64.
43. Calvin Coolidge, "Enemies of the Republic," *Delineator*, June and July, 1921.
44. Ishbel Ross, *Silhouette in Diamonds: The Life of Mrs. Potter Palmer*, New York, 1960.
45. Ross, p. 24.
46. Ibid., p. 115.
47. Ibid., pp. 44–45.
48. Ibid., pp. 33–36.
49. Ibid., pp. 46–47.
50. Ibid., pp. 55–56.
51. Ibid., pp. 58–61.
52. Ibid., pp. 62–65.
53. Ibid., pp. 78–80.
54. Ibid., pp. 165–99.
55. Fairfax Downey, *Portrait of an Era as Drawn by C. D. Gibson*, New York and London, 1936, p. 100.
56. Ibid., p. 154.
57. Quoted in Downey, pp. 164, 198.
58. E. M. Halliday, "Shairistiké Anyone?" *American Heritage*, June 1971, pp. 49–54.
59. Reproduced in Downey, pp. 261–62.
60. Ibid., pp. 243–47.
61. Percy Lubbock, *Portrait of Edith Wharton*, New York, 1947, pp. 1, 5.
62. Edith Wharton, *A Backward Glance*, New York, 1934, pp. 50–57, 60.
63. Quoted by Leon Edel, *Henry James*, vol. III, *The Middle Years: 1882–1895*, Philadelphia, 1962, pp. 378–79.
64. Quoted by Louise Hall Tharp, *Mrs. Jack, A Biography of Isabella Stewart Gardner*, Boston and Toronto, 1965, pp. 109, 140.

65. Ibid., p. 104.
66. Ibid., pp. 176–77, 208–9.
67. Ibid., pp. 226–33.
68. Ibid., pp. 266–67.
69. Henry Wise Miller, *All Our Lives: Alice Duer Miller*, New York, 1945, pp. 3–11.
70. Ibid., p. 30.
71. Ibid., p. 6.
72. Ibid., pp. 60, 63, 88.
73. Ibid., p. 94.
74. Ibid., p. 31.
75. James Bryce, *The American Commonwealth*, II, 589–90.

Eleven

The Double Bed

Wild nights—Wild nights!
Were I with thee,
Wild Nights should be
Our luxury!

"My Husband"
Women say
Stroking the melody
                    Emily Dickinson

It is extremely difficult to get an accurate picture of the sex lives of nineteenth-century women. There were no Kinseys, no Masterses and Johnsons. The traditional view accepted by a number of modern social historians is that women were sexually inhibited to a point where they found sex in marriage merely something to be endured. That this was not uniquely American is suggested by the classic joke about the English mother advising her about-to-be-married daughter to lie quiet during intercourse and think about the British empire.

Nevertheless, it must not be forgotten that until the twentieth century the double bed was *de rigeur* for married couples. Emily Dickinson described *Wife* as "title divine" and clearly envied the way married women stroked the term, "My Husband."

However there can be little doubt that on both sides of the Atlantic prudishness in speech and writing reached extreme heights, or depths, during the Victorian era. In 1884 Henry James wrote

> In the English novel (by which of course I mean the American as well), more than in any other, there is a traditional difference between that which people know and that which they agree to admit that they know, that which they see and that which they speak of, that which they feel to be a part of life and that which

they allow to enter into literature. There is the great difference, in short, between what they talk of in conversation and what they talk of in print.[1]

For this reason the nineteenth-century novel in England and America is a highly unsafe source of information about the sexual life of the period. In *Pendennis*, Thackeray admitted that he had to omit a part of his hero's life which an eighteenth-century novelist could have treated frankly. In 1873 Anthony Comstock persuaded Congress to institutionalize this reticence in a statute signed by President Grant. It provided "That no obscene, lewd, or lascivious book, pamphlet, picture, paper, print, or other publication of an indecent character, nor any article or thing designed or intended for the prevention of conception or procuring of abortion, . . . nor any written or printed card, circular, book, pamphlet or notice of any kind of information . . . shall be carried in the mail. . . ."[2]

Under this statute Comstock instituted prosecutions not only of the writers on free love and contraception but kept such novels as Harold Frederic's *The Damnation of Theron Ware* (1896) out of the mails, and tried to ban Shaw's *Mrs. Warren's Profession* (1905). In 1877 a guest editor of Lucy Stone's *Woman's Journal* praised Anthony Comstock. As late as 1915 the *New Republic* published an editorial stating, "No one who doesn't know how such things [obscene publications] were thrust on young people forty or fifty years ago and how difficult and risky the trade has been made nowadays can realize the vast amount of good Mr. Comstock has accomplished."[3] President Wilson appointed him as delegate to an International Purity Conference.

There is evidence that Comstock represented a counter-revolution of middle-class conservatives against the advocates of free love and easier divorce, and against the essayists and novelists who questioned the traditional pieties. It probably reflects the nice-Nellyism of an increasingly urban society, especially of that part of it striving for social gentility, the kind of people who said *limbs* instead of *legs*. This drive for gentility was characteristically feminine. It is reflected in the books of etiquette and in Lydia Howard Sigourney's *Letters to Young Ladies* which, appearing in 1836, ran through many editions. The drive for gentility was satirized as early as 1828 by Margaret

Bayard Smith, who very properly places it in an urban setting. It will be remembered that women used to farm life, like Abigail Adams and Mercy Warren, were not given to prissy language.

It is almost certain that sexual mores, at least on the surface, became more rigid after the eighteenth century. Abigail's letters to John suggest that they had become sexually intimate before marriage. In a study of the records of Braintree and Groton from 1751 to 1777, Charles Francis Adams found that among 200 persons, 66 confessed to having had premarital relations.[4] In 1721 the Spy Club at Harvard debated "Whether it be fornication to lye with one's sweetheart before marriage."[5] Chastellux, who traveled in America between 1780 and 1782, found that in Connecticut a seduced girl was not ruined; her misfortune could be remedied by finding a husband. After his marriage—probably a common-law marriage—Benjamin Franklin took his illegitimate son, William, into his home and later got him appointed to various offices. William moved in aristocratic circles in Philadelphia and in 1763 was appointed Governor for His Majesty of the Province of New Jersey. It was in that century that Franklin could publish in the *Pennsylvania Gazette* the satirical "Plea of Polly Baker" in which this fictional character justified the bearing of five bastard children.

The reasons for the growth of prudery on both sides of the Atlantic during the nineteenth century are beyond the scope of this study. It is obviously related to the spread of an evangelical religion which preached the sinfulness of sex, dancing, alcohol, tea, coffee, and card playing. Prudery is more characteristic of the middle classes of the small town or provincial city than of farmers, laborers, and aristocrats. Nor is it necessarily a measure of chastity. From the time of Burns's *Holy Fair* the religious camp meeting was notorious for sexual shenanigans. One of Lincoln's anecdotes was of the man who said he had no father: "I was just a camp meeting baby." It was not until the loosening of literary taboos in the 1890s that this folk custom got back into literature when Harold Frederic in the *Damnation of Theron Ware* described a camp meeting.

It may well be that the off-color joke, with all its exaggerations, is a better indication of nineteenth-century sexuality than is the novel. The traveling salesman and the farmer's daughter were not entirely figments of the imagination. The diary excerpts quoted in Chapter 4 show that actual courting customs were far different from those described in novels.

In real life people knew that young girls were not sexless. Dr. Elizabeth Blackwell wrote:

> . . . in the attraction of one sex to the other, the young woman is unconsciously impelled under the inexorable law of race perpetuation towards the accomplishment of her special race work, by a force out of proportion to her intellectual development or her worldly experience. She is led in the direction of this great mission of motherhood not by the conscious craving of abnormal appetite, but by the far stronger and more irresistible might of creative energy working through her.[6]

Her remarks on the legitimacy of sexual passion have already been quoted (pp. 102–3).

Elizabeth's sister Anna wrote to her advocating free love, and said "when women are fully developed their passion will be as great as man's."[7] In 1860 a story in *Harper's* by Nora Perry included the remark, "When girls say that they do not like caresses from any man, they do not speak the truth."[8] She said that such denials grew out of a false notion of delicacy or a special fear of emotions even the purest women sometimes feel. Even Susan B. Anthony gave a left-handed acknowledgment of the fact that women enjoyed sex. When Mrs. Stanton in her forties again became pregnant, Susan wrote to Nettie Blackwell complaining that this was "For a *moment's pleasure* to herself or her husband."[9]

Lucy Stone, very possibly reflecting her own views, wrote to her brother saying that Angelina Weld advocated sexual intercourse only for the begetting of children, with a three-year interval advisable. Frank Stone replied that he thought people did not "cohabit for the sake of children only, but because they want to. . . . I will say that my wife is as well now as Mrs. W. is after she has gone three years and then had one"[10]—a rather clear indication that Frank and his wife were making love because they wanted to.

Nineteenth-century novels give only rare glimpses of sexuality in women. The seduced girls in the sentimental Richardson tradition are victims of man's lust. So too was the girl in George Lippard's

The Quaker City or *The Monks of Monk's Hall* (1844), a vastly popular and, for its time, pornographic novel. It was based on an actual case in which a Philadelphian killed his sister's seducer. The slayer was acquitted to the satisfaction of his fellow citizens. Lippard embellished his account with scenes in an elaborate bordello and gambling house, including one in which a husband discovers his voluptuous wife naked in bed with her lover, but the narrative is chiefly a picture of male lust.

A rare glimpse at the other side of the coin is given in an anonymous pamphlet, apparently of 1849, in the Library Company of Philadelphia: *A Guide to the Stranger, or Pocket Companion to the Fancy, containing A List of The Gay Houses and Ladies of Pleasure in the City of Brotherly Love and Sisterly Affection.* Similar guides were published in New York, Boston, and other cities. But along with the names and addresses of bordellos in Philadelphia there is a list of houses of assignation, one of which is described thus: "The landlady has everything very comfortable for the accommodation of married ladies, sly misses and their lovers." Another "has the reputation of being a No. 1, in point of cleanliness, quietness and privacy. Great resort for married ladies."

Oddly enough it was Hawthorne who in mid-century most nearly approached the subject of women's sexuality. Certainly *The Scarlet Letter* (1850) is not a sexy novel, but it shocked the prudes, and mothers forbade their daughters to read it. Nevertheless Hawthorne did represent Hester as saying to Arthur Dimmesdale, "We are not the worst of sinners. What we did had a kind of consecration of its own." And in *The Blithedale Romance* (1852) Zenobia is so sexy that Miles Coverdale felt compelled to close his eyes sometimes "as if it were not quite the privilege of modesty to gaze at her." He could not help thinking that she was a woman "who had lived and loved," to whom wedlock "had thrown wide the gates of mystery." It is significant that Zenobia committed suicide; she did not fit into the society of her time.[11]

Laura Hawkins in Twain's and Warner's *The Gilded Age* muses about the man who had tricked her into a bogus marriage: "Was not her love for George Selby deeper than any other woman's could be? Had she not a right to him? Did he not belong to her by virtue of her over-mastering passion?"[12] However Laura is probably drawn partly from Victoria Woodhull—hardly a typical nineteenth-century woman. In fact Laura supports her case by a recollection of Victoria's views on love and marriage.

And of course there was De Forest's Mrs. Larue who "was tolerably well accustomed to drunken gentlemen, was not easily offended by love making, no matter how vigorous." Characteristically, Howells remembered her as "a very lurid Mrs. Leroy, of whom I cannot think without shuddering."[13]

Characters like Zenobia, Laura Hawkins, and Mrs. Larue are not heroines in the usual meaning of the term. Wasserstrom's generalization about the sexlessness of the usual heroine is valid. Because of the love story convention of the time she was a young girl; married women appear in the novels but chiefly as mothers, grandmothers, or aunts. In fact, a large proportion of Jamesian heroines seem to have no visible mothers. In the novels of Howells, mothers are likely to be moronic. Married women in the novels had their problems: husbands who drank, gambled, or were unfaithful; sons who went astray; financial disaster; illness; and death. But it is difficult to name a novel before 1890 which represented a respectable married woman's sexual drives.

Apparently all children were born by immaculate conception. In the approximately 170,000 words of *The Portrait of a Lady* one sentence is devoted to the birth and death of Isabel Archer's child—events which normally occupy a considerable amount of a woman's attention. In *Their Wedding Journey* Isabel March is chiefly concerned with bending her husband to her whims and with a concern that she avoid the little public demonstrations of affection indulged in by the other brides at Niagara Falls.

As has been recorded, Howells regarded marriage as more of an ordeal than a joy. Page Smith makes the unsupported generalization that "There is substantial evidence that the vast majority of American marriages, at least in the larger cities of the East and Middle West in the nineteenth century, were minor disasters."[14] However, it might be that marriage to a man with Howells's views on women and sex could be a major disaster.

As one of his rare bits of "substantial evidence," Smith cites Harriet

Beecher Stowe's husband, Calvin Stowe, as "a typical nineteenth-century husband, fussy, tyrannical, tormented by piles, a depressive . . . who treated his wife like a serving woman." [15] Even if this were all true of Calvin Stowe, it would not prove that the typical husband was fussy, tyrannical and had piles. However the evidence suggests that Calvin Stowe was not all that bad.

In the first place, no Beecher can have been easy to live with. In public life at least, the Beechers were constantly involved in controversies. And there is no doubt that Calvin Stowe had spells of depression when he would take to his bed. At other times he had a sense of humor. He was inept at physical chores, so Harriet moved furniture, put up curtains, and hammered nails. But three weeks after her marriage Harriet wrote, "It is a wonder to myself. I am tranquil, quiet, and happy." [16] When Calvin left for Europe to buy books for Lane Seminary, Harriet wrote him a diary letter, posting it once a month.

In her day the bearing of children did not necessarily reflect a woman's sexual desires, but frequent childbirth does suggest a certain amount of marital cooperation. At the end of a year of marriage she bore twins, and two years later, a son. With three babies on her hands she wrote to her sister: "Well, Georgy this marriage is—yes, I will speak well of it after all; for when I can stop long enough to discriminate my head from my heels, I must say that I think myself a fortunate woman both in husband and children. My children I would not change for all the leisure, and pleasure that I could have without them." [17] Not an ecstatic account of marriage but certainly not a report on a disaster.

Eventually she bore six children, one of whom died of cholera, then a recurrent scourge in Cincinnati. With a nursemaid to look after the children, Harriet wrote three hours a day. It was Calvin who told her, "My dear you must be a literary woman." On a visit to Hartford after the birth of her fourth child she and Calvin exchanged affectionate letters. In one of them she said, "There are a thousand favorite subjects on which I could talk with you better than anyone else. If you were not already my dearly loved husband, I should certainly fall in love with you." [18]

Page Smith may be right in suggesting that a nineteenth-century method of birth control was for a wife to go off by herself for a time. After the birth of her fifth child Harriet spent a year in a sanitarium in Battleboro, Vermont, taking water treatments, but also dancing, sledding, snowballing, and skating. Soon after she got home she was again pregnant.*

After the early success of *Uncle Tom's Cabin*, Mrs. Stowe wrote to her husband saying, "It is not fame nor praise that contents me. I seem never to have needed love so much as now. I long to hear you say how much you love me."[19] Calvin accompanied her to Europe where crowds lined the streets to see her. However he began to recognize that the uproar was anti-American, a national orgy of self-righteousness. Her biographer suggests that Harriet left England because she was frightened by her feelings about Ruskin. In the light of his warm letters to her she could not have known how safe any woman would be with him.

No doubt the Stowes' marriage had its difficulties, but it could hardly be described as even a minor disaster. As for male tyranny, the chapter on the crusaders shows that the husbands of Lucretia Mott, Elizabeth Stanton, Antoinette Brown, and Lucy Stone aided and abetted them in their crusade for woman's rights. The marriage of James and Lucretia Mott was almost notoriously happy, so too was Sarah Hale's; the biographer of Mrs. Stanton states that her

* It must be remembered that until the twentieth century many female ailments which are now routinely treated by surgery must have interfered with sexual life. Beginning in the 1870s the advertisements for Lydia Pinkham's "Extract" claimed: "It will cure entirely the worst form of Female complaints, all ovarian troubles, Inflamation and Ulceration, Falling and Displacements, and the consequent Spinal Weakness, and is particularly adapted to the Change of Life.

"It will dissolve and expel tumors from the uterus. . . ." (Gerald Carson, "Sweet Extract of Hokum," *American Heritage*, June 1971, pp. 21–22.)

The vast sales of this quack remedy indicate that many women suffered from one or more of the listed ailments. In *Fat and Blood* (1877) Dr. S. Weir Mitchell described the neurotic invalid who lay on the sofa or bed most of the day. "If the case did not begin with uterine troubles they soon appear. . . ." Mitchell's recommendation was to build up a woman's general health. He warned against "the mischievous role of bromides, opium, chloral, and brandy" (*Fat and Blood*, Philadelphia, 1877, pp. 17–18). It's worth noting that Lydia Pinkham's Extract originally contained 17.9 percent alcohol—about the same amount as sherry.

In an era when physicians prescribed opium and its derivatives for ailments they could not cure, addiction was not uncommon. Coleridge, Elizabeth Barrett Browning and Louisa May Alcott were all victims of this medical practice. Mitchell said that the wives of physicians were especially prone to addiction because their husbands found it so easy to relieve their pains.

diary and memoirs show that hers to Henry Stanton was a happy one. Four years after the marriage of Theodore Weld and Angelina Grimké, and after the birth of two children, he wrote her from Washington, "Beloved, I miss you more than I can express. I can't think of you or talk of you without my heart and eye filling."[20] As has been mentioned, the marriage of Alice Freeman and George Herbert Palmer was idyllic. She wrote a sonnet sequence about it, and after her death he wrote a starry-eyed biography of her.

The sexual record of unmarried women crusaders and educators is less happy. Henry James, whose *The Bostonians* is a caricature of the woman's rights movement, did catch one valid element—the tendency of married crusaders to develop crushes on other women, often younger than themselves—frequently with unhappy results. In the novel, Olive Chancellor, on the second meeting with Verna Tarrant, asks, "Will you be my friend of friends, beyond every one, everything, forever and forever?" Verna, basically heterosexual, says, "Perhaps you like me too much." For his time James is amazingly clear about the lesbian implications of Olive's behavior. She longs to kiss Verna; she holds the girl's hands; she speaks of "the closeness and sanctity of our union"; she hopes with all her soul that Verna will never marry: "don't fail me—don't fail me, or I shall die."[21]

The passionate attachment of Dorothea Dix and Anne Heath, and that of Susan B. Anthony to Anna Dickinson, young enough to be her daughter, and of M. Carey Thomas to Mamie Gwinn and Mary Garrett have already been mentioned. Miss Anthony opposed the marriages of Antoinette Brown and Lucy Stone. Anna Dickinson refused numerous offers of marriage and may have blackmailed General Butler by threatening to publish his letters to her.[22] During her life she had occasional nervous breakdowns, and may have become an alcoholic before ending up in the State Hospital for the Insane at Danville, Pennsylvania. Her biographer describes her as a profoundly unhappy woman. Carey Thomas's apparently lesbian attachments and her violent rejection of friends who married have also been recorded.

To what extent, if any, these attachments involved physical relationships is not important. What is significant is that some of these unmarried women preached a hatred of men and proclaimed war between the sexes. Then as now that tactic did not help the cause of women. Anna Howard Shaw, who was president of the National American Woman Suffrage Organization after Susan B. Anthony, was so anti-male that she antagonized men who otherwise would have voted for suffrage.[23]

As late as 1913 the slogan of the militants was "Votes for Women, Purity for Men." In his history of American feminism, William O'Neill argues that the nineteenth-century feminists closed their eyes to the sexual elements in women's lives.[24] This is too sweeping: as the foregoing account shows people like Frances Wright, Elizabeth Blackwell, Elizabeth Stanton, and certainly Victoria Woodhull did not ignore the sexual elements in women's lives. However, this charge could be made against a number of the unmarried crusaders like Susan Anthony. For them lust was a male aberration. Catharine Beecher proposed "mothergardens" where pregnant wives could go to protect themselves against their husband's lusts.[25] According to O'Neill it was the sexual views of the older feminists which after World War I made it difficult to understand or speak to a new generation.[26]

All this is not a justification for male chauvinism from Saint Paul to Norman Mailer. The arguments of the opponents of higher education for women, of women in medicine, and of woman suffrage seem very silly today. Apropos of an address at Wellesley, Alice Freeman, no man hater, remarked: "It does seem impossible for a man to come here and speak in a sensible way to sensible women. As usual, our orator talked in a superior way about woman's nature and condition, health, etc. He said he "knew the depths of a woman's heart." If I live to be a thousand years, I hope I never make that remark about any man."[27] One often gets the same feeling about the pronouncements of modern social historians about the sexual frigidity of nineteenth-century women. In the 1870s Victoria Woodhull, addressing a Spiritualist convention in Chicago, said that "Every man should have thundered in his ears the need for the female orgasm."[28] Speaking in Steinway Hall in New York, she said, "Yes I am a free lover! I have an inalienable, constitutional, and natural right to love whom I may, to love as long or as short a period as I can, to change that love every day if I please."[29]

Victoria and her sister Tennessee went in for sexual adventure, but the Free Love movement as a whole was largely a revolt against the restrictions of traditional marriage which made a woman the property of her husband and which made divorce almost impossible even from a drunken or brutal husband. The roots of the movement go back to rationalistic and anticlerical writers like Godwin, Mary Wollstonecraft, and Shelley. Robert Dale Owen and Frances Wright, pioneer advocates of marriage reform, published Shelley's *Queen Mab* in 1831 from the London edition.[30]

From the 1830s through the 1870s Free Love was hotly debated in the press. A considerable number of publications carried the propaganda—especially Robert Dale Owen's *Free Inquirer*, Ezra Hervey Heywood's *The Word*, and *Woodhull & Claflin's Weekly*. Horace Greeley, who opposed free love, nevertheless opened the pages of the *Tribune* to a debate on the subject. Because of the relationship to marriage reform and divorce, free-love doctrines impinged on the woman's rights movement. As reported in the *Newark Call*, Elizabeth Stanton said, "The men and women who are dabbling with the suffrage movement for women should be at once . . . and emphatically warned that what they mean logically if not consciously . . . is next Freedom or in a word Free Love, and if they wish to get out of the boat, they should for safety get out now, for deeps are dangerous." Late in life she said, "We are all free lovers at heart though we may not have thought so."[31]

It will be remembered that both Elizabeth Stanton and Susan Anthony defended Victoria's participation in the National Association. The other persecuted women cited by Mrs. Stanton: Mary Wollstonecraft, Fanny Wright, George Sand, and Fanny Kemble, had all been accused of sexual immorality—Fanny Kemble because of her divorce from Pierce Butler and her appearance on the stage. On a lecture tour Mrs. Stanton said that when the men kept themselves pure "then we will demand that every woman who makes a constitutional argument on our platform shall be as chaste as Diana."

She suggested that men "trouble themselves as much about the virtue of their own sex as they do about ours. . . ."[32]

The marriage reformers constantly pointed out that prostitution was one of the results of conventional views on chastity and marriage. Robert Dale Owen published a report of the New York Magdalen Society whose statistics for 1830 gave an estimate of twenty thousand prostitutes in New York City, equally divided between those in groups and free-lance operators. Even discounting the figures by fifty percent, Owen estimated that if each received three visits daily this came to ten million a year. To him it was disgusting that love could be bought and sold. This could not be the case if human affections were free.

In the 1870s *Woodhull & Claflin's Weekly* published an editorial on prostitution. It deplored midnight raids and the rents which churches received from whorehouse properties and it recommended police licensing and religious visitation. "This is not authorizing sin by statute. It is simply recognzing social and physiological facts."[33]

Although Victoria Woodhull was the most flamboyant spokesman for free love, her articles and speeches were largely written by her ex-husband, Colonel Blood, and by Stephen Pearl Andrews, who may have been one of her lovers. Andrews was the Pantarch of a group of intellectuals calling themselves a Pantocracy who advocated a kind of state socialism, free love, and state control of children.[34]

In journalistic debate Andrews took on Horace Greeley and Henry James, Sr., pointing out that the latter's position was equivocal: James talked about perfect individual freedom, but wanted to preserve marriage.* Did he mean pure marriage without the sanctions of church and state or did he mean conventional marriage? If the latter, then his lengthly abstruse writings on the subject were meaningless. With considerable justice Andrews said "he cuttlefishes."[35]

The long debate on the subjects of marriage and free love which had begun in the late 1820s with the writings of Robert Dale Owen and Frances Wright did not produce a sexual revolution. Despite

* In the course of the debate James wrote: "No doubt there is a very enormous clandestine violation of the marriage bond at the present time; careful observers do not hesitate to say an unequaled violation of it . . ." (letter to the *New York Observer*, November 13, 1852).

such typical charges as the one in the Indianapolis *Indiana Journal* which said of Owen's New Harmony society, "it would be no breach of charity to class them all with whores and whoremongers, nor to say that the whole group will constitute one great brothel,"[36] there is little evidence that many of the communal and Fourieristic experiments developed into free-love communes. This practice may have been true of Fanny Wright's short lived Nashoba Community in Tennessee, and it was definitely true of John Humphrey Noyes's Oneida Community between 1847 and 1879, at which time it abandoned "complex marriage."[37]

One thing the fifty-year controversy did produce was sex education for American women. They were told that sexual desires were normal, even desirable, and that monogamous marriage was not ordained by God. They were given information about contraceptive techniques.

It is of course impossible to find statistics on the effect of these revelations, but the sales of some publications on these subjects are revealing. Without the knowledge of either Fanny Wright or Robert Dale Owen, their press carried a prospectus for *Every Woman's Book*, a birth-control treatise by Richard Carlile, an English radical. Owen's *Free Inquirer* carried articles on the population question, and in October 1830 announced that a little treatise on the physiology of the subject would be published. This was his *Moral Physiology, or a brief and plain treatise on the population question*. Owen was more concerned with the sociological aspects, but his work did carry about a half-dozen pages on the physiological and emotional aspects of contraception. By 1874 *Moral Physiology* had an estimated circulation of some sixty thousand copies.[38]

Influenced by Owen's work, Dr. Charles Knowlton in 1832 published *Fruits of Philosophy, or The Private Companion of Young Married People*, which gave considerably more physiological information. Ditzion asserts that Knowlton was merely giving sanction to practices already in use by the American and British middle classes. This view at least as it applies to America is in accord with the account of the Scottish traveler, David Macrae. In the late 1860s he reported a vice "almost unknown in England" but

... so prevalent in Chicago—so prevalent, indeed, in certain circles all over the North. . . . I mean the practice among women of resorting to medical aid to avoid the trials and responsibilities of maternity. It is impossible for anyone to travel in the States, without becoming aware of the frightful prevalence of this practice. The papers swarm with advertisements of the requisite medicines; and the books and pamphlets giving instruction in this diabolical art are openly advertised and sold. . . . A medical man in one of the large cities of the North enumerated thirty practitioners in that one city who, to his own knowledge, devoted themselves to this species of murder. In all these cities there are establishments called by such names as "Invalid Retreats" but well enough known to be reserved almost exclusively for cases of this description. The practice is not confirmed to those who wish to hide their sin; it is resorted to by thousands of married ladies to prevent the interruption of a life of gaiety and to escape the trouble of bringing up a family.[39]

Apparently Macrae was writing about both abortion and contraception, for he quoted *The Serpent in the Dove's Nest* by a clergyman who declared his belief that there was scarcely a woman in America who did not know of a friend "practising this iniquity."

Such estimates by moralists like Macrae and his quoted sources are always suspect, but accurate or not, they do reveal that a considerable trade in abortion and contraception was flourishing. Macrae's remark about what women knew about their friends is a useful reminder that any discussion of published works gives a very inadequate notion of the amount of information in circulation by word of mouth. One of the results of giving any group an inferior status is to produce a subculture with its own rituals, secrets, and esoteric knowledge. Some of this underground information, especially the prescriptions for producing abortions, was undoubtedly worthless, but many a girl must have learned from a married friend or older sister the recipe for a douche or the recommendation to use a sponge dipped in vinegar as a pessary.

Also such information as there was in print was likely to be passed from hand to hand. Ditzion suggests that because no copy of the first edition of Knowlton's pamphlet can be found, it was literally read to death. By 1877 it went through a tenth edition. In England a reprint by Charles Bradlaugh and Annie Besant sold 300,000 copies in three years. In the year of its original publication, Knowlton was fined at Taunton and sentenced to three months at hard labor.

In addition to writing on contraception, Knowlton had further infuriated the prudes by arguing that sexual desire was a normal bodily appetite and should be honored as such. It should be indulged within reason for health and satisfaction; denial was probably harmful and it led to prostitution and solitary vice.[40]

These themes were picked up by Ezra Heywood in *Cupid's Yokes* (1876). In Princeton, Massachusetts, Heywood and his wife Angela ran the Cooperative Publishing Company which printed all sorts of reform pamphlets and a paper called *The Word* with the slogans "free labor," "free land," "free love," "anti-monopoly," "anti-taxes." In the outspoken *Cupid's Yokes*, Heywood wrote that "Pen cannot record, nor lips express, the enervating, debauching effect of celibate life upon young men and women. . . . Yet they are now compelled to choose between the suicidal evils of abstinence and the legalized prostitution of marriage."[41]

Heywood deplored the fact "that sexual intercourse is yet an Ethiopia, an unexplored tract of human experience . . . due to the prevailing impression among religious people, that it is 'unclean,' and among free thinkers that it is uncontrollable. . . ." He listed three phases of sexual morality which had emerged in the modern Christian church: "Shakerism, or the utter proscription of sexual intercourse; Mormonism, or sanctified polygamy; and the Oneida-Perfection with its free love and omniogamy." He thought the views of the Oneida community were sounder than those of any other Christian sect. "Whether the Oneida scheme succeeds or fails, as an experiment it is doing great service to civilization. . . ."[42]

However, Heywood deplored birth control by methods then in use: "abortion, the fashionable method of single persons and very many married people . . ., the Shaker-Malthus method which forbids sexual intercourse. . . . The French-Owen method of barriers, withdrawal &c. . . ."[43] Heywood favored a highly dubious version of the rhythm method.

In the 1877 printing of *Cupid's Yokes* Heywood listed the pamphlet as being in its twentieth thousand. Partly because the pamphlet contained an attack on the Comstock law of 1873, Comstock instituted legal action in 1878. Heywood was sentenced to two years at hard labor, but his friend Laura Cuppy Smith, a woman's rights advocate, got President Hayes to grant a pardon on the grounds that Heywood's life was in jeopardy because of poor health. (He lived twenty-five years longer.) He was again arrested in 1822 on a variety of counts, including one that he had printed in *The Word* quotes from Whitman's *To a Common Prostitute* and *A Woman Waits for Me*. This time he was acquitted, but in 1890 he was sentenced to two years in jail where he died.[44]

The prosecutions under the Comstock law may indicate that America was becoming more puritanical in the last quarter of the nineteenth century, or that the prudish and pious members of society were instituting a counter revolution. The second of these possibilities seems the more likely. Despite attacks by the clergy and the conservative press against contraception the remarkable decline in the birth rate suggests that it was widely practiced. In 1830 for white women between the ages of fifteen and forty-four the birth rate was 240 per thousand; in 1860 it was 184, and by 1900 only 130 or slightly over half what it had been seventy years before.[45] This is all the more remarkable in view of the tremendous increase in people from the Catholic countries of the old world. The figures for old stock, middle-class American women would undoubtedly be even more dramatic.

The taboos represented by the Comstock law and enforced by that indefatigable snoop were an inhibiting force on frank discussion on art and in fiction. In 1887 Comstock raided the Knoedler Art Gallery in New York and in 1906 took action against the Art Students League. Thus it was not until 1962 that Mark Twain's views on women's sexuality could be published.

In his *Letters from the Earth* Twain commented on the irony of man's omission of sexual intercourse from his pictures of heaven. "From youth to middle age all men and all women prize copulation above all other pleasures combined."[46] As an example of man's reasoning powers Twain commented:

He observes certain facts. For instance, that in all his life he never sees the day that he can satisfy one woman; also that no woman ever sees the day that she can't overwork and defeat, and put out of commission any ten masculine plants that can be put to bed with her. He puts these striking suggestions and luminous facts together, and from them draws this astonishing conclusion: the Creator intended woman to be restricted to one man.*[47]

Granted Mark Twain's penchant for "embroidery," this testimony about women's sexuality from a nineteenth-century man who had knocked about the continent and been a devoted husband cannot be dismissed as a mere jape. *The Letters from the Earth* are satire in the Swiftian mode—a surface jocularity masking a deadly serious view of society.

Needless to say, Twain's view of the sexuality of women ran counter to the nineteenth-century myth that man was the lustful sex to be tamed by woman's purity. That is one reason why prostitutes in fiction were treated sympathetically: they were the victims of man's lust and of economic exploitation. Stephen Crane's Maggie in the novel *Maggie, A Girl of the Streets* (1893) is not motivated by sex but by desperation when she briefly becomes a prostitute. This was generally in accord with the theories of the woman's rights crusaders who spoke and wrote on the subject. Even the more sensational *Susan Lennox* by David Graham Phillips shows the heroine using prostitution as an escape from the squalor to which the mass of humanity was condemned. Even so, Crane had to publish *Maggie* privately, and *Susan Lennox, Her Fall and Rise* was not published until 1917, six years after Phillips's death. Like Dreiser's *Sister Carrie* (1900), *Susan Lennox* was at first suppressed.

An important reason for the squeamishness of the public and the publishers was explained by Howells in *Criticism and Fiction* (1891). An American novelist could not write a story like *Anna Karenina* or *Madame Bovary* because, unlike the continental audience of men and married women, the novelist in America addressed a mixed company, the majority of whom were ladies, many of them young girls. The writer should not cut himself off "from the pleasure—and it is a very

---

* He cited the Hawaiian princess who died in 1866, and whose funeral was attended by her harem of thirty-six splendidly built young men. A song about her said it had been her boast that she kept them all busy, and that "more than one of them had been able to charge for overtime."

high and sweet one—of appealing to these vivid, responsive intelligences, which are none the less brilliant and admirable because they are innocent."[48] It was this sort of attitude which led mothers to hide *The Scarlet Letter* and M. Carey Thomas to forbid *Tom Jones* to Bryn Mawr freshman and sophomores.*

The simplistic explanation of all this, the one which flourished in the Mencken era, is that it was a manifestation of American puritanism. If so, it was a pathological condition which affected the England of Swinburne and Hardy, the Norway of Ibsen, and even France, for both Flaubert and Baudelaire were prosecuted for indecency. Nevertheless, Howells had a point about the young girl. In other societies she was hedged in to a degree rare in America. In England if she belonged to the aristocracy, the gentry, or the wealthier middle class, she was guarded by nannies and governesses; she went to a sex-segegated school. In Catholic countries she had a convent education. When she reached an age for courtship she was rigorously chaperoned. In the United States only the rich who aped European manners required a young girl and her escort to be chaperoned. Outside of the cities even young people's social affairs were often conducted without adult supervision.

In several of his novels, Henry James pictures the European jeune fille as far more innocent of the world than her American contemporary. Europeans were shocked at the freedom given to American girls; Americans were shocked at the freedom exercised by European married women. It may well be that the attempt to censor reading matter by official action was the American way of doing what European parents and schools did privately. One cannot imagine Mlle. Jeanne de Vionnet of *The Ambassadors* being allowed to choose her own books; she could not even choose her husband. Young Mamie Pocock of the same novel would certainly consult her own taste about both.

Of course the attempt to keep girls from a precocious knowledge of sex could go to absurd lengths. Lucy Stone turned her daughter Alice into such a puritan that she was ashamed to look at a ballet, and thought Fitzgerald's *Rubaiyat* should have been kept locked up in a

---

* Harold Frederic in *Mrs. Albert Grundy* 1896 satirized a British mother who hides a copy of Hardy's *Tess* from her daughter.

foreign tongue.[49] Mary Roberts Rinehart (1876–1948) remembered that when an acquaintance had an illegitimate baby, she was not allowed to look in the girl's direction.[50]

However it is probable that most American girls were not kept in ignorance for long. By the time she was seventeen Mary Roberts was nursing in the men's ward of a Pittsburgh hospital. Even there among the injured steel workers she never heard a coarse word or suggestive remark.[51] The women who nursed in Civil War hospitals never complained of offenses to their modesty. But as has been said, Elizabeth Stanton could not say the same thing of conversations at Miss Willard's seminary.

In *Rose of Dutcher's Cooley* (1895) Hamlin Garland, after telling how a farmer's daughter learned about barnyard sex, commented that "these happenings have a terrible power to stir and develop passions prematurely." In the story, children write obscene words on fences and little girls scream them at each other. Early marriages were the result of "the mere brute passion which seizes so many boys and girls of that age [in their teens]." After some sort of rural sexual experience Rose goes to the University of Wisconsin, where she discovers she has a mind. There she meets Dr. Isobel Herrick who "knew men as polygamous by instinct, insatiable as animals." As has been noted, this was the first novel to represent a woman's college experience. But despite Garland's recognition of female sexuality, he did not explore his heroine's mature sexual experience. As Dr. Herrick's views indicate, the novel adheres to the male lust tradition.[52]

The late nineteenth-century shift from the seducer to the seductress was a kind of left-handed recognition of women's sexuality. De Forest's Mrs. Larue is an early example. Then came Harold Frederic's *Seth's Brother's Wife* (1887) and *The Damnation of Theron Ware* (1896). In the first Isobel, a bored wife, carries on a dangerous flirtation with her naive young brother-in-law, Seth. The husband, Albert, coming home unexpectedly, interrupts a seduction scene. When Albert is murdered for money he was carrying to bribe politicians to nominate him for Congress, Isobel incorrectly assumes that Seth did the murder. Even so, in order to hold onto him she tries to break up his engagement to a childhood sweetheart. In *The*

Damnation of Theron Ware, a truly fine novel, Frederic portrayed a young Methodist clergyman temporarily deserting his wife to chase off after the tremendously and willfully seductive Celia Madden, who had been merely amusing herself by trying her wiles on him.

In one scene she plays Chopin for Theron in her candlelit apartment, which is decorated with nude statues and pictures of the Virgin. She herself is robed like a Rossetti enchantress "in some shapeless, clinging drapery, lustrous and creamy and exquisitely soft like the curtains. The wonderful hair hung free and luxuriant about her neck and shoulders, and glowed with an intensity of fiery color which made all other hues of the room seem pale and vague." After playing sensuous music she gives Theron a glass of Benedictine, something he had never tasted. In their conversation she gives her version of the Greek ideal of life: "Absolute freedom from moral bugbears for one thing. The recognition that beauty is the only thing in life that is worth while."[53]

Frederic links Celia's behavior with the new freedom for women. Celia says that it is an old fashioned idea "that women must belong to somebody, as if they were curios, or statues, or race-horses. . . . I am myself, and I belong to myself, exactly as much as any man." She says that she will never marry, but when Theron deplores her sacrifice of love, she answers, "When did I say I should never know what love meant?" Eventually she tells him that she finds him a bore.

The novel deals only superficially with Celia Madden's emotional life; after all it is a study of the intellectual and emotional conflicts of a young clergyman in a bigoted and hypocritical community. Celia is only one of the forces operating on Theron. To that extent she is symbolic of the growing hedonism of American society. It is significant that Frederic represents this in the person of a woman.

It is also significant that Celia Madden, like Mrs. Larue, is not an Anglo-Saxon Protestant; she is a second generation American whose father, starting as a laborer, made a fortune. Thus both women differ from the traditional national types portrayed by most novelists including Howells and James. Catholics were supposed to be less bound by puritan morality. As this was hardly true of the Irish, Frederic puts a strain on credibility in making Celia an Irish Catholic.

With her knowledge of art and music, her emancipated ideas, and merely nominal religious affiliation she seems much more French.

Thus the best nineteenth-century American novel about a woman's sexual awakening represents the heroine as a Kentucky Presbyterian thrown into the Creole society of Louisiana. Very appropriately titled *The Awakening*, this novel by Kate Chopin appeared in 1899 and aroused a storm.

In many ways Kate Chopin (1851–1904) was a more interesting character than her heroine: possibly her inner life was that of her heroine, Edna Pontellier. Kate was born in St. Louis to an Irish father, Thomas O'Flaherty, and a mother of French Creole descent, Eliza Faris. French was the language spoken in the home. In her grandmother's circle a knowledge of the French classics was taken for granted, but Kate also read widely in English literature. She played the piano well and loved to go to concerts—St. Louis in the 1860s had a Philharmonic Society and two opera companies.[54]

On graduation from school she became a popular belle, but noted in her diary, "What a nuisance all this is—I wish it were over. I write in my book today, the first time for months: parties, operas, concerts, skating and amusements ad infinitum have so taken up my time that my dear reading and writing that I love so well have suffered from neglect."[55]

As this suggests, she was trying her hand at writing. Significantly one of her early efforts was "A Life Fable" about a caged animal who gets out. "So does he live, seeking, finding, joying and suffering."[56] About this time she met and fell in love with Oscar Chopin, a native of Louisiana who worked in a St. Louis bank. On a train from Philadelphia to New York during her honeymoon she met Tennessee Claflin* who entreated her not to fall into the useless degrading life of most married ladies—but to elevate her mind and turn her attention to politics, commerce, etc. Kate said she would do so.

That Kate was rather unlike the conventional women of her time is suggested by the fact that she smoked cigarettes, and while traveling in Europe, stopped off for a beer. After the Franco-Prussian War sent the Chopins home, Oscar became a cotton factor in New

---

* Seyersted thinks this was Victoria Woodhull, but Kate refers to her as "Miss Clafflin."

Orleans. Later they moved to Cloutierville, Louisiana, where he managed some small plantations. Kate's biographer says that the marriage seems to have been a happy one. However, in 1883 Oscar died of swamp fever, leaving her with six children to bring up.

For about a year she managed the plantations, then moved back to St. Louis. Here she had a close friendship, possibly a liason with an Austrian obstetrician, Dr. Kolbenheyer, who got her interested in Darwin, Huxley, and Spencer. At this time she began to write stories, working in the living room with her children swarming around her. Her discovery of Maupassant was a revelation: "Here was life not fiction." Between 1894 and 1899 she turned out nearly forty stories.[57]

In her day she was less well known than such local-colorists as Mary E. Wilkins Freeman and Sarah Orne Jewett, who wrote stories about the minor tragicomedies of aging New England spinsters. They used such themes as the displacement of a choir singer whose voice was failing; the ruin of a party dress shared by two elderly sisters; the purchase of unfashionable hair pieces by two naïve old ladies. These were the kind of nice safe subjects preferred by the editors of the genteel tradition.

Kate Chopin wrote about women in the full tide of life. Some of her stories were too advanced for her time. In *Two Portraits*, Alberta gives herself "when and where she chooses." This was unpublished during her lifetime; even the *Yellow Book* turned it down. *Lilacs*, which hinted that Mme. Farival had affairs, and *A Vocation and a Voice*, telling of a woman who turned a boy into her lover, were rejected by many editors. Eventually *Lilacs* was published in the *New Orleans Times-Democrat*, and *A Vocation* in Reedy's *Mirror*, a radical paper which some years later first published Masters's *Spoon River Anthology*.

Apparently she never attempted to publish *The Storm*, a lighthearted story about a casual adultery. Alcée, a former suitor of Calixta's, stops off at her home for shelter during a storm. Calixta's husband Bobinôt and little son are marooned in a distant store. The lovemaking of Alcée and Calixta is described in lush detail. "When he touched her breasts they gave themselves up in quivering ecstasy, inviting his lips. And when he possessed her, they seemed to swoon together at the very borderland of life's mystery." After the storm he rides away and Bobinôt comes home, bringing some shrimp. Calixta gives him a smacking kiss and plans a feast. Alcée writes his wife saying she may stay a month longer at Biloxi. She is charmed by her husband's letter. "So the storm passed and everyone was happy."

The characters in *The Storm* are all Creoles and therefore outside the Puritan tradition. Even George W. Cable in his stories of Louisiana spoke of this absence of puritanism, but he usually adhered to the literary tradition that it was the men who strayed. In her masterpiece, *The Awakening*, Kate Chopin placed an Anglo-Saxon Protestant in unfamiliar Creole society. "A characteristic which distinguished them and which impressed Mrs. Pontellier most forcibly was their entire absence of prudery. Their freedom of expression was at first incomprehensible to her."

Mrs. Pontellier, who is twenty-eight, is married to a man interested only in business and his club. "She had all her life long been accustomed to harbor thoughts and emotions which never voiced themselves." She meets Robert, two years younger, who is something of a ladies' man. In a series of skillfully drawn incidents she is sensually awakened by music, by the sea, and by the presence of Robert. "The voice of the sea is seductive . . . the touch of the sea is sensuous, enfolding the body in its soft, close embrace." [58]

A mutual friend tells Robert to let Edna Pontellier alone because she is unlike Creole women, who do not take a flirtation seriously. After a moonlight swim and a near seduction, Robert leaves for Mexico to get away from temptation. Mrs. Pontellier realizes she is in love with Robert, and remembers "the glint of the moon upon the bay: and could feel the soft gusty beating of the south wind. A subtle current of desire passed through her body." A more unscrupulous ladies' man, Alcée Arobin, makes a play for her. He admires her paintings and talks in a way that at first caused her to blush, then "in a way pleased her at last, appealing to the animalism that stirred impatiently within her." [59]

When Arobin kisses her, she realizes, "It was the first kiss of her life to which her nature had really responded. It was a flaming torch that kindled desire." However, she feels a pang of regret "because it was not the kiss of love which had held this cup of life to her lips."

When Robert returns, she confesses her love. He again runs away, this time leaving a note saying it is because he loves her. She puts on a bathing suit and swims out to drown herself.

No other nineteenth-century American novel is so frank about a woman's sexual longings. No doubt countless women had, like Mrs. Pontellier, been accustomed to harboring thoughts and emotions which never voiced themselves. Without question the nineteenth century was a reticent era: even diaries and private letters are almost never explicit about sex. But as sophisticated people know, the people who talk most about sex are not necessarily the best in bed. Reading between the lines of nineteenth-century letters, diaries, memoirs, and considering the amount of public discussion of sex and marriage, one finds considerable evidence that the women of that era were not as sexless as most writers of fiction represented. Kate Chopin may be one of the few novelists who told the truth.

NOTES

1. Henry James, "The Art of Fiction."
2. As reported in E. H. Heywood, *Cupid's Yokes, or The Binding Forces of Conjugal Life*, Princeton, Mass., 1877, p. 11.
3. *New Republic*, III (June 19, 1915), pp. 160–61.
4. Wasserstrom, *Heiress of All The Ages*, pp. 124–25.
5. Charles A. Wagner, *Harvard, Four Centuries of Freedoms*, New York, 1950, p. 63.
6. Quoted in Page Smith, *Daughters of the Promised Land*, pp. 228–29.
7. Wilson, *Lone Woman*, p. 145.
8. Wasserstrom, p. 74.
9. Page Smith, p. 118.
10. Lerner, *The Grimké Sisters*, pp. 308–9.
11. *The Complete Novels . . . of Hawthorne*, pp. 464, 466.
12. Mark Twain and Charles Dudley Warner, *The Gilded Age*, Hartford, Conn., 1874, p. 353.
13. William Dean Howells, *Heroines of Fiction*, New York, 1901, p. 157.
14. Page Smith, p. 132.
15. Ibid., pp. 132, 136.
16. Johnston, *Runaway to Heaven*, pp. 136–37.
17. Ibid., p. 149.
18. Ibid., pp. 163, 162.
19. Ibid., p. 229.
20. Lerner, p. 305.
21. Henry James, *The Bostonians* (Dial), New York, 1945, pp. 72, 118, 132.
22. Chester, *Embattled Maiden*, p. 232.
23. O'Neill, *Everyone Was Brave*, pp. 121–22.
24. Ibid., p. 32.
25. Page Smith, p. 228.

26. O'Neill, p. 34.
27. Palmer, *The Life of Alice Freeman Palmer*, p. 111.
28. Johnston, *Mrs. Satan*, p. 206.
29. Ibid., p. 133.
30. Sidney Ditzion, *Marriage, Morals and Sex in America: A History of Ideas,* New York, 1953, p. 73.
31. Page Smith, p. 235.
32. Sachs, *The Terrible Siren*, pp. 78–79.
33. Ibid., p. 69.
34. Ibid., p. 65.
35. Ditzion, p. 164.
36. Arthur Eugene Bestor, *Backwoods Utopias*, Philadelphia, 1950, p. 233.
37. Ibid., p. 53, and Ditzion, pp. 220–26.
38. Ditzion, pp. 88, 114–16.
39. David Macrae, *The Americans at Home*, pp. 440–41.
40. Ditzion, pp. 320–21.
41. Heywood, *Cupid's Yokes*, p. 8.
42. Ibid., pp. 17, 11–12.
43. Ibid., p. 21.
44. Ditzion, pp. 173–74.
45. *Historical Statistics of the United States*, prepared by the Bureau of the Census with the cooperation of the Social Research Council, Washington, 1961.
46. Mark Twain, *Letters from the Earth*, ed. by Bernard DeVoto, New York and Evanston, 1962, p. 10.
47. Ibid., p. 41.
48. William Dean Howells, "Criticism and Fiction," in *My Literary Passions*, New York, 1895, p. 263.
49. Hays, *Morning Star*, pp. 272, 298.
50. Mary Roberts Rinehart, *My Story*, New York, 1931 and 1948, p. 17.
51. Ibid., pp. 61–63.
52. Hamlin Garland, *Rose of Dutchers Cooley*, Chicago, 1895, pp. 22, 62, 288.
53. Harold Frederic, *The Damnation of Theron Ware*, introduction by Henry Raleigh, New York, 1960, pp. 201, 205.
54. Per Seyersted, *Kate Chopin, A Critical Biography*, Baton Rouge, 1969, pp. 14–19.
55. Ibid., p. 24.
56. Ibid., p. 31.
57. Ibid., pp. 49–68.
58. Ibid., pp. 940, 960.
59. Kate Chopin, *The Awakening*, in *The Complete Works of Kate Chopin*, Baton Rouge, 1969, p. 897.

Epilogue

The evidence presented in the foregoing chapters suggests that with rare exceptions novelists before World War I presented a picture of American girls and women quite different from the living and breathing people of the era. As the diaries, memoirs, and biographies show, a large number of women did not fit the nineteenth-century stereotype of the fragile, timid innocent, with little learning but a heart of gold. To an astonishing degree the novelists failed to represent an Abigail Adams or a Jane Addams; they neglected the women who served in Civil War hospitals, held important jobs, went to college, or influenced affairs of state. When the novelists pictured crusaders for woman's rights or career women, the portraits tended toward caricature. The sexlessness of nineteenth-century heroines in English and American literature has become a cliché.

There were a variety of reasons for the failure to give an adequate fictional picture of women from 1776 to the early twentieth century. Among them were an extreme prudishness of a reading public made up largely of middle-class women, and the editors who catered to this class; the baleful influence of the sentimental heroines of Richardson, Scott, and Dickens; the power of a Calvinistic clergy which preached the evils not only of tobacco and alcohol, but of dancing, card playing, and novel reading.

In 1726 Cotton Mather had set the pattern, charging that poets were the most dangerous authors in the library of the Powers of Darkness, and adding: "Most of the Modern Plays, as well as the Romances and Novels and Fictions, which are a kind of Poems, do belong to the Catalogue of this cursed library." The Oberlin condemnation of novel reading has already been mentioned. In many homes young people hid novels from their parents and read them on the sly. The more realistic the novel the more it came under censure—witness the banning of *Huckleberry Finn* from numerous public libraries, a fate also suffered by the early novels of Dreiser. Anthony Comstock's raids on publishers and his success in keeping novels like *The Damnation of Theron Ware* out of the mails were possible because of wide public approval of his efforts.

Obviously the forces of prudishness, literary tradition, and Calvinism are related. The puritanical distrust of pleasure naturally involved a tendency to regard sex as evil except for the procreation of children. The novelists, aware of ecclesiastical disapproval, leaned over backward to incorporate moralistic teachings in their stories. More often than not these sermons were put into the mouths of angelic heroines. It is a literary tradition that goes back to Richardson. Society—especially the male segment of it—agreed with Howells that women were "the sex which is supposed to have purity in its keeping."[1]

Therefore Kate Chopin's *The Awakening* was especially disturbing to the moralists because it represented the sexual feelings of a respectable woman. That was more shocking than Stephen Crane's *Maggie* (1896), in which the daughter of a drunken slum mother was seduced by a bartender, and after being abandoned, turned prostitute for a brief period before killing herself. Conventional morality triumphed. Dreiser's *Sister Carrie*, published in 1900 and then withdrawn until 1907, was also about a lower-class girl, one who used her two lovers as a means for obtaining the luxuries she craved. It was not sex which motivated her: "And now Carrie had attained that which in the beginning seemed life's object. . . . She could look about on her gowns and carriage, her furniture and bank account." That she is vaguely dissatisfied is not because of sexual desires but the discovery that possessions and acclaim do not bring happiness.

Kate Chopin was, of course, part of a literary revolution which began in the late 1880s and the 1890s with John De Forest, Ed Howe, Harold Frederic, Stephen Crane, and Hamlin Garland, and which continued in the early 1900s with Dreiser and Edgar Lee Masters— writers who violated the taboos about the representation of sex. At long last the novelists were discarding the sentimental feminine stereotypes stemming from Richardson, Scott, and Dickens.

This attempt to give a more realistic picture met a roadblock set up by a literary establishment of elderly editors and critics represented by such people as Henry Mills Alden (1836–1919), editor of *Harper's*; Thomas Bailey Aldrich (1836–1907), of the *Atlantic*; Richard Watson Gilder (1844–1909), of *Century*; Richard Henry Stoddard (1825–1903), literary editor of the *New York Mail and Express*; Hamilton Wright Mabie (1845–1916), namby-pamby essayist and critic; Edmund Clarence Stedman (1833–1908), poet and anthologist; and of course William Dean Howells (1837–1920), who occupied "The Easy Chair" of *Harper's* until his death. It must remembered that this was a period when writers of fiction, including Howells and James, found a profitable market in the magazines for their stories and serialized novels.

It was this literary establishment which in the 1880s rejected Whitman but published the verse of Gilder, Stedman, S. Weir Mitchell, and numerous less able versifiers. *Harper's* did accept one poem of Whitman's but refused four or five others; the *Atlantic* and *Scribner's* turned down his work, the latter with an offensive note. "I think Stedman likes me as a critter," Whitman told Horace Traubel, "but when it comes to my books he shies some." According to Walt, Gilder felt as Stedman did about his work.[2]

When Ellen Glasgow began to write in the 1890s, she fought shy of this establishment. "They constituted the only critical judgment. ... When they were not ... encouraging one another in mediocrity, they were gravely preparing work for one another's praise.... They were elderly, but they were not yet mature. One and all, in their sunny exposure, they had mellowed too quickly. And this ever-green optimism spread over the whole consciousness of America."[3]

It was her discovery of Maupassant, Flaubert, and Tolstoy which helped her to break out of the trap of the sweetness-and-light tradition. She thought *Madame Bovary* was the most flawless novel she had ever read, and *War and Peace* affected her "as a revelation from heaven." Then she came upon Chekhov. But for her, *Anna Karenina* and *War and Peace* were the "two greatest of all novels." Other American writers and critics were making similar discoveries.

Ellen Glasgow charged that when Hamlin Garland left the West and came to New York, he was tamed of his wildness, as well of his originality, by Mr. Howells. Thus, although she respected Howells, she would not let herself "come within the magic circle of his influence. For more than one generation all the well-thought-of fiction in America was infected by the dull gentility of his realism, and broke out in a rash of refinement."[4] She forgot that Howells had championed Twain, De Forest, Crane, and Garland.

However, as late as 1913 in "The Easy Chair" he was attacking the rather timid short stories of the time for indelicacy: "As yet their authors have not conceived of decently leaving to the reader to suppose the clasping and kissing which perhaps goes on in life, and which their illustrators graphically report in embraces frank as those of the lovers on the benches in the park—'shows of tenderness' from which the witness turns away ashamed."[5]

The uproar over the franker treatment of sex by Theodore Dreiser, David Graham Phillips, Edgar Lee Masters, James Branch Cabell, Carl Van Vechten, Floyd Dell, Sherwood Anderson, and other writers of the first quarter of twentieth century is testimony to the strength of the taboos.

In *Points of View* (1924) Stuart Sherman, one of the "New Humanists," spoke of "an ominous buzzing of 'Freudians.' Whatever was most unwholesome in the fiction of Russia, France, Germany, and the younger England was cried up by our criticasters and seized upon for imitation. . . ."[6] Understandably, Sherman became one of Mencken's chief targets.

The *Atlantic* for November 1925 published "The New Paganism" by an alarmed woman, Ellen Duvall, who charged: "Misled in part perhaps by Freudian psychology,—which is no psychology at all, but simply a dull materialistic theory of life based on animal instinct only,—our pagan fiction seems chiefly interested in man because of his capacity for concupiscence. . . ." Such literature, she said, belonged on the other side of the Channel with *Madame Bovary* and *L'Ile des pengouins*.

It was not only prudery about sex which distorted the picture of American life: it was, as Ellen Glasgow recognized, a lack of maturity, an "ever-green optimism." Howells himself had argued that American novelists should represent "the more smiling aspects of life." In this spirit Walter Hines Page, senior partner of Doubleday,

Page and Company, wrote to Dreiser in 1900, saying that the choice of characters in *Sister Carrie* was unfortunate. "I think I told you personally, this kind of people do not interest me and we find it hard to believe they will interest the great majority of our readers."[7]

It is obvious that this literary establishment catering to relatively conservative readers would not be much interested in crusaders, career women, or college girls, except perhaps as these were satirized —witness the drawings of Charles Dana Gibson. For instance, *Poole's Index* noted only one article in the *Atlantic* on woman suffrage— and that hostile—during the editorships of Howells and Aldrich—that is from 1871 to 1900. During the decade between 1882 and 1892 *Poole's* has no entries on woman suffrage for *Harper's* or *Scribner's*. In the 1890s the controversy heated up. *Century* for August 1894 published a long debate on the subject. Of all the general magazines, the *North American Review* under Allen Thorndike Rice carried the most material on woman's right to vote. But as late as 1903 the *Atlantic* had an article, "Why Women Do Not Want the Suffrage." Five years later, Richard Watson Gilder, still editor of *Century*, presided at an antisuffrage meeting in New York. Nicholas Murray Butler, president of Columbia, also spoke.[8]

The opposition to suffrage reflects the traditional concept of women as too pure to be sullied by the polling place, and too ignorant of public affairs to vote intelligently—a concept embodied in generations of novels. This is of course the reiterated view of William Dean Howells.

Henry James, a vastly greater novelist, is to be faulted in his picture of American women—especially young girls—not so much because of distortions of reality as for a limited canvas. Undoubtedly Daisy Millers did exist—possibly even Isabel Archers—but his heroines represent the American girl in a restricted type of social milieu and tend to run to a single type—the brash innocent. When he dealt with a crusader like Miss Birdseye or a newspaper woman like Henrietta Stackpole, he resorted to caricature. He could deal with adultery as in *The Ambassadors* and *The Golden Bowl*, or with the brief sexual interlude of Kate Croy and Merton Densher in *The Wings of the Dove*—significantly all written after 1900—but there is almost no sense of physical passion.

E. M. Forster wrote, "James has a very short list of characters and besides being few in number, they are constructed on personal lines. They are incapable of fun, of rapid motion, of carnality, and nine-tenths of heroism. Their clothes will not take off. . . ."[9] To the extent that Forster is correct, this rules out most of the qualities of the American girls and women discussed in this study.

Implicit in this whole discussion is the theory that the limited or distorted fictional picture of American women is not merely a critique of the novel, but that it has colored our whole concept of what the real women were like before World War I. They were vastly more lively, able, full blooded, and interesting human beings than we have been led to suppose.

NOTES

1. Howells, "Criticism and Fiction," *My Literary Passions*, p. 262.
2. Horace Traubel, *Walt Whitman in Camden*, New York, 1915, p. 170
3. Glasgow, *The Woman Within*, pp. 139–40.
4. Ibid., pp. 141–42.
5. *Harper's Magazine*, CXXVII, No. 766 (March 1913), 625.
6. Stuart Sherman, *Points of View*, New York, 1924, p. 191.
7. *Letters of Theodore Dreiser*, ed. by. Robert H. Elias, Philadelphia, 1969, pp. 55–56.
8. *Outlook*, Dec. 19, 1908, p. 849.
9. Quoted by Herschel Bickell, "Aspects of the Novel," *Virginia Quarterly Review*, XXI, No. 1 (Winter, 1949), 96.

Index